# THE WORK OF SARTRE

## Volume One

# *Search for Freedom*

HARVESTER PHILOSOPHY NOW

GENERAL EDITOR Roy Edgley, Professor of Philosophy, University of Sussex

English-speaking philosophy since the Second World War has been dominated by the method of linguistic analysis, the latest phase of the analytical movement started in the early years of the century.

That method is defined by certain doctrines about the nature and scope both of philosophy and of the other subjects from which it distinguishes itself; and those doctrines reflect the fact that in this period philosophy and other intellectual activities have been increasingly monopolized by the universities, social institutions with a special role. Though expansive in number of practitioners, these activities have cultivated an expertise that in characteristic ways has narrowed their field of vision. As our twentieth-century world has staggered from crisis to crisis, English-speaking philosophy in particular has submissively dwindled into a humble academic specialism, on its own understanding isolated from substantive issues in other disciplines, from the practical problems facing society, and from contemporary Continental thought.

The books in this series are united by nothing except discontent with this state of affairs. Convinced that the analytical movement has spent its momentum, its latest phase no doubt its last, the series seeks in one way or another to push philosophy out of its ivory tower.

# THE WORK OF SARTRE

## Volume One

## *Search for Freedom*

### ISTVÁN MÉSZÁROS

*Professor of Philosophy, University of Sussex*

## THE HARVESTER PRESS

First published in Great Britain in 1979 by
THE HARVESTER PRESS LIMITED
*Publisher: John Spiers*
17 Ship Street, Brighton, Susex


© István Mészáros, 1979


*British Library Cataloguing in Publication Data*

Mészáros, István
  The work of Sartre.
  Vol. 1: Search for freedom.
  1. Sartre, Jean Paul – Criticism and interpretation
  I. Title
  848' .9'1209          PQ2637.A82Z/

ISBN 0-85527-861-7
ISBN 0-85527-752-1     Pbk.

Printed in Great Britain by
Redwood Burn Limited, Trowbridge and Esher

'A man carries a whole epoch within him,
just as a wave carries the whole of the sea.'

*The Purposes of Writing*

'I depend only on those who depend only on God,
and I do not believe in God. Try and sort this out!'

*Words*

'It is not my fault if reality is marxist.'

*Sartre quoting Che Guevara*

'*The* fundamental question is: what have you made
of your life?'

*La Question*

# Contents

# Contents of Volume Two

## The Challenge of History

# INTRODUCTION

> *Without falling into manicheism, one ought to
> intensify intransigence. At the extreme limit any
> Left position – in the measure that it is contrary to
> what they try to inculcate to the whole of society – is
> found to be 'scandalous'. This does not mean that
> one should look for scandal – that would be absurd
> and inefficacious – but that one should not dread it:
> it has to come, if the position taken is right, as a
> side-effect, as a sign, as a natural sanction against a
> Left attitude.*[1]

JEAN-PAUL SARTRE is a man who lived half his life in the
limelight of extreme notoriety. An intellectual who already
in 1945 had to protest against attempts aimed at
institutionalizing the writer, turning his works into 'national
goods', exclaiming: 'it is not pleasant to be treated in one's
lifetime as a public monument'[2].

What must be equally unpleasant is to be constantly
subjected to abuse. And the fact is that no writer in his
lifetime has been the target of so many attacks, from the
most varied and rather powerful quarters, as Jean-Paul
Sartre.

What are the reasons? How should we approach the work
of this man, our contemporary?

## 1

In October 1960 a mass demonstration of war veterans on
the Champs-Elysées marches to the slogan: 'Shoot Sartre'.
In the same period, *Paris-Match* carries an editorial with the
title: 'Sartre, civil war machine'.

Some of the demonstrators or readers of *Paris-Match*

1

mean business: his flat is bombed on 19 July 1961, and again, a few months later, on 7 January 1962. For how could one leave in peace a 'civil war machine'?

Nor is October 1960 the first time he is called a 'war machine'. In June 1945—that time from the opposite side of the barricade—he is attacked as 'manufacturer of war machine against marxism'.[3] The irony of it all. Is it Sartre who has changed so much? Or is it, perhaps, that this passionate advocate of every individual's full responsibility in the midst of the forces of impersonal institutionalization is deemed irrecoverable and thus, by a curious logic, must be declared to be an alien body, a machine—indeed, a mythical war machine at that? How revealing is the shared, bombastic imagery? Why is it that powerful institutions in their confrontations with solitary individuals represent the relation of forces 'upside down' and denounce the voice of dissent as sinister sounds of a powerful enemy's war machine?

In 1948 no less a power than the Soviet Government takes an official stand against Sartre: its diplomatic representatives in Helsinki try to pressurize the Finnish Government to forbid the performance of Sartre's play: *Les Mains sales* (*Dirty Hands*). It is supposed to be 'hostile propaganda against the USSR'—nothing less, nothing more!

Who is this man, this 'machine de guerre', armed with such mythical powers? During the war, when Churchill tried to back his own arguments by making references to the Pope, Stalin remarked with a sense of realism and candid cynicism: 'How many Divisions, did you say, the Pope had?' Did the ageing Stalin think, in 1948, that Sartre was about to launch an invasion, with many more divisions at his command than the Pope could ever dream about?

And while we are talking about the Pope, we should recall that in the same year, on 30 October 1948, a special decree of the Holy Office puts the whole of Sartre's work on the Index. It is in the spirit of this Index that sixteen years later, in October 1964, on the occasion of Sartre's rejection of the

Nobel Prize, the gentle Gabriel Marcel, spokesman of Christian existentialism, thunders against him in a very non-Christian voice, calling him 'inveterate denigrator', 'systematic blasphemist', man of 'pernicious and poisonous' views, 'patented corrupter of youth', 'grave-digger of the West'.[4] Thus the decree of the Holy Office under the reign of Pope Pious XII—the same man who blessed Hitler's arms in their 'Holy Crusade'—becomes the licence to open the floodgates of unholy venom, in the name of Christianity and as upholding the 'values of the West'.

It seems, then, that Sartre is responsible for inflicting a mortal offence not only on the great powers of this world of ours, but also on the earthly representatives of the world of beyond. No mortal is likely to accomplish much more.

## 2

Yet, every coin has two sides, and Sartre's case is no exception to the rule. And the rule is that institutions also try to neutralize—absorb, recuperate, assimilate (Sartre)—their rebels.

To describe in any detail the 'temptations' extended towards Sartre would fill too many pages. We must be content with mentioning just a few.

Characteristically, offers of integration arrive from both directions. Not long after being declared an enemy of the Soviet Union, Sartre is elected Vice-President of the Association France–USSR (a post he keeps up to his resignation following the events of Hungary in 1956), and he is received with the greatest honours on his journey to Russia. Once denounced by Stalin's literary spokesman, Fadeev, as the 'Hyena of the pen', now his books—products of the same pen—are published, and some of his plays performed, in the USSR. Even *Les Mains sales*—once the subject of a diplomatic exchange between the Soviet and the Finnish Governments—is performed in the East, though not in Russia but in Prague. Ironically: not before but *after* the

Soviet intervention of 1968. Equally, his relations with the French Communist Party—notwithstanding some major setbacks, as in Hungary in 1956—are on the whole quite good between 1949 and 1968. Until, that is, Sartre's evaluation of May 1968 leads to a complete, and it seems irreparable, rupture.

As to the other side, the number of offers is literally legion; from that of the Légion d'Honneur to the award of the Nobel Prize.

In 1945, in recognition of his merits during the resistance, he is offered the order of the Légion d'Honneûr, but declines it. In 1959, though—almost as a clumsy attempt to take back an offer that has not been accepted—Malraux accuses Sartre of collaboration, on the absurd ground that he allowed the performance of his anti-fascist play, *Flies*, during the German occupation, while in fact it all happened in complete agreement with the Resistance group of writers.[5]

In May 1949, following Mauriac's attack on his political position,[6] Sartre turns down in public Mauriac's offer to get a seat for him among the selected few living 'immortals'— the forty members of the *Académie française*—insisting, in a tone of irony, that he is not going to 'learn equality' in the company of those who display their own 'sense of superiority'.[7] In the same spirit, he rejects the idea of joining another pinnacle of French culture, the *Collège de France*, though his former friend, Maurice Merleau-Ponty, gladly did so.

Sartre's stature has to be recognized even as high as the very apex of the institutional pyramid: several Presidents of the French Republic address him with respect. Vincent Auriol, in 1952, confides in Sartre that he finds Henri Martin's sentence excessive, but he cannot reduce it until he is allowed to get off the hook of political protest in which Sartre plays a prominent part. (Sartre, characteristically, does not oblige.) Giscard d'Estaing, twenty three years later, hastens to assure him that he had found much spiritual nourishment and inspiration in Sartre's writings on freedom.

And even the proud General de Gaulle, who considered himself France's destiny, calls Sartre *'Mon Chèr Maître'*, to which the latter retorts: 'It is to mark well, I believe, that he intends to address himself to the man of letters, and not to the president of a tribunal [the Bertrand Russell tribunal on Vietnam—I.M.] which he is determined not to recognize. I am no "Master", except for the waiter in the café who knows that I write.'[8] There cannot be much left to be said after that.

But perhaps the most 'scandalous' of Sartre's refusals is his public rejection of the Nobel Prize,[9] in 1964. Though he makes it amply clear in his letter to the Nobel Prize Committee that he would turn down with equal firmness the Lenin Prize, in the unlikely event it was awarded to him, André Breton accuses him of performing a 'propaganda operation in favour of the East bloc'.[10] Sartre is condemned for an allegedly premeditated, calculated publicity stunt (as if he were in desperate need of publicity, like surrealism gone stale), although he writes privately to the Swedish Academy the moment the rumours start to circulate that he might be awarded the Prize, trying to *prevent* a decision in his favour, thus rendering unnecessary all publicity. This confirms against Fichte's wisdom, namely that when the facts do not fit the preconceived ideas, 'umso schlimmer es für die Tatsachen': 'all the worse for the facts'.

The only institution that remains curiously aloof from this race for Sartre's soul is the church. But then the church has a well established tradition of first burning the alleged heretics—as Jeanne d'Arc's fate reminds us—elevating them to the ranks of sainthood long after they are dead and gone.

3

Thus no one can deny that Sartre generates intense passions. And when he rejects the generous offers of integration, he is attacked with all the greater indignation: for what could be more wicked than biting the hand that wants to spoonfeed you?

There is another stratagem: pretended indifference, but this is not of much use with Sartre as his old adversary Mauriac illustrates very well. When Sartre assumes responsibility for the persecuted Maoist group's journal, *La Cause du Peuple*, Mauriac writes in a tone of superiority: 'The *thirst for martyrdom*\* which Sartre possesses is no reason for putting in prison this *incurably inoffensive character*'.[11] Sartre answers a few weeks later to all those who take up Mauriac's line of approach: 'They often say, for the ruse of the bourgeoisie is like this, that I want to be a martyr and get myself arrested. But I don't care at all for being arrested—*quite the contrary*! What I am interested in is that one should not arrest me, for in that way I can *demonstrate*, and my comrades with me, Louis Malle or someone else, that there are *two weights, two measures*'.[12]

Here we can clearly see how Sartre, surrounded by the establishment chorus of self-complacent laughter, succeeds not only in extricating himself from a difficult situation—despite the uneven odds that characterize nearly all the confrontations in which he is involved—but also, a somewhat unlikely outcome, in ending up on top. For if they arrest him, there will be an outcry the world over for imprisoning Sartre for a *crime of opinion* (i.e. a *political*, and not a *criminal* offence); and if they do not arrest him, fearing the consequences in world opinion, it is a humbling admission that the crime of those who are prosecuted by the Government is in fact a *political* 'crime'. A *crime of opinion* which can lead to imprisonment only in the form of trumped-up charges, under the conspiracy of silence (often condemned by Sartre) of liberal public opinion.

This is how Sartre squeezes victory out of what is supposed to be a hopeless position of defeat. The positive outcome does not just happen: Sartre is highly conscious of the paradoxical constituents of his precarious position. It is by no means accidental that he returns time and again to the

*All italics in quotations are mine, I.M.

problem of 'winner loses'. He explores the complex dialectic of defeat and victory in order to grasp and lay bare the ways through which one can reverse the prefabricated odds: so as to show how it does come about that Loser wins; indeed that at times loser takes all.

## 4

How is it possible for a solitary individual, whose pen is his only weapon, to be as effective as Sartre is—and he is uniquely so—in an age which tends to render the individual completely powerless? What is the secret of this intellectual who defies, with immense pride and dignity, any institution that interposes itself between him and the realization of the values he cares for?

The secret is no real secret: Sartre loudly speaks it out when he defines the essence of living literature as *commitment*. All the controversy, indeed scandal, follows from such a definition. It is this passionate commitment to the concerns of the given world; the 'Finite' (as against the fictitious pursuit of literary 'immortality'), that acts as a powerful catalyst in the present, and a measure of achievement linking the present to the future. Not the remote future over which the living individual has no control whatsoever, but the future 'at hand', the one within our reach which therefore shapes and structures our present life. Other than such commitment to one's own, however painful, temporality, there is only the world of evasion and illusion. 'This is the measure we propose to the writer: as long as his books arouse anger, discomfort, shame, hatred, love, even if he is no more than a shade, he will live. Afterwards, the deluge. We stand for an ethics and art of the finite' says Sartre.[13] And in every sense he lives up to his own measure.

He is a strange 'grave-digger of the West' for one could hardly even imagine a writer more intensely concerned with moral values than this 'systematic blasphemist' and 'corruptor of youth'. This is how he sees the writer's task:

> The most beautiful book in the world will not save a child from pain: *one does not redeem evil, one fights it*. The most beautiful book in the world redeems itself; it also redeems the artist. But not the man. Any more than the man redeems the artist. We want the man and the artist to work their salvation together, we want the work to be at the same time an act; we want it to be explicitly conceived as a weapon in the struggle that men wage against evil.[14]

If talking in such terms means grave-digging for the West, who can say that the West does not deserve the fate of being buried forever?

The work, as we can see, is defined in its total setting, and emphatically not on its own. It is its dimension of being an *act* in the struggle against *evil* that compels the reader to define his own position on the issues at stake, and since the *act* is always clearly in evidence in Sartre's works, no one can bypass him with indifference. They can reject the moral intensity of his measure but they cannot ignore it. Throughout his development he applies with great consistency his criteria of commitment in literature, even though he changes 'inside permanence'.[15] Almost twenty years after writing the passage quoted above, he asks the question: 'Do you think that I could read Robbe-Grillet in an underdeveloped country?' And he answers it with a self-critical affirmation: 'Facing a dying child *Nausea* has no weight.'[16]

It goes without saying, the literary world recognizes, with hostility, its own indictment and 'defends' Sartre against himself (not to mention Robbe-Grillet). For did they not try, as long ago as 1945, to praise Sartre's first work, *Nausea*, as his 'literary testament',[17] so as to lock him into the walls of this 'national good', produced by its author at the age of thirty?

5

It is not easy to lock Sartre into anything, let alone into the prison cell of timeless literary excellence. His view of the writer's commitment is a *total* one:

> If literature is not *everything*, it is worth *nothing*. This is what I mean by 'commitment'. It wilts if it is reduced to innocence, or to songs. If a written sentence does not reverberate at every level of man and society, then it makes no sense. What is the literature of an epoch but *the epoch appropriated by its literature*? . . . You have to aspire to everything to have hopes of doing something. [18]

This conception of literature as a 'critical mirror' [19] of man and the epoch shared by the writer with his fellow men sounds outrageous—a scandal—to all those whose sensitivity has been modelled on *l'art pour l'art* and on the self-contemplating irrelevance of various 'isms'. Goethe could still take for granted that every poem was a *Zeitgedicht*, a poem of its time, but that was before the ravages of alienation succeeded in inducing the writer to fall back upon his own inner resources. And while this isolation of the writer from his epoch and from his fellow men is the real scandal, as a result of the general acceptance of alienation by prevailing literary opinion, Sartre's passionate rejection of it appears as unforgivable scandal, as betrayal, indeed as blasphemy.

To challenge established opinion, with all its institutions and institutionalized values, requires not only a set of firmly held beliefs but a very strong *ego* as well. And Sartre undoubtedly possesses them both. The articulation of his lifework is characterized by immense pride and dignity. For what could he accomplish with humility in a hostile environment? 'An insane pride is necessary to write—you can only afford to be modest after you've sunk your pride in your work', writes Sartre. [20] And he is by no means alone in this. His vision of total commitment reminds us of a great poet's words:

> Pushing aside intruding Graces,
> I didn't come to be an 'artist',

> But to be *everything*,
> I was the Master;
> The poem: fancy slave.[21]

In Sartre's view, 'Art in its totality is engaged in the activity of a *single man*, as he tests and pushes back its limits. But writing cannot be critical without calling everything into question: this is its content. The adventure of writing undertaken by each writer *challenges the whole of mankind*.'[22] To take upon oneself the burden of this challenge, and consciously so, as happens to be the case with Sartre, is far from being an easy decision. But once the writer's fundamental project is defined in such terms, he cannot shrink from the magnitude of his task without losing his own integrity (or authenticity). He has to articulate the concerns of the whole of his epoch, and follow them through, no matter what.

His vision of the *whole* carries with it a constant reminder of his own responsibility for it *all*. Even if they want to absolve him of this responsibility, he must by calling *everything* into question assert and reassert his own inalienable right to assume the burden of *total responsibility*. For 'the whole of his epoch' and 'the whole of mankind'. This is why he cannot help being *intransigent* in an age dominated by evasion and subterfuge, compromise and escape; in short by reified institutional self-assurance, in place of facing and tackling the contradictions which in their chronic non-resolution ultimately foreshadow the prospect of collective suicide. And since this unflattering truth cannot be brought home to ears deafened by the self-complacent noise of comforting compromise except by the loudest cry of the voice of intransigence, uncompromising moral and intellectual intransigence (not to be confused with the quarrelsome pursuit of narrow self-interest) becomes the fundamental virtue of the epoch, a *sine qua non* of significant achievement.[23]

6

Yes, every man 'carries a whole epoch within him, just as a wave carries the whole of the sea.' But there are waves and waves, as there are seas and seas. The sea which is our own epoch is far from being a quiet one, even in its most peaceful moments; it is the turbulent sea of a make or break age of transition from one social order to another, and Sartre is a giant wave of this mighty sea. He can express many aspects of the dynamic turmoil, following its changes in many different ways, but he categorically refuses to assume the shape of entertaining ripples on the surface of the sea so as to hide under some cheerful diversion the gathering storm.

It is not comforting to be reminded of the coming of the storm, but Sartre cannot help being a constant reminder: one would look in vain for playful serenity in his massive *oeuvre*. No one in this century has summoned up with greater intensity the combined resources of philosophy and literature in order to demonstrate the possibilities and the limitations of the individual as situated at this crucial juncture in human history. If the tormented articulation of his vision is disturbing, it is not his fault. Nor is it surprising that precisely the most valid and farsighted elements of this vision—as we shall see later—should meet with the greatest incomprehension and hostility, leading to isolation: the ironical predicament of 'lonely notoriety'. In this again he shares the fate of the poet József, who says:

> No easy comfort for men:
> My words are rising mould.
> Clear and heavy to bear
> I am, like the cold.[24]

Comfortless, cold clarity pervades many of Sartre's works, and no reader can assume in relation to them the attitude of cool detachment. There are two principal factors which make such detachment impossible: the *organic* connection of the methods of literature and philosophy and the careful situation of every *detail* in relation to the complex *totality* to which they all belong.

From the beginning, Sartre's work has been characterized by a conscious effort to combine philosophy and literature in order to intensify the powers of persuasion and demonstration. We shall see later the specific forms of this effort across his development. The point here is simply to stress the *purpose* behind this method. It arises out of the author's conviction that against the power of prevailing myths and vested interests the force of analytical reason is impotent: one does not displace an existing, firmly rooted, 'positive' (in the Hegelian sense) reality by the sheer negativity of conceptual dissection. If the weapon of criticism is to succeed, it must match the *evocative power* of the objects which it opposes. This is why 'the real work of the committed writer is . . . to *reveal, demystify, and dissolve myths and fetishes in a critical acid bath*'.[25] The imagery clearly displays the nature of the enterprise. It is to prevent opting out with 'cool detachment'. What is at stake is nothing less than a general assault on the well established positions of cosy comfort, whether they appear as the 'complicity of silence' or in any other form. Sartre wants to *shake* us, and he finds the ways of achieving his aim, even if in the end he is condemned as someone constantly in search of scandals.

The other point, the concern with *totality*, is equally important. Sartre insists that '*the beauty of literature lies in its desire to be everything*—and not in a sterile quest for beauty. *Only a whole can be beautiful*: those who can't understand this—whatever they may have said—have not attacked me in the name of art, but in the name of their *particular commitment*.'[26] Indeed, the real character of a particular commitment is not recognizable without laying bare its links with the given totality. *Particularism* can and must claim the status of *universality* in the absence of a comprehensive frame of reference, since to be in perspective necessarily transforms particularism itself into *its own perspective*, and thus into the measure of everything else. Any attempt to reveal the proper connections with totality must therefore clash with the interests of the prevailaing particularisms. At the same time, the unveiling of particularisms does not leave only their champions naked but suddenly exposes also the vulnerability of all those who were previously able to find self-assurance and (however illusory) comfort in the sheltered corners of various particularisms.

But there is no other way, The 'critical mirror' cannot fulfil its functions if it is fragmented into a thousand pieces. Such a broken mirror can only show distorting details even when they appear to be faithful in their immediacy: distorting because severed from the whole which alone can confer upon them their full (i.e. true) significance. The choice is therefore unavoidable. Either one abandons the aim of bearing witness to the age in which one lives, and thus ceases to be a critical mirror; or one appropriates the epoch in the only way in which this can be done through writing—by the uncomforting, cold clarity of a work which 'reveals, shows, demonstrates' the connections of the part with the whole, demystifying and dissolving the fetishes of the seemingly rock-solid, established immediacy in the dynamic framework of constantly changing totality. There can be no doubt of which is Sartre's choice.

## 7

The focus of Sartre's grappling with totality is his search for *freedom*. Everything appears in relation to this concern. He calls his novel cycle *Roads to Freedom*: a title that might well sum up the character of his work as a whole. (This applies as much to his literary as to his philosophical-theoretical work.) And precisely because his work has the focus it does have, Sartre never gets lost in the socio-historical totality of which he is a tireless explorer.

Of course, his preoccupation with freedom goes through many metamorphoses. There is a world of difference, even if accomplished 'a l'intérieur d'une permanence' (inside permanence), between saying that 'man is free so as to commit himself, but he is not free unless he commits himself so as to be free'[27] and recognizing that 'no one is free unless everybody is free . . . Freedom is conditioned—not metaphysically but practically—by protein.'[28] The first quotation offers a solution only in the form of a verbal paradox; the second, by contrast, assumes a more modest posture, but indicates some tangible targets for human action. All the same—and this is why he is right to talk about change 'inside permanence'—the organizing centre and structuring core of Sartre's work remains his all-embracing concern for freedom. The removal of hunger and exploitation do not appear as ends in themselves but as necessary stepping stones towards the liberation of man, towards the realization of his freedom.

Sartre's work covers an enormous area and shows an immense variety: from occasional articles to a novel cycle, from short stories to massive philosophical syntheses, from film scripts to political pamphlets, from plays to reflections on art and music, and from literary criticism to psychoanalysis, as well as monumental biographies, attempting to grasp the inner motivations of unique individuals in relation to the specific social-historical conditions of the age which shaped them and which in their turn they helped to transform. Yet one cannot say that the trees hide the wood. Quite the contrary. It is Sartre's lifework as a whole that predominates, and not particular elements of it. While one can undoubtedly think of unique masterpieces among his numerous writings, they do not account by themselves for his true significance. One might go as far as to say that it is his total 'fundamental project', with all its manifold transformations and permutations, which defines the uniqueness of this restless author, and not the accomplishment of even his most disciplined work. For it is an integral part of his project that he constantly changes and revises his previous positions: the many-faceted work articulates itself through its transformations, and 'totalization' is achieved through ceaseless 'de-totalization' and 're-totalization'.

Success and failure thus become very relative terms for Sartre: they turn into one another. 'Success' is the manifestation of failure and 'failure' is the reality of success: 'in the domain of expression, success is necessarily failure',[29] and he quotes his friend, Giacometti, according to whom when failure reaches its climax and 'all is lost, at this point . . . you can throw your sculpture in the rubbish bin or exhibit it in a gallery'.[30] The reason is (though this is not quite how Sartre puts it, tending at this point towards a timeless explanation) that the writer and the artist in our age have to assemble their work from fragmented pieces. For fragmentation and compartmentalization (or, at another level, isolation and privatization) are not mere figments of the intellectuals' imagination but objective characteristics of contemporary socio-historical reality. And this makes the work, even when it consciously aims at totalization—inherently problematical.

There are many different ways of facing up to this problem; the names of Proust and Thomas Mann indicate two clearly contrasting attempts. But neither Proust's ordered subjectivity, nor Thomas Mann's disciplined and restrained objectivity can be compared to Sartre's project. The relevant comparison is Picasso, whatever their differences: both devour, with insatiable appetite, everything that comes their way, and produce not so much 'representative works' as *a representative lifework*.

Thus it does not matter that particular works are not paradigm summations of the artist, in the sense in which *À la recherche du temps perdu* and *The Magic Mountain* certainly are. It does not matter that the particular works (even *Guernica*) are more problematical than the ones which, by contrast, are constituted on the basis of a most careful sifting and elaboration of the given moments of reality. If Picasso and Sartre have to move on from a particular kind of synthesis to something on the face of it *quite different*, it is because what is involved in their quest is a type of totalization which always refers to the artist's lifework as its immediate ground. Theirs is a singular form of subjectivity in comparison to Proust and Thomas Mann. The former produces his synthesis by dissolving the world of objects in his interiority and subjectivity; the latter makes the writer's subjectivity recede quietly behind a carefully reconstructed objectivity. In both Sartre and Picasso, subjectivity is always in evidence but uses as its vehicle the world of objects, not to subjectivize it but to 'nihilate' it (to use Sartre's expression) in the course of depiction. As a result of this dialectical process of 'objectivation-nihilation'—a first cousin of Brecht's *Verfremdungseffekt*—the lifework is enriched, paradoxically at the expense of the particular work which it uses 'to stand on its own shoulders', so to speak. We are captivated by the *process* of nihilating objectification that produces the lifework, and not necessarily by particular *results*. Just how many individual works survive in the long run is irrelevant. What matters is the constitution of a representative lifework: a singular fusion of subjectivity and objectivity.

The great variety and mass of Sartre's particular projects readily combines into a coherent whole. The extraordinary coherence of his lifework is not preconceived. It is not the result of an original blueprint which is imposed on every detail as time goes by: that would be an artificial, external unity. Here we have to do, on the contrary, with an *inner unity* that prevails through the most varied manifestations of formal divergence. This is an *evolving* unity that *emerges* through more or less spontaneous *explorations* of the 'roads to freedom'—or, for that matter, of the manifold obstacles to freedom—whatever they happen to be. The unity is therefore *structural* and not *thematic*: the latter would be far too restrictive for a lifework. (Some of Sartre's works are, though, characterized by an attempt to achieve a thematic unity, and by no means always with a happy result, most notably his novel cycle; but this is another matter.) Thus Sartre is right in rejecting suggestions that his conception of commitment in literature leads to thematic restriction and political illustration as well as to a paralysis of artistic spontaneity.

But to stress how the exploration of the 'roads to freedom' produces the structural unity of Sartre's work is not enough to take hold of its specificity. It is equally important to put into relief the structuring role of Sartre's conception of the *individual* in his work as a whole. For *freedom* does not appear in its *generality*—that would be thematically restrictive political illustration or abstract symbolism, both rejected by Sartre—but always as manifest through particular *existential predicaments,* whether the subject is from Greek antiquity or from Modern France. It is in this sense that he is and remains an existentialist.

Kant asserted the *primacy of practical reason* (i.e. the supremacy of moral judgment) in the architectonic of his system, and he carried through this principle with exemplary consistency. Sartre—not only as a young man, but also as the author of an ethical work written at the age of sixty[31]—quotes Kant's 'you ought to, therefore you can', and insists on the primacy and centrality of *individual praxes vis-à-vis* collective and institutional structures. Such a statement clearly assigns a prominent place to the world of morality. This could not be otherwise without undermining the inner unity and consistency of Sartre's work. For, as he remarks in 1944, 'Morality is . . . my dominant preoccupation; it always has been.'[32] And so it has remained ever since, directly or indirectly, in theoretical and in literary forms. It is this primacy and centrality assigned to *individual praxes*, in close relation with the problematics of freedom, which defines the specificity of Sartre's fundamental project through all the variety of its manifestations.

8

The point of reading a contemporary is to recognize and examine ourselves in his critical mirror. This is not a one-way business for reading is interpreting and thus necessarily implies not only an examination of ourselves, but at the same time also a critical examination of the mirror and of its relationship to the epoch which it reveals. As Sartre puts it, recognizably in terms of his own central concerns, 'the reader freely allows himself to be influenced. This fact alone is enough to quash the fable of his passivity. The reader invents us: he uses our words to set his own traps for himself. He is active, he transcends us'.[33]

This is particularly true of reading a contemporary author. For there are many crucial junctures of experience which we share with him. This confers a privileged position on the reader in his critical dialogue with his living contemporary. But saying that only accounts for the credit side of the equation. The debit side consists in the particular difficulties of evaluating the lifework of a living contemporary. 'All my works', says Sartre, 'are facets of a *whole* whose meaning one cannot really appreciate until I'll have brought it all to an end.'[34] This is true enough. But not quite. Were it categorically true, evaluation of a contemporary author would be *a priori* impossible. The job of the critic would oscillate between *arbitrary subjectivity* ('inventing' the author entirely out of one's own concerns, using his words only as a pretext for pseudo-objective self-exhibition) and the *dead objectivity* of mere description of the works reviewed: a superfluous and hopeless venture.

To be sure, evaluation can proceed only from the *whole*, which is, by definition, *incomplete* so long as the lifework has not been brought to its end. All the same, when one deals with a significant author, whose individual works are 'facets of a whole', new and possible additions are not capricious attempts at a radical break, but additions which are *possible* in relation to the given and self-evolving whole. In other words, all modifications represent change 'à l'intérieur d'une permanence', in accordance with the dialectic of continuity and discontinuity. The *structuring* elements of an original lifework are clearly visible at a relatively early age; and the *tendencies* of a writer's quest are displayed through the *type* of varietions the particular works represent in relation to one another.

And there is a crucial—one might say strategic—point of reference: the stubborn recurrence of some basic concerns which assume the form of *incomplete* or *unfinished* (for within the given writer's project, *unfinishable*) works. When a writer's lifework is suddenly brought to its end, what happens is that the former incompleteness is elevated to the level of completion. Paradoxically, in the shape of works unfinishable *for inner reasons* we find anticipations of the completed lifework; and we find these in particular abundance in Sartre's *oeuvre*. A closer look at them—not in isolation but in relation to the rest—may help to provide the vantage point from which a critical assessment of a living contemporary becomes possible.

# PART ONE

# The Unity of Life and Work:
*Outline of Sartre's Development*

*'The important thing is not what
one is but what one does'.*[35]

## Chapter 1

# THE WRITER AND HIS SITUATION

### 1

A WRITER creates his work from the raw material of experience given to him by the contingency of his situation, even if, as in Kafka, the end result seems to have very little in common with the immediate ground from which it emanates. Some writers, like Villon, throw themselves right in the middle of the turmoil of their epoch, and live through the events with great intensity at the level of particularized human conflicts and adventures. Others, like Schiller or Hegel, leave the ground of their direct experience much more radically behind them when they articulate in works their view of the meaning of their age. And, of course, there can be a virtually endless number of variations between the two extremes.

The interchange of life and work of which Sartre is intensely aware—it is enough to mention *Saint Genet* and *The Idiot of the Family* on Flaubert—constitutes the writer's life in the interest of his work and *vice versa*; he makes his work and his work makes its author. But, of course, it all happens within a given social framework which constitutes both the *horizon* and the *ground* of human achievement. The writer does not lead a life of 'double book-keeping'. He reaches out for experience in the spirit of his work in the course of its articulation, and he transforms the acquired experience into work. Thus he turns contingency into necessity—within the broad framework of his social reality: the ground and the horizon of a 'free' and 'conditioned' work—and at the same time he turns the necessity of this ground and horizon into the new contingency of a somewhat modified starting point for his contemporaries, who are now challenged to define themselves also in relation to his work.

23

Three important questions arise in this context: (1) How and why does a writer choose writing as the specific form in which the interaction of life and work is carried out? (2) Given his original choice, how does he erect from the scraps of contingency at his disposal the structured necessity of his work? For no man comes in direct contact with the 'World Spirit', not even Hegel who thinks to glance at it in the shape of Napoleon on horseback on the battlefield of Jena. (3) What is the spectrum of his possible work, that is, what can be successfully accomplished in the framework of his fundamental project, given the dialectical interchange between the sum of the writer's lived experience and the particular projects on which he embarks? In other words, what kind of works can he make while 'being made' by them?

The first question concerns the nature and constitution of the writer's 'fundamental project'. In a generalized form (i.e., asking the same sort of question about individuals in general, to whatever walk of life they may belong) it can be phrased like this: 'By what activity can an "accidental individual" realize the human person within himself and for all?'[36] This makes it clear that the form in which we encounter the problem in so many of Sartre's works (*Words, Saint Genet*, 'Of rats and men', *The Idiot of the Family*, for example) is a searching confrontation of a typically modern problem rendered increasingly acute by a certain type of social development: a process of individualization and privatization inseparable from the advancement of alienation. As Marx puts it, 'The present condition of society displays its difference from the earlier state of civil society in that—in contrast to the past—it does not integrate the individual within its community. It depends partly on chance, partly on the individual's effort etc., whether or not he holds on to his station'.[37] The 'accidental individual', divorced from his 'universal being', must therefore embark on a project of great complexity: a journey of discovery how to realize the human person 'within himself and for all'. A journey that ends only by death: either the 'suicide' of a self-complacent coming-to-a-halt (for example, the institutionalized and 'recuperated' writer) or the natural death which is the completion of life. Thus, the fundamental project and its articulation through particular projects become the same, and the originally envisaged discovery assumes the form of a constant rediscovery of authentic self-renewal in accordance with the individual's changing situation, in the interest of realizing the human person within himself and for everyone else. Accordingly, Sartre's often recurring examination of the constitution of a writer's project—whether his own or someone else's—which might appear to the superficial observer as a narcissistic obsession, is in fact concerned with the meaning of every individual's enterprise. A quest for a meaning in a society in which he cannot help being an 'accidental individual' but which he must in a way transcend if he is to snatch back his own humanity—for himself and for all—from the powers of alienation.

2

To answer the second question in detail is a truly forbidding undertaking, for it involves the collection and evaluation of a virtually infinite number of data. And once infinity enters an equation—whether in quantum theory or in the Sartrean project on Genet and on Flaubert (not to mention those abandoned, after some hundreds of pages, on Mallarmé and on Tintoretto) the whole equation becomes methodologically problematical to an extreme degree. It is by no means accidental that *Saint Genet,* originally intended as a short preface to a volume of Genet's writings, grows into a massive work of 573 pages, only to be dwarfed later by the several thousand—and still incomplete—pages of the study on Flaubert, also originally envisaged as a much more limited project. If one adds to these the considerable mass of Sartre's abandoned works of this kind there is clearly something to be explained. This will be attempted in its proper context, in Volume Two (Chapter 8), for it is inextricably linked to Sartre's conception of history as singular and 'non-universalizable'; a conception that seeks to demonstrate the 'dialectical intelligibility of the singular' and 'the dialectical intelligibility of that which is not universalizable'.[38] Here the point is simply to emphasize the relevance of the question to an understanding of Sartre himself in two respects. First, Sartre always combines the investigation of a writer's 'fundamental project' with an enquiry, *in extenso,* into the concrete ways in which he squeezes necessity out of the contingencies of his situation, thus producing the exemplary validity of a work whose constituents are, in principle, readily available in each and every one of us. Secondly, turning into necessity the scraps of contingency as encountered in everyday circumstances is much in evidence in Sartre's own development. This is the sense in which the unity of his work emerges, not out of some mythical original blueprint, but on the basis of a *totalizing determination* which aims at integrating the elements of transformed 'facticity' into a coherent whole. We can only indicate a few particular events and circumstances as *types* of such transformations, thus violating Sartre's own rule about the 'non-universalizability of the singular'.

In 1940-41, while prisoner of war, Sartre obtains the works of Heidegger—a *persona gratissima* with the Nazis—and gives a course on his philosophy to some fellow-prisoner military chaplains. Naturally, Kierkegaard is also an integral part of their discussions which, in their intensity, lay the foundations of *Being and Nothingness,* drafted a year later. Around Christmas, in the same company, Sartre writes his first play, *Bariona – or the Son of Thunder.* Both events acquire a major significance for his future. The experience of writing *Bariona* and its reception by his comrades determine Sartre's view that the theatre 'ought to be a great collective religious experience'[39]—a view reaffirmed on many occasions, stressing the organic connection between theatre and myth. (The idea goes well beyond theatre only, as we shall see in the next chapter.) Similarly, the integration of Kierkegaard and Heidegger into Sartre's world of ideas and images carries far-reaching consequences. *Saint Genet* adopts as its structure (for interpreting Genet's 'metamorphoses') the Kierkegaardian stages: the 'ethical', the 'aesthetic' and the 'religious', though the 'third metamorphosis' is now identified as the predicament of 'the Writer'. But as we learn in many places, 'in my imagination, literary life was modelled on religious life. . . . I had transposed religious needs into literary longings'.[40] Also, the depth of his contact with Kierkegaard can be measured with Sartre's innumerable references to 'the singular', or indeed to 'the singular universal'. The same goes for Heidegger. His role cannot be overestimated in the formation of Sartre's structure of thought. It would be useless to speculate what would have happened had Sartre been given the experience of a Russian instead of a Nazi prisoner of war camp, with the works of Marx and Lenin on the shelves. Useless not only because of the inherent sterility of counterfactual conditionals but also because his first acquaintance with Heidegger's writings, though not very deep, predates the war experience by some ten years. In any case, Sartre puts Heidegger to his own use. It would be as mistaken to read Sartre through Heidegger's eyes as the other way round. All the same, one cannot build a crystal palace from stone. Thus, while Sartre is right in defending himself against sectarian attacks on account of Heidegger's Nazi past, his arguments on the real issue are far from convincing. He says: 'And then Heidegger, so what? If we discover our own thought à propos of another philosopher, if we ask him for techniques and methods susceptible to make us accede to new problems, does that mean that we marry all his theories? Marx had borrowed from Hegel his dialectic. Would you say therefore that *Capital* is a Prussian work?'[41] The point is not only that Sartre borrows from Heidegger much more than 'techniques and methods' but also—and this is far more important—that he *never* submits Heidegger's work to that radical 'settling of accounts' which characterizes Marx's relationship to Hegel.

What we can see in all these instances is that contingency is in a sense 'superseded'. Not that the writer can do whatever he pleases. (As a matter of fact, Sartre has to pay a high price for adopting a great deal from Heidegger's truncated ontology which can found only itself and therefore must coil back into itself. More about this later.) Contingency does not give way to some mystical freedom emanating from the intellectual's subjectivity but to a structured necessity. What happens before our very eyes is that the *accidental* character of contingency is transcended and 'metamorphosed' into the necessity of *inner determinations*.

3

The third question raised above—the spectrum of a writer's possible work—is directly linked to the range of his personal experiences. In 1959, after praising Françoise Sagan for producing 'something new' on the basis of 'personal experience',[42] Sartre indicates that one of the main factors in his decision to abandon writing novels was his awareness of the deficiencies (*manque*) in his own personal experiences. In a more generalized sense, his decision is linked to a definition of the novel as 'prose which aims at the *totalization of a singular and fictive temporalization*',[43] and since his own personal experiences cannot provide the ground of the kind of representative totalization required by the novel form, Sartre has to adopt in the end someone else's 'singular temporalization' by producing, in *The Idoit of the Family*, what he calls a 'true novel'.[44]

This is not as simple as it looks. To be sure, Sartre's life is not very adventurous. In fact, most of it is spent on a demonic dedication to work. The sheer mass of his production is staggering. Some five or six million words already published, and perhaps another two to three million sunk in manuscripts lost or abandoned, or yet to be published: more than enough to keep half a dozen scribes busy all their life during the Middle Ages just to copy out such an amount. When asked about his extraordinary wealth of production, he explains half-apologetically: 'One can be productive without too much work. Three hours in the morning, three hours in the evening: this is my only rule. Even on journeys. I carry out little by little a consciously elaborated plan of work'.[45] It is daunting to learn that six hours of intensive work, every day, 'even on journeys', is considered 'little by little'. The whole truth, however, is even more daunting, for we know from other sources (primarily from Simone de Beauvoir's memoirs) that often he writes 'day and night', and is prepared to spend twenty-eight hours in one stretch on revising a single article.[46] Nor is such intensity reserved for rare occasions. On the contrary, it seems to be the rule rather than the exception. Many of Sartre's literary works are written in a few days or weeks. More amazing still, his two monumental theoretical works, *Being and Nothingness* and *Critique of Dialectical Reason* were each written in a few months.[47] Moreover, François Erval tells me, often whole chapters are rewritten from beginning to end just because Sartre is dissatisfied with some details. If one adds to all this the endless number of hours spent on discussions, correspondence, interviews, rehearsals of plays, lectures, political and editorial meetings, and so on, clearly there cannot be much time left over for 'personal experiences'. One book authors, like Sagan, may abundantly afford them; not Sartre, who just 'cannot stop, to take life as it comes: he must be active all the time'.[48]

In any case, the meaning of a writer's personal experience is dialectical; it should not be turned into a frozen fetish. Does not Sartre always insist, rightly, that 'the work makes its author while he creates his work'? This dialectical interchange between work and experience could not find a clearer manifestation than in Sartre. We can sense it already in his first original piece of theoretical writing, a letter contributed to an enquiry among students published in *Les Nouvelles Littéraires* at the beginning of 1929. There is only one earlier theoretical work by Sartre, an essay entitled 'The theory of the state in modern French thought',[49] but that is a very different proposition. It shows nothing of Sartre's future path. It merely puts a few sultanas of originality in the insipid dough of academic conventionality. By contrast, in the letter to the *Nouvelles Littéraires* we get the first glimpse of the real Sartre: a formidable figure. It is not *what* he says but the *way* he approaches the problem that makes this letter a truly original beginning, well worth a longer quotation:

> It is a paradox of the human mind that Man, whose business it is to create the necessary conditions, cannot raise himself above a certain level of existence, like those fortune-tellers who can tell other people's future, but not their own. This is why, at the root of humanity, as at the root of nature, I can see only sadness and boredom. It is not that Man does not think of himself as a being. On the contrary, he devotes all his energies to becoming one. Whence derive our ideas of Good and Evil, ideas of men working to improve Man. But these concepts are useless. Useless, too, is the determinism which oddly enough attempts to create a synthesis of existence and being. We are as free as you like, but helpless. . . . For the rest, the will to power, action and life are only useless ideologies. There is no such thing as the will to power. Everything is too weak: all things carry the seeds of their own death. Above all, adventure—by which I mean that blind belief in adventitious and yet inevitable concatenation of circumstances and events—is a delusion. In this sense, the 'adventurer' is an inconsequential determinist who imagines he is enjoying complete freedom of action.[50]

No doubt this is already a synthesis—however preliminary: the result of much questioning and dissecting. It is the summation of all the personal experiences which made possible such reflection and generalization in the relatively trivial context of a student enquiry. The mark of a commanding and imposing personality is well evidenced by the fact that he elects to voice precisely such 'heavy-going' metaphysical fundamentals on such an occasion, when others might be content to complain about digs and catering. This is not simply an occasional piece, though it is that too. What matters more is that it is a project of life, whatever the implications it may carry for the personal as well as literary-intellectual development of its author. He grasps a major paradox, which in turn takes hold of him, and thus he gets involved in the lifelong project of reaching the roots of *being* (italicized by Sartre) through questioning *Man* and *nature, mind* and *existence, humanity* and *ideology, good* and *evil, freedom* and *adventure, death* and *determinism.* What a maiden speech for a student learning to fly in the world of ideas!

This quest for the roots of being is of necessity a project of totalization *par excellence.* It is the whole that predominates in so far as the elements and details of reality must be always brought into relation with their foundation: being. Thus the overriding characteristic of the work must be synthesis and not analysis: the latter can only assume a subordinate position, as a well marked preliminary stage to the emerging synthesis. This is why Sartre considers himself diametrically opposed to Proust, despite his great admiration for this French classic writer, insisting that Proust takes delight in *analysis* while the inherent tendency of his own work is *synthesis.*[51] Sartre's description of his 'religious model of literature'—conceived as an all-encompassing and all-fulfilling enterprise—is only another name for this synthesizing, which profoundly affects every facet of life and work, from character to work method, from personal relations to the writer's perception of and attitude to the world of objects, and from the 'style of life' to the structure and style of the work itself. And since the ultimate point of reference is 'being', with its existential bearing on everything, the surveyed facets of the whole cannot be approached with detached objectivity (we are always inside the perimeters of the quest: integral parts and not sovereign observers of it) but with a powerful *fusion* of subjectivity and objectivity, more often than not under the predominance of the former. Kierkegaard spoke of 'infinite compelling subjectivity';[52] In Sartre we are faced also with 'compelling subjectivity' (sometimes identified as 'voluntarism'), even if with a more restrained form than in his great predecessor. No matter how abstract a problem may be in itself, it is always converted into a 'lived idea' in the course of its situation in relation to being.

4

A few examples must suffice to illustrate this inter-penetration of subjectivity and objectivity. Take the concept of space and distance. We are told by Sartre that distance was '*invented* by man and has no meaning outside the context of *human space*; it separated Hero from Leander and Marathon from Athens, but does not separate one pebble from another'. The point is hammered home by describing a personal experience of 'absolute proximity' in a prison camp where 'my skin was the boundary of my living space. Day and night I felt the warmth of a shoulder or a thigh against my body. But it was never disturbing, as the others were a part of me'. This is contrasted with his return home: 'I had rejoined bourgeois society. Where I would have to learn to live once again "at a respectful distance" '.[53] And all this is to prepare the ground for an exploration of Giacometti's handling of space and distance, in relation to the 'plenitude of being' and the 'void of nothingness'.

Simone de Beauvoir writes of Sartre that 'if it had been necessary, he would have been willing to remain anonymous: the important thing was that his ideas should prevail'.[54] This is all very well, except that *anonymity* and the prevalence of Sartre's ideas—*lived* ideas—is a contradiction in terms. Ideas like those of Sartre must be dramatically asserted, if necessary through the most extreme manifestations of 'compelling subjectivity'. Thus 'notoriety' and 'scandal' are necessary concomitants of his all-embracing project towards being, and 'anonymity' must remain at most some momentary longing for peace under the strain of scandal and notoriety.

Sartre's relations to people, works of art, everyday objects and so on, are sketched, in his works as much as in real life, with dramatic colours. He does not simply like or dislike what he sees in the Prado but loathes and detests Titian and admires Hieronymous Bosch. One look at a gathering in an Oxford college is enough to make him detest the snobbery of Oxford society and never to set foot in that city again. It is part of the economy of life that he has to make up his mind about everything with great speed and intensity, always looking for an overall evaluation which can be integrated into his totalizing search. Similarly with personal relations, even some of the closest friendships have to be terminated dramatically (for example those with Camus and Merleau-Ponty) as soon as he perceives that continued friendship would interfere with the realization of his aims. He orders all his personal relations, including the most intimate ones, in such a way that he shall never be diverted from his single-minded dedication to the central concerns of his life. He refuses to accept the responsibility and burden of family life precisely for this reason. He refuses to be trapped by the conditions of bourgeois comfort and tries to banish money and possessions from his personal life.

Equally, he explores, with great passion and imagination, modes of experience which to a less compelling subjectivity would appear to be, in principle, a book closed forever. Thus he gets involved in a passionate discussion of *Negritude,* totally indifferent to the possibility that his 'eidetic analysis' of it (since it cannot be other than that) might be, as it has been, dismissed as 'disastrous'[55] by those who experience it from the inside. Problematical as such a venture might be, how could he do without it in his totalizing quest for being when racism looms so large, with the most devastating implications, in the totality of our predicament? Thus, paradoxically, 'compelling subjectivity' is the necessary condition of some degree of objectivity (the objectivity of facing up to the problem with real concern), whereas the 'objectivity' of modest withdrawal—the acknowledgement of a white man's inadequacies to such a task—would mean the worst kind of subjectivity, that of evasive complicity.

A similar manifestation of Sartre's compelling subjectivity is when he tells Daniel Guérin that 'he doesn't understand anything of his own book'.[56] Preposterous as such a statement must appear from the point of view of the criticized author, the relative justification for it is that the context into which Sartre inserts Guérin's account of the French Revolution (a dialectical assessment of the 'ontological structure of history') imposes a significantly different angle on the particular events discussed and thus it puts into focus dimensions which remained hidden or secondary in the original context. One may thoroughly disagree with Sartre's conception of the ontological structure of history, born out of his own specific concerns and clearly exhibiting the marks of his compelling personality, but it is impossible to deny that it throws radically new light on our understanding of the structures and institutions we can identify in the course of historical development.

The 'I' is in the foreground of virtually everything Sartre writes, and his subjectivity is carried, if necessary, to the point of belligerence. He emphatically refuses to withdraw into the background and assume the role of an objective guide whose function is merely to point at objects, works, and events, or at some well established connections between them. In his view, just like 'distance', objects must be brought to life by presenting them through the writer's subjectivity before they can be inserted into meaningful human discourse, otherwise they remain dead things and fetishes. Critics have often wondered why Sartre does not write lyric poetry, not noticing that he does it all the time, though not as a separate genre, but as diffuse throughout his work. What could be more lyrical than his description of Giacometti's handling of distance as linked to his own homecoming from prison camp to live life at a respectful distance?

Sartre's *style* is determined by the great complexities of his overall project of totalization. Talking about his *Critique of Dialectical Reason,* he admits that its length (nearly 400,000 words) could be somewhat reduced if he could spend on it much time and effort, but he adds: 'All the same, it would very much resemble the work as it is now. For, basically, its sentences are so long, so full of parentheses, quotation marks, of "in so far as" etc., only because every sentence represents the *unity of a dialectical movement*'.[57] It is impossible to convey the unity of a dynamic movement, with all its complexities, by using static devices such as short root sentences, simplified meaning, or by concentrating on one aspect, for the sake of clarity, while neglecting many others. The deceptive translucency of analytic dissection, disregarding the need for meaningful synthesis, produces only irrelevance or misrepresentation. Style and method must match the full complexity of the task itself, otherwise they are prefabricated devices artificially superimposed on any subject matter, irrespective of its specific nature and inner demands. Sartre consciously opposes to this practice of Procrustean superimposition (frequently witnessed in modern art and thought from philosophy to sociology and from economics to anthropology) his own method of capturing movement and intricacy. If sharply focusing on one aspect at the expense of others represents distortion, since only the proper conjunction of the one with the many constitutes the relevant whole, he aims at clarifying and revealing *indeterminacy,* paradoxical as this may sound. This is what he praises in Giacometti, stressing that it should not be confused with *vagueness*—the result of failure. For 'the indeterminate

quality that comes from lack of skill has nothing in common
with the *calculated* indetermination of Giacometti, which
could more accurately be termed *overdetermination*
(*surdetermination*)'.[58] It is the adoption of this principle of
overdetermination, corresponding to the structure of totality, in conjunction with what Sartre terms 'the principle of
individuation',[59] which defines the specificity of his style
and the vitality of his method as arising from the soil of his
totalizing quest for being. The whole is grasped through the
simultaneity of 'calculated indetermination' (overdetermination) and the shifting presence of graphic individuation whereby even absence becomes tangible as a vital
dimension of totality (see for example the discussion of
Pierre missing from the café in *Being and Nothingness*).
Thus movement and rest, the whole and its parts, the centre
and the periphery, the premier plan and the background, the
determinations from the past and the anticipations of the
future converging on the present, all come to life in the
synthetic unity of a dialectical totalization in which
subjectivity and objectivity are inextricably fused.

5

As we can see then, the work carries the marks of the
writer's personality in every respect, from the choice of
astonishing subject matter (like Negritude) through modes
of analysis and depiction to the style and method of writing.
Viewed from the other side, the inner determinations of a
certain overall project determine in their turn a 'belligerent
character', a compelling subjectivity, a writer's own way of
defining himself in relation to institutions, people and
property; in short, his style of life and the experiences he will
embark on in accordance with his vision of the world and of
his own place in it. Thus we can see 'the singularization of
the work by the man and the universalization of the man by
the work'.[60]

In Sartre's case the spectrum of his possible work is

circumscribed by that all-encompassing quest for being we have already seen in the groping words of the student confronting man and nature, mind and existence, humanity and ideology, good and evil, death and determinism. Since the target is being itself, conventional forms will not provide the ways of its unfolding; and since Sartre's works always aim at revealing being, or at indicating the roads towards it, they must *a priori* exclude anything whatsoever to do with naturalism. Symbolism is also excluded as it would merely inflate isolated chunks of the given immediacy into some abstract and static generality, instead of reproducing the dynamic multiplicity of relations which characterize the whole. What is called for, then, is some form of *mediation* capable of conveying the 'plenitude of being' and the 'void of nothingness' without falling into abstract symbolism. He finds the mediation he needs in what he calls 'myth': a *condensation*[61] of traits of character (in line with the 'density' or 'plenitude' of being) that elevates the perceived and depicted reality to the level of being without abandoning the grounds of sensibility. Thus 'condensation' provides the ground on which 'calculated indetermination' and graphic 'individuation' can flourish as truly creative principles.

We shall see in the next chapter the place of myth in Sartre's work in general. Here we are interested in its implications for our present context: the range of works the author can successfully accomplish on such grounds in the framework of his totalizing quest. The first is his novel cycle, *Roads to Freedom*. Considered not in isolation but in the totality of his development, *Roads to Freedom* is a failure in the sense of being a blind alley from which there can be no exit, no further explorations, no branching out, no roads—not even a footpath—to freedom. Despite its partial accomplishments, numerous and impressive though they may be, this work remains completely *peripheral* in Sartre's lifework. He has to tear himself away from it, as late as 1949, extricating himself from the consequences of a false choice, in order to continue his quest in other directions. Ten years after abandoning work on the fourth volume, he gives his reasons as follows:

> The fourth volume was to speak of the Resistance. The choice was simple in those days—even if one needed much strength and courage to stand by it. One was for or against the Germans. The choice was black or white. Today—since 1945—the situation is complicated. One needs less courage, perhaps, to choose, but the choices are much more difficult. I could not express the ambiguities of our epoch in a novel situated in 1943'. [62]

These are what Sartre calls elsewhere his 'internal difficulties' [63] for abandoning *Roads to Freedom*.

In reality the issue is much more complicated, for it is not only the fourth volume which is problematical but the project as a whole. Reaching 1943 means that things become more visible, at a point of climax, but they are there from the beginning. The problematic character of the work manifests itself structurally in a disturbing tension between straightforward everydayness, depicted in its immediacy, and an abstract rhetoric which tries to project everydayness onto the plane of universality. [64] In other words, it is the missing intermediary of 'myth' or 'condensation' that renders the work structurally abstract and problematical in the framework of Sartre's totalizing quest. The perception of a whole epoch within the parameters of an extremely simplified conflict of 'black or white' is in fact the *consequence* of this abstract structure, rather than its massively objective *cause* as Sartre curiously suggests— very much out of character with his dialetical conception of subject and object, author and work, cause and effect in literature. Examining the conditions under which *Roads to Freedom* was written we find that Sartre allowed himself to be manoeuvred into the adoption of its abstract structure, first, by the scandal [65] that followed the pervasive negativity of his early short stories and *Nausea*, making him unwisely promise a positive continuation, secondly (more understandable but artistically just as problematic), by the 'abstract heroism'[66] of his perception of the Resistance movement in which he cannot assume more than a very peripheral role, no matter how hard he tries. While it is true to say that his dramatic work as a whole is free from this structural abstractness, it would be quite wrong to see as the reason for it simply that here we are concerned with a novel—with 'prose which aims at the totalization of a singular and fictive temporalization'. It is the *type* of prose which is in question: one that resists the necessary condensation of characters and situations and thus tempts the author to intervene repeatedly, in the form of abstract rhetoric, in order to compensate by producing some 'philosophical condensation'. Prose showing affinity with Kafka, or with the works of E. Th. A. Hoffmann, as a much earlier example, would be a very different proposition. However, as things stand, the structure of *Roads to Freedom* opposes that 'calculated indetermination' which is so vital to the realization of the Sartrean project.

We find the exact opposite in *Huis Clos* (*No Exit*). Written in a fortnight in the Autumn of 1943 and first staged in Paris in May 1944 (and banned by the censor in England in September 1946), *Huis Clos* is a most suggestive 'pièce de circonstance'. The occasion that calls it into being is a friend's request for a play easy to stage, with few actors, by a travelling theatre company. And since Sartre wants to create roles of equal weight for his friends who are the principal actresses, he devises a situation in which they must remain together on the stage all the time. First he thinks of a bomb shelter, with its exits caved in, offering no escape. The time of writing is not far from the completion of *Being and Nothingness*,[67] and Sartre wants to explore in the medium of drama the conflict inherent in interpersonal relations, the threat to freedom represented by 'the other'. Thus the setting of a bomb shelter would, clearly, produce, a failure. Such a situation would offer at least as much room for the display of human solidarity and 'fusion' towards a shared end as for the intended manifestation of reciprocally paralysing enmity. Sartre's brilliant inspiration to locate the stage in *hell,* from which there can be no exit, turns the work into a masterpiece. Elevating a human situation of consuming conflict to the level of a *myth*—a myth in which the devastating negativity and all-consuming character of the conflict is intensified, to a degree inconceivable in whatever other form, by giving a dimension of *eternity* to destruction and consumption, which are normally paradigms of temporal limitation and determination, bringing things to a predictable end—Sartre creates a tangible intermediary in which the concerns of everyday life and some of the most fundamental dimensions of the structure of being converge. In such a medium of extreme condensation sentences like 'hell is the other' arise spontaneously from the situation, whereas they could be superimposed only in the form of abstract rhetoric in the medium of, say, *Roads to Freedom.* Calculated indetermination, graphic individuation, multiple layers of ambiguous meaning, condensation and over-determination, claustrophobic enclosure and its negation through the totality of being, constitute the hypnotic unity of movement and paralysis which characterizes *Huis Clos.* It is certainly *No Exit* for Inés, as well as for Estelle and Garcin; but many roads lead from it towards the realization of Sartre's project. It illustrates very well how much the very nature of his overall quest for what might appear at first sight as mere abstraction—the plentitude of being and the void of nothingness—brings with it forms of mediation through which even the most abstract ontological determinations can be conveyed as tangible manifestations of human destinies.

## Chapter 2

# PHILOSOPHY, LITERATURE, AND MYTH

## 1

THE IMPORTANCE of 'myth' is by no means confined to Sartre's conception of *Huis Clos*. He sees in the same terms *Bariona, Flies, The Trojan Women* and *Kean*, as well as *Lucifer and the Lord, Altona,* and others. Concerning Altona, which he describes as a kind of *Götterdämmerung* ('crépuscule des dieux'),[68] he stresses his aim as demystification through inflating its subject matter to the proportions of a myth.[69] And in a conversation with Kenneth Tynan he reveals that he would like to write a play on the Greek myth of Alcestis in such a way as to be able to condense into it the drama of women's liberation.[70]

Equally, he praises the works of his contemporaries in the same key. In an article entitled 'Forgers of myths—the young playwrights of France'[71] he singles out Anouilh's *Antigone,* Camus's *Caligula* and *Cross Purposes,* and Simone de Beauvoir's *Useless Mouths* as examples of the same approach to character and situation that animates his own plays. And twenty years later, in December 1966, he gives a lecture in Bonn with the title 'Myth and reality of the theatre' in which he counterposes the form of drama he stands for to the 'bourgeois realist theatre whose aim was the direct representation of reality'.[72] In the same spirit, shortly after his lecture he characterizes Georges Michel as a truly original playwright who succeeded in transcending realism through a 'deformation towards the myth',[73] sharply contrasting this with the abstract symbolism of Ionesco's *Rhinoceros*.

As we can see, ever since the time of writing *Bariona*—when Sartre reaches the conclusion that theatre must be a great collective religious experience—he remains consistent

41

to a conception of drama as myth. 'The function of the theatre is to present the individual under the form of myth'[74] says Sartre in an interview. And he reiterates the same point again and again, with variations in stress and with clarifications. He insists in the conversation with Tynan that the theatre must transpose all its problems into mythic form, and he spends much time clarifying his position in the interview given to *New Left Review:*

> For me the theatre is essentially a myth. Take the example of a petty-bourgeois and his wife who quarrel with each other the whole time. If you tape their disputes, you will record not only the two of them, but the petty-bourgeoisie and its world, what society has made of it, and so on. Two or three such studies and any possible novel on the life of a *petty-bourgeois couple* would be outclassed. By contrast, the relationship between *man and woman* as we see it in Strindberg's *Dance of Death* will never be outclassed. The subject is the same, but taken to the *level of myth*. The playwright presents to men the *eidos* of their daily existence: their own life in such a way that they see it as if externally. This was the genius of Brecht, indeed. Brecht would have protested violently if anyone said to him that his plays were myths. Yet what else is *Mother Courage*—an anti-myth that despite itself becomes a myth?[75]

It does not matter here that Sartre's assessment of the possibilities of the novel is highly debatable. What is important is the definition of myth in drama as 'the *eidos* of daily existence'. This makes it clear that the issue at stake transcends the limits of the theatre, and leads us right into the heart of Sartre's overall quest. Indeed, this is the key that opens not only the door of his literary vision but also of his conception of art in general, and beyond.

In an earlier essay on Giacometti, Sartre emphasizes the totality of this artist's vision, saying that his characters are 'complete wholes', arising fully made in an instant and 'gushing forth in my field of vision as an *idea* in my spirit'. He adds: 'only the idea possesses such immediate trans-lucidity, only the idea is in one blow all that it is'. Giacometti accomplishes 'the unity of multiplicity' as the 'indivisibility of an idea'.[76] His myth as *eidos* is not some mysterious, hidden absolute but the visible absolute, grasped as the 'unity of the *act*', in evidence as 'appearance in situation'.[77] Similar considerations are applied to the work of Masson, which is described as 'mythological in its essence' so that 'the project of painting does not distinguish itself from the project of being man'.[78] And there is no contradiction whatsoever between the concern with myth and the absolute on one hand and our historical predicament on the other. On the contrary, just like Giacometti, who grasps the absolute as 'appearance in situation' Masson's 'monstrous universe is nothing else than the comprehensive representation of our own universe'.[79] For the absolute cannot be taken hold of except precisely through the well defined temporality of human existence. 'How to make a man out of stone without petrifying him'—this is the great question for the sculptor. It is a question of 'everything or nothing'[80]—just like the question of literature, as we have seen above. This applies everywhere, even when the medium is not representational, like Calder's mobile constructions which 'traversed by an Idea' capture live movements and 'are, that's all; they are absolutes . . . strange beings, midway between matter and life'.[81]

2

From this brief survey of Sartre's conception of his own work as well as of the work of those he values highly it becomes clear that the crucial terms of reference are: myth, drama, absolute, idea, act, totality, conflict and situation. Philosophy fits organically into this picture.

> Today I think that philosophy is dramatic in nature. The time for contemplating the immobility of substances which are what they are, or for laying bare the laws underlying a succession of phenomena, is past. Philosophy is concerned with *man*—who is at once an agent and an actor, who produces and plays his drama while he lives the contradictions of his situation, until either his individuality is shattered or his conflicts are resolved. A play (be it

epic, such as Brecht's, or dramatic) is the most appropriate vehicle
today for showing *man* in action,—i.e. *man full stop*. It is with this
man that philosophy, from its own point of view, should be
concerned. That is why the theatre is philosophical and philosophy
dramatic.[82]

Thus philosophy is not abstract self-reflection and detached
contemplation but total involvement in the drama of being.
The 'project' is concerned with choice and 'original choice'
is 'absolutely' the same as 'destiny'.[83] Exploring 'human
destiny'[84] at its greatest intensity is not confined to Sartre's
plays but characterizes all his synthesizing attempts, from a
general definition of contemporary European culture as only
one aspect of a much greater problem, 'the whole destiny of
Europe',[85] to his fundamental works on philosophy. Both
*Being and Nothingness* and *Critique of Dialectical Reason*
are centrally concerned with conflict as inherent in the
ontological structure of being as manifest in human destiny.
The same drama is indicated in Sartre's definition of the core
of his moral philosophy, structured around a fundamental
antinomy:

> In the choice I make of my freedom, the freedom of others is
> reclaimed. But when I find myself on the plane of action, I am
> compelled to treat the other as means and not as end. Here we are
> evidently in the presence of an antinomy, but it is precisely this
> antinomy which constitutes the moral problem. I shall examine this
> antinomy in my *Morale*.[86]

The fact that after 2,000 pages of examination Sartre remains
dissatisfied with the solutions he arrives at and abandons the
project does not mean that he changes his mind about the
fundamental underlying drama, but, on the contrary, that he
finds it even more overpowering than originally thought, as
the evidence of his later work clearly shows.

The conflict and drama in question is not the quarrel
between the petty-bourgeois and his wife: philosophy and
theatre in his view do not operate at that level. The drama of
philosophy is the same as that which makes him conclude

that plays are the most appropriate vehicle today for showing man in action: 'man full stop'. The difference is that while philosophy, being a discursive form, can address itself *directly* to the fundamental question of being, theatre, a representational form, must proceed *indirectly,* through the presentation of individuals under the form of a myth, and thus producing an adequate artistic *mediation* between sensible reality and the most general determinations of being. They are similar in that they represent the highest level of synthesis or 'condensation', and thus they get the closest to the heart of being. This is why drama, in its Sartrean conception, is the most appropriate—in Hegel's term the most *representative*—literary form today; and is why philosophy, if it wants to be relevant, must be dramatic.

3

Naturally, philosophy and drama do not comprehend everything. More precisely, they cannot take hold of all levels of the human totality. In fact, according to Sartre, the sphere of 'singular individuality'[87] is beyond their reach. 'Philosophy is dramatic but it does not study the individual as such'.[88] Nor does drama, for that matter. Consequently, if Sartre wants to study Flaubert as an individual, he cannot do it in drama, nor in philosophy. We have seen his definition of the novel as the totalization of a singular and fictive temporalization. Accordingly, he could tackle this task in the form of a novel, incorporating as best he can all the available factual evidence needed for a satisfactory totalization of the singularity of a *historical* individual. The consequence of this approach would be an inevitable overflow of the factual documentary material and a tendency to subdue the novelistic elements. Alternatively he could proceed from the available material and fill in the gaps as they appear with the novelist's imagination. Paradoxically, the more he seeks to present a total portrait, the more inadequate the documentary evidence must appear, and consequently the more the fictional elements will tend to predominate. Thus, he either abandons full portrayal, or accepts its consequences for the nature of his work. This dilemma is expressed in the curious answer he gives to the question: 'Why have you personally stopped writing novels?'

> Because I have felt no urge to do so. Writers have always more or less chosen the imaginary. They have a need for a certain ration of fiction. Writing on Flaubert is enough for me by way of fiction—it might indeed be called a novel. Only I would like people to say that it was a *true novel*. I try to achieve a certain level of comprehension of Flaubert by means of hypotheses. Thus I use fiction—guided and controlled, but nonetheless fiction—to explore why, let us say, Flaubert wrote one thing on the 15th March and the exact opposite on the 21st March, to the same correspondent, without worrying about the contradiction. My hopotheses are in this sense a sort of invention of the personage. [89]

The beginning of the answer—which is simply 'I don't feel like it'—gives way to a redefinition of fiction in general, leading to the conclusion that his Flaubert, in the course of his kind of totalization, turned out to be an 'invented personage' and thus a form of novel or fiction.

All this is inherent not in some *a priori* determination of the relationship between philosophy and drama, and philosophy and fiction in general, but in their characteristically Sartrean conception. The crucial determining factor is the conception of his overall quest into which everything is integrated with great vigour. In this vision the overriding determinations are *levels of generality*—dramatic philosophy and philosophical theatre at one pole and the totalization of individuality at the other—and this tends to blur the lines of demarcation between the discursive and the representational forms in Sartre's work. There are three clearly distinguishable forms of manifestation of this tendency:

1. In his shorter essays—for example, on Giacometti,

Nizan, Merleau-Ponty, Gorz's *Traitor*—discursive and representational forms are often fused in lyric passages and in a conscious effort to give an *evocative unity,* a forceful *Gestalt,* to the essay as a whole, no matter how abstract the problems tackled in particular contexts.

2. Representational elements abound in his major philosophical works (e.g. the treatment of 'bad faith' in *Being and Nothingness*), and philosophical elements in his plays and novels.

3. Perhaps the most significant: fictional totalization tends to turn into philosophical discourse, to the point of forcing him to abandon it (see *Roads to Freedom,* especially the fourth volume), and his most important critical monograph, on Flaubert (and this is by no means the only one) tends to turn into fiction.

These characteristics cannot be isolated from the innermost nature of Sartre's totalizing quest. For the concern with singular universality cannot stop at that level but must strive through totalization towards universality or the 'absolute', whatever formal transformations may necessarily follow from such movement. On the other hand, the Sartrean absolute is not some rarefied abstraction occupying a mysterious sphere of its own, but is existentially situated and therefore must always be rendered tangible through the evocative power of condensation and individuation at the writer's disposal. This is why, despite his boundless admiration for Kafka, the latter's fictional style and method of representation, with its hidden yet threateningly mysterious omnipresent absolute, constitute an altogether different universe of discourse which cannot conceivably be adopted by Sartre as the model of his novels.

Problematical as some of the formal characteristics of Sartre's work may at times appear, they are necessary manifestations of his overall vision in particular contexts, and thus cannot be properly weighed up without comprehending the nature of the whole. Significantly enough, his closely integrated conception of philosophy and literature appears at a very early age. The same year that he writes the letter contributing to the student enquiry (1929) he also conceives *The Legend of Truth*:[90] a strange mixture of philosophy, myth and literature of which only a fragment has been published. It is a kind of 'Urnebel' (the Kantian 'primeval fog') from which the later creations emerge, through manifold differentiations and metamorphoses. What is clearly in evidence from the very beginning is that for Sartre '*form* and *meaning* are always linked',[91] indeed in an organic fashion. The overall configuration of meaning determines the form, and the articulation of form carries with it the concrete definition of meaning.

The not very happy symbiosis of *The Legend of Truth* soon gives way to the primarily philosophical or predominantly literary works of the 1930s, without completely abolishing the reciprocal interpenetration. Nevertheless Sartre feels that there are certain things in his overall quest which are 'too technical' and therefore prescribe a 'purely philosophical vocabulary', and he promises to 'double up, so to speak, every novel with an essay'.[92] This is still a rather naive diagnosis of the problem, characteristic of the avid learner of the new philosophical vocabulary of German phenomenology and existentialism. Once he has behind him this period of learning and succeeds in elaborating his own vocabulary, he soon discovers not only that there can be no 'doubling-up' between philosophy and novels, except for a short transitory period, but also that the real affinity for him is between philosophy and theatre, not between philosophy and fiction. Furthermore, in the course of articulating his original philosophical concepts in *Being and Nothingness* he realizes that they need not—indeed cannot—be kept in separate compartments, but call for the unity of philosophy and literature in the service of his monumental quest for man. Already *Being and Nothingness* is unthinkable without his conscious appeal to the idea of such a unity.

4

The specificity of Sartre's work cannot be understood without focusing attention on the network of terms and usages he introduces in the course of his development. They constitute a coherent set of closely interconnected concepts, each with its own 'field of radiation' and points of link-up with all the others. This is obvious if we think of such examples as 'authenticity', 'anguish', 'bad faith', 'the spirit of seriousness', 'contingency', 'nausea', 'viscosity', 'facticity', 'negation', 'nihilation', 'freedom', 'project', 'commitment' ('engagement'), 'possibilities', 'responsibility', 'flight', 'adventure', 'chance', 'determination', 'seriality', 'fused group', 'temporalization', 'totalization', 'detotalization', 'condensation', 'overdetermination', 'mediation', 'progression-regression', 'singular universal', 'irreducibility', and so on. However, we are talking about an omnipresent characteristic which comes to the fore even in the most unsuspected places and forms. Whether it is a direct confrontation of a major philosophical issue or of an apparently everday matter, Sartre's terms of analysis and evaluation are always typically his own, and from any particular point of detail they link up with the main supporting pillars of his thought structure. Take the term 'invention'. Talking about the intellectual, of his 'vain yearning for universality', he makes his point like this:

> I remember seeing a puppy after the partial removal of the cerebellum. He moved across the room, rarely colliding with the furniture, but he had become thoughtful. He established his itinerary carefully. He pondered before going around an object, requiring a great deal of time and thought to accomplish movements to which he had previously paid no attention. In the language of the time, we said that the cortex had assumed for him certain functions of the lower regions. He was an intellectual dog. I don't know whether this made him very useful or harmful to his kind, but we can quite well imagine that he had lost what Genet, another exile, has so well named, 'sweet natal confusion'. To sum up, he either had to die or reinvent the dog.

So we others—rats without cerebella—we are also so made that
we must either die or reinvent man. Moreover, we know perfectly
well that man will make himself without us, through working and
fighting, that our models become obsolete from one day to the next,
that nothing will remain of them in the finished product, not even a
bone, but that also, without us, the fabrication would take place in
the dark, by tinkering and patching, if we, the 'debrained', were not
there to repeat constantly that we must work according to
principles, that it is not a matter of mending, but of measuring and
constructing, and finally, that mankind will be the concrete
universal, or that it will not be. [93]

To suggest that the dog 'reinvents the dog' is, of course,
most unusual, to say the least. And yet it does not matter in
the slightest whether or not Sartre's description would
match an objective scientific account. For the point is not
about the dog but about man who has to be 'reinvented'.
And, again, 'invention-reinvention' is by no means the term
that would most naturally present itself in the context. But,
is the idea less unusual than the term of which Sartre avails
himself to convey it? How can one 'reinvent' man without
falling into extreme voluntarism? Obviously one cannot if
the term is taken in its literal sense, but that is not how it is
intended. Nor is it intended as a poetic image. The meaning
is conceptual, not figurative. But it is conceptual in the
sense of the earlier discussed totalizing 'condensation-
overdetermination,' that is it derives its full meaning from
the multiplicity of structural-contextual interconnections. It
would be relatively easy to find some terms that could
express in a more literal and univocal form the central idea of
the passage on 'reinvention'. But at what price? It would
mean not only the loss of the writer's characteristic style, but
of a great deal of the meaning as well. Sartre deliberately
chooses a term which keeps the central idea somewhat 'out
of focus', in order to bring a multiplicity of allusions and
connections into a *joint focus*. For the depth as well as the
field of radiation of any particular concept is determined by
the totality of interconnections it can summon up whenever
it appears on its own. The difference between a profound

thinker and a shallow one is that the former always operates with a whole network of organically interpenetrating concepts, whereas the latter contents himself with isolated terms and one-sided definitions. Thus the first establishes connections even when he has to single out specific contexts and draw lines of demarcation, while the second loses even the most obvious connections when he sacrifices complexity to analytical percision and to the univocal clarity of oversimplification in place of overdetermination.

Let us consider briefly the field of Sartre's concept of 'invention'. We have already quoted one of the contexts in which he suggests that 'The reader invents us: he uses our words to set his own traps for himself.'[94] This is not paradox for the sake of paradox. It underlines a firm belief that 'inventing' is not a sovereign activity, carried out from a safe distance, but a complex relationship of being inside and outside simultaneously, like man who makes and reinvents himself by being both at one with his own projects and at some distance from them. (As we can see, the idea of *distance* is an integral part of these considerations, both as it appears in Sartre's discussion of Giacometti and in his references to Brecht's vision of the simultaneity of inside and outside achieved through his *Verfremdungseffect*.) Talking about Genet, Sartre brings another aspect into the foreground. 'Genius is not a gift but an outcome one invents in desperate situations.'[95] Here invention is response to a situation in which everything seems to be lost—it is like the sudden leap and escape of the cornered animal above the head of its pursuers. Similarly, authentic feelings, essential to the production of good literature, are not just 'given, in advance: every one must invent them in his turn'.[96] Thus, again paradoxically, the spontaneity of authentic feeling is an 'invented spontaneity'. Nor is this an isolated instance. The liberation of Paris in 1944 is described as 'the explosion of freedom, the rupture of the established order and the invention of an efficacious and spontaneous order'.[97] We are thus presented with invention as a fusion of negativity and positivity: 'invented discipline' triumphs over 'learned discipline', and Apocalypse is defined as 'a spontaneous organization of the revolutionary forces', foreshadowing a central problem of Sartre's *Critique of Dialectical Reason*. Invention is the key term also when, in 1947, he speaks about the need to 'invent the road to a socialist Europe'[98] in order to secure humanity's survival. And in 1968, appealing for 'Power to the imagination', he recalls that 'in 1936 [the working class] invented the occupation of factories because that was its only weapon to consolidate and to exploit its electoral victory'.[99] In a similar vein, he talks about the task of 'inventing a university whose aim is no longer the selection of an elite but the transfer of culture to all'.[100]

One could go on giving further examples from different fields of Sartre's thought, from his ontology to his theory of language, but there is no need. The instances we have seen so far are amply sufficient to indicate the nature of the conceptual interconnections earlier referred to. Linking 'invention' to a paradox is not a formal stylistic device but a recognition of objective constraint, to be transcended by the act of invention which itself is the paradoxical result of such constraint. (A 'cunning of history' against its own determinations, if you like.) Thus freedom and order, discipline and spontaneity, negation and self-affirmation, etc., are brought into play as necessary dimensions of invention as a human enterprise. All these dimensions must be simultaneously recalled, by means of the 'condensation' of a multiplicity of interrelations into a joint focus, in order to be able to link the part to the whole and thus to confer upon it its full significance. This is how, starting out from Sartre's invention of the dog which 'reinvents the dog', we arrive at the roots of the human enterprise: man 'reinventing man' and thus producing the 'concrete universal'.

But we must note not only the structure of conceptual interconnections but also its 'sign': not unproblematically positive attainment but prevalent *negativity*. For the way in which 'invention' articulates itself through its linkages is dominated by distance and constraint, determination and anguish from which 'invention' extricates itself only for an ecstatic moment. In such moments, when 'freedom explodes' and 'imagination assumes power' (or 'genius' commutes a man's death sentence into his life-imprisonment as a writer), the ecstatic fusion of human interchange manifests itself as the doomed temporality of 'Apocalypse which is always defeated by order'[101]—by the 'established order', that is, to which 'invented discipline' and 'spontaneous order' do not seem to be able to provide a lasting answer. This is why in the end the positive moment of invention cannot be envisaged by Sartre except as a radical negation of the powers of alienation and negativity. Thus positivity appears only on the distant horizon, in the form of a passionate 'ought'. The inventive task of 'making humanity' is spelled out 'not as the *construction* of a system (be it the socialist system) but as the *destruction* of all systems'.[102]

## 5

It is necessary to introduce here another complex of problems: Sartre's conception of *temporality* as one of the most fundamental constituents of his system of ideas, determining the articulation of many of his specific concerns.

In a very early piece on 'L'Art, cinématographique' (1931),[103] Sartre contrasts the temporality of science—its conception of irreversible order and absolutely determining march forward, which would be unbearable as a feeling if it went with all our actions—with the sudden movements and spontaneous manifestations of life perceived by the individual. He suggests that the arts of movement (music, theatre, cinema) have the task of representing this irreversible order 'outside us, painted in things'. He talks about the 'fatality' of musical progression in the melody; of tragedy's 'forced march towards the catastrophe', and of a kind of

fatality also in the cinema. He characterizes music as
abstraction and tragedy as 'strongly intellectual . . . a
product of reason . . . a logical deduction starting from
certain principles proposed right at the beginning'. While the
unfolding of action in the cinema too is described as 'fatal', it
is contrasted with the theatre in that it has not got the
'abstract and cut time of the tragedy'. According to Sartre, it
is the cinema which represents 'by nature the civilization of
our epoch'. Cinema is the art form which is 'the closest to
the real world' which captures best the 'inhuman necessity'
of the *durée* of our life, and teaches us 'the poetry of speed
and of the machines, the inhumanity and splendid fatality of
industry'. What saves the cinema from the abstract and cut
time of the theatre as well as from its intellectualism is its
*simultaneity* and *overimpression* (or *overprinting,*
'surimpression'—the predecessor of Sartre's concept of
'overdetermination). He refers to Abel Gance's *Napoleon*
in which the imagery of a 'tempest at the Convention' is
intensified by the scenes of a tempest on the Mediter-
ranean. The two themes are cut into each other in such a way
that they 'accuse and enlarge themselves and in the end they
fuse with one another'. Just as in Giacometti, the
particular themes do not convey their meaning individually
but only if they are taken together in a combined unity.
Thanks to the formal characteristic of 'overimpression' the
artist can 'develop several themes simultaneously' and
thus achieve a 'cinematographic polyphony'.

Many points of this analysis are changed in the course of
Sartre's subsequent development. Yet, the enrichment and
concretization of his views proceeds from the concepts first
spelled out in this article. As he discovers the theatre for
himself through his own practice, he changes his views on
'abstract time' and 'intellectualism' as necessarily inherent
in all theatre. That is to say, in the light of his own dramatic
work he identifies the intellectual type of drama with a
certain form of classical tradition which he continues to
oppose. Talking about *Flies* he insists that he aims at

creating 'the tragedy of *freedom* in opposition to the tragedy of *fatality*'.[104] Also, he retains his aversion to intellectualism when he criticizes Orson Welles's film, *Citizen Kane*, as 'an intellectual work, the work of an intellectual',[105] which shows that the affirmation of spontaneity is a 'Leitmotif' of his work, from its earliest inception. And in terms of formal criteria, he retains and expands the idea of simultaneity linked to 'overimpression' (overdetermination) and the polyphony of integrated multiplicity (condensation and joint focus), as we have seen.

But this is as far as we can go in identifying similarities. Sartre's 'tragedy of freedom' is inconceivable on the basis of his youthful conception of temporality and causation, since it accepts necessity and fatality as the guiding principle of all three art forms he refers to. Consequently the characteristics of simultaneity and polyphony can only soften the blow; they cannot transcend the fundamental determination and limits of fatality. Characteristically, he has to ask us to admire cinema's *inflexible but supple* concatenation ('enchainement inflexible, mais souple'),[106] which is not much more than a consolation prize in the form of a verbal-paradoxical 'solution'. *Ex pumice aquam*—one cannot squeeze spontaneity and freedom out of fatality by calling it 'supple'.

We can witness in Sartre's youthful article on the cinema a tension between his passionate adherence to spontaneity, the surprise of life, and the acceptance of a conception of temporarility as absolute concatenation in the world around us (which inevitably means that the cinema, 'closest to the real world', representing 'real man in a real countryside', 'real mountains and real sea',[107] etc., is essentially trapped and only marginally free). This is a fertile tension because it is not simply a conflict of ideas but a contradiction between a restrictive theory and an existential striving towards freedom. In order to extricate himself from this contradiction he has to get rid of Bergson—whose 'liberté intérieure', with its evasion of the question of 'destiny', is, as

Sartre later recognizes, an illusory freedom, remaining always merely theoretical and intellectual',[108] but not real (existential)—and elaborate a conception of temporality in affinity with his own quest.

This new conception of temporality is clearly formulated in an essay on Faulkner, written in 1939, in which Sartre analyses *The Sound and the Fury*,[109] concentrating on the question of time. The contrast between affective (emotional) and intellectual order of time found in the youthful essay is recognized in Faulkner's novel as treated in favour of the affective order, to Sartre's great satisfaction. What bothers him is the absence of the future. 'Nothing happens, everything has already happened . . . the present is only . . . *past future*' (p 68). 'Proust and Faulkner have simply decapitated time, they removed its future, that is the dimension of acts and of freedom'.[110] The way Quentin's suicide is treated shows that he has no 'human possibilities'; what we are confronted with is not 'a human enterprise, it is *fatality*'.[111] The whole problem hinges on the future: 'If the future is real, time moves away from the past and brings nearer the future; but if you suppress the future, time is nothing but what separates, that which cuts off the present from itself'.[112] But is it true, asks Sartre, that human time is devoid of future? The temporality of the nail, of a lump of earth, of the atom, is '*perpetual present*. But man, is he a thinking nail?' Faulkner, in accordance with his vision of time, represents man as a creature 'deprived of possibilities'. He defines man as 'the sum of all that he has'.[113] To this Sartre opposes his own definition of man as 'the totality of all that he does not yet have, of all that he could have'.[114]

In *History and Class Consciousness* (1923), Lukács analyses 'possible consciousness' as the consciousness of a historically progressive class which has a future ahead of it and therefore has the possibility of objective totalization. In our epoch, according to Lukács, only the proletariat has proper temporality, inseparable from the possibility of socio-historical totalization, for the bourgeoisie has lost its future—its temporality, as Sartre puts it about Proust and Faulkner, has been 'decapitated'—in that its fundamental aims as a class are radically incompatible with the objective tendencies of historical development. Given this fundamental contradiction between aim and reality, the class without future cannot realize the 'unity of subject and object' but must, instead, produce a dualistic-antinomous structure of thought, centred around individualism and subjectivity, and dominated by the conditions of 'reification' which it can oppose only in and through subjectivity, thus exacerbating the contradiction between subject and object. Heidegger, facing the Lukácsian problematic, proposes a 'solution' by transcending Lukács towards his youthful essay, 'The metaphysics of tragedy' (1910) published in the volume *Soul and Form,* in which nearly two decades before Heidegger Lukács had spelled out some of the central themes of modern existentialism.[115] Heidegger offers a conception of temporality which *ascribes possibility* (projection towards the future ultimately identified with death, in the spirit of 'The metaphysics of tragedy') to *consciousness in general.* Thus, by turning possibility into an ontological dimension of *consciousness as such,* Lukács's Marxian critique of bourgeois class consciousness is theoretically liquidated, and a project of unified ontology is announced, on the basis of the Heideggerian reconstruction of subjectivity. Significantly, however, the project is never brought to its conclusion. And twenty-five years after publishing *Being and Time*—originally intended as the founding preliminary to the overall project—Heidegger is forced to make an admission: 'While the previous editions have borne the designation "First Half", this has now been deleted. After a quarter of a century, the second half could no longer be added unless the first were to be presented anew'.[116] This sounds very reasonable, except that no reasons are given for the failure to complete, not just in twenty-five years but ever since, the whole project. Clearly we are not concerned with Heidegger's Nazism—which is more like a consequence than the cause—but with the nature of the project itself: the extreme subjectivism of its temporality and being. *Ex pumice aquam*—one cannot squeeze the foundation of being out of a mythically inflated subjectivity by calling it 'Fundamental ontology'.

Sartre adopts some elements of Heidegger's conception when he writes: 'The nature of consciousness implies that it throws itself forward by itself into the future . . . it determines itself in its present being by its own possibilities: this is what Heidegger calls "the silent force of the possible" '.[117] At the same time, right from the beginning, he goes well beyond Heidegger, putting the German philosopher to his own use. Proceeding from his own existential quest for freedom and spontaneity, he finds support in Heidegger's conception of temporality against fatality and inertia. But this is only the *negative* side of his overall view. The positive aspect is clearly exemplified in a beautiful concluding passage of the essay on Faulkner.

> How comes it that Faulkner and so many other authors have chosen an absurdity which is so little in character with the novel, and so little true? I believe we have to look for reasons in the social conditions of our presentday life. It seems to me that Faulkner's despair precedes his metaphysics: for him, as for us all, the *future is barred.* Evertything we see, everything we live through, incites us to say: 'It cannot last', and meanwhile change isn't even conceivable except in the form of a *cataclysm.* We live in the epoch of *impossible revolutions,* and Faulkner employs his extraordinary artistry to describe this world which is dying of old age, and our suffocation. I love his art, and I don't believe in his metaphysics: *a barred future is still a future.*[118]

The phrase 'a barred future is still a future' (which becomes the model of many a Sartrean paradox, like 'refusal to commit oneself is a form of commitment', or 'failure to choose is itself a choice') does not mean much, if anything, in and by itself. What breathes life into this abstract formal tautology is the context (or situation) into which it is inserted. The subjectivism of the Heideggerian conception of temporality helps him negate the 'barred future' of an epoch torn by the inherent contradiction of the necessity of change and the impossibility of revolutions. Yet—and this is what decides the issue—the whether or not of 'impossible revolutions' is a question of *real temporality* which is being decided in the *actual* socio-historical arena. Thus while the abstract temporality of 'a barred future is still a future' negates the real temporality of social inertia (determined by the temporal-historical conditions of alienation and reification), this subjectivist temporality of *abstract possibility* is also being negated by the *real possibility* of actual revolutions.

Heideggerian purists would no doubt describe the way Sartre inserts the adopted concepts into the context seen above as 'eclecticism'. In fact, such 'eclecticism' constitutes Sartre's exemplary originality and philosophical significance. He succeeds in freeing himself of the tension manifest in his youthful conception of temporality by acquiring a much greater tension. The latter is not only much greater but it is incomparably more fertile as well. From now on, even if he does not yet know it (perceiving change in his own development as commitment initiated by the war) he is situated right in the turmoil of real temporality which he cannot just contemplate from the sideline, from the 'temporalité intérieure' of literary withdrawal. Indeed, his act of commitment during the war becomes possible within the framework of this new conception and intensified existential tension which are suitable to provide the basis of articulating a rich lifework. For without the changed framework he might well respond to the inhumanity of the war and the fatality of falling bombs in terms of the same decadent aestheticism of 'interiority' with which he once raved about the 'poetry of speed, of the machines' and about the 'inhumanity and splendid fatality of industry'. But 'cataclysm' arrives and is followed by upheavals and revolutions—some unfinished, others defeated, others still

partially successful, or delayed, frustrated, brutally inter-
fered with, but all painfully real. Could it be that they all
should have no major consequences for the other side of the
contradiction locked up in Sartre's new existential tension?
Hardly, as his subsequent development clamorously
proves.

6

This is not the point to anticipate Sartre's later development,
but to lay bare the structure of his thought as the inner
necessity that constitutes a vital condition of such development. In this sense, we have to indicate another fundamental
dimension: the way in which Sartre becomes a moral
philosopher *malgré lui*. The problem arises out of the
characterization of the present as an *inert totality:* a world
dying of old age, an epoch of 'impossible revolutions',
spreading and intensifying the feeling of paralysis even
through the consciousness of 'cataclysm' as the only feasible
form of change. How can the abstract proposition of 'barred
future is still a future' effectively negate such gloom and
doom? Only if it is turned into a categorical absolute which
necessarily transcends all given temporality, no matter how
suffocatingly real. And who is the subject of this 'barred
future'? If it is the individual, the proposition is clearly false,
because barred future for the individual is inexorably
*barred.* On the other hand, if the subject is mankind, the
proposition is absurd, because mankind cannot possibly
have a 'barred future' except by barring it for itself in the
form of a collective suicide, in which case there is no future,
barred or unbarred—nor indeed mankind, for that matter.
Paradoxically, the existential (non-tautological) meaning of
the proposition is produced by *conflating* the individual and
the collective subject. Its meaning is thus not what it literally
suggests (a tautology or a banality at best), but the functional
meaning of a *radical negation* which cannot point at tangible
historical forces as carriers of its truth and therefore must

assume the form of a categorical imperative: the *moral ought*.

This dimension of Sartre's structure of thought, as inextricably linked to the question of individual and collective subject, remains a fundamental characteristic of his work throughout his development. Not that there can be no changes in this respect for the rest of his life, for there are many. The point is that such changes as they arise must always affect this whole set of relations, notably the problems of temporality and morality as articulated in terms of subject and object, the individual and the collective subject. These problems are discussed at length in chapter 6 (Volume Two); here the point is simply to stress the necessary interconnection between Sartre's conception of temporality and the paradoxical *specificity* of his moral philosophy. The truth is that the latter is not an explicit but a *latent* moral philosophy—and it remains so no matter how hard he tries in some unfinished (unfinishable) manuscripts to turn it into an explicit one. To some extent it resembles his writing lyric poetry: he cannot write it because he does write it—in a diffuse form—*all the time*. It is inherent in all his analyses, as the positive standpoint of the future which assumes the form of a radical negation while it is unable to identify itself with a historical subject. In the specific works which he is forced to abandon his attempts at rendering explicit his moral principles are necessarily frustrated because he tries to accomplish the task while remaining within the confines of his phenomenological-existential ontology, which renders redundant such explicitness.

Paradoxically, in order to remain a moral philosopher his moral philosophy must remain latent. In order to spell out his latent moral philosophy in a fully developed form, as he tries to again and again, he would have substantially to modify the structure of his philosophy as a whole, including the function of the categorical moral ought in it. But such modification would radically displace—indeed, possibly render superfluous—precisely the moral ought in the

structure of his thought. Thus he could produce his *Morale*
only by ceasing to be a moral philosopher at all. This
explains why, curiously, his conscious efforts aimed at
transcending his earlier posititions result in their strongest
possible reaffirmation as the necessary precondition of the
'impossible enterprise' he is involved in: the deduction of a
socially oriented moral philosophy from the ontological
structure of individual praxes. No text is nearer to his
original system as spelled out in *Being and Nothingness* than
'Determination and freedom', a lecture delivered twenty-
three years later, in May 1966, at the Gramsci Institute in
Rome, and part of a substantial recent manuscript on his
*Morale*. It could be inserted into the pages of the early work
without too much difficulty. By the same token, if he wants
to transcend some of his earlier positions, he has to do it
'without really trying'. That is, he has to transcend through
expansion, by bringing into the picture new ontological
structures—as indeed he does, in *Critique of Dialectical
Reason*—which objectively *imply* a certain supersession,
even if he does not spell it out in what is intended again as a
first volume. This means that the old and new structures
must be left side by side, without integration. For as soon as
the task of integration is attempted, in the second volume or
in some related work, the inherent difficulty of moving from
latency to explicitness presents itself with renewed intensity, and we are back to the world of *Being and Nothingness*
through the route of 'Determination and freedom'.

We can see, then, how right Sartre is when he
characterizes his concern with morality as his 'dominant
preoccupation'. With one necessary qualification. This
concern enters his horizon *malgré lui*, in a paradoxical form,
via his definition of temporality and transcendence as
opposed to his earlier conception. Up to the time of writing
'L'Art cinématographique', and for a few years thereafter,
there can be no room for morality in his world of sheltered
'interiority' which laughs off man's concern with Good and
Evil as 'useless ideology' and aesthetically reconciles itself

with the 'splendid fatality' of capitalist inhumanity, without realizing the enormity of such pronouncements. Thus when Paul Nizan, his closest friend, notes while reviewing *Nausea*[119] that Sartre's thought is 'entirely alien to moral problems', he is correct in characterizing an early phase in Sartre's development, although it is highly debatable whether one should include *Nausea* in it. (Nizan is no doubt influenced by the memory of their college discussions.) In any case, it is a very limited phase. By the time *Nausea* is published, it is certainly over, thanks to Sartre's investigation of the nature of emotion and imagination, and thanks to his radical redefinition of temporality.

7

Sartre's network of concepts constitutes an amazingly coherent whole in which the particular elements are organically linked. The way he uses 'invention', for instance, might appear at times rather subjective, perhaps even capricious, so long as it is not related to the conceptual framework as a whole. But as soon as we become aware of the related concepts, as we have seen above, the one-sided impression of subjectivity disappears. The Sartrean concept of invention would indeed seem extremely voluntaristic and utterly futile even within his own youthful vision of temporality. Not so in his later conception. Once the fatality of absolute determination and irreversible concatenation is banished from his picture, 'invention' and 'imagination' can come into their own and acquire a major importance in his system of ideas. Conversely, too, his preoccupation with the *Imagination* and *L'Imaginaire* (translated into English as *The Psychology of Imagination*) greatly contributes to the elaboration of his conception of temporality.

'Past' becomes associated with the 'intellectual order'—a sombre condition, 'without surprise', ruled by the one-sided causality of concatenation—with inertia, lifelessness, despair. 'In *Citizen Kane* the game is over. We are not involved in a novel but in a story in the past tense . . . Everything is analysed, dissected, presented in the intellectual order, in a false disorder which is the subordination of events to the rule of causes; everything is dead.'[120] The same goes for Zola with whom 'everything obeys the narrowest kind of determinism. Zola's books are written from the past, while my characters have a future'.[121] And when he realizes that the future is locked out from some of his own works, he does not hesitate to condemn them. Talking about *Men Without Shadows* (*Morts sans sépulture*: 'Unburied Dead') he insists that 'It is a failed play . . . the destiny of the victims is absolutely determined in advance . . . The cards are already on the table. It is a very sombre play, without surprise'.[122] Similarly with volume IV of *Roads to Freedom*, which he abandons. Simone de Beauvoir echoes Sartre's own strictures and imagery of gambling when she comments: 'For his heroes, at the end of *Drôle d'amitié* [the chapter published from volume IV] the game is over'.[123] It is the future that gets his approval, expressed with great consistency in the positive connotation of its field of associated concepts, from 'hope' and 'authenticity' to 'surprise' and 'life', and from the 'affective order' (the opposite of 'intellectual order') to 'dialectical totalization' which brings to life the object of its synthesis, instead of dissecting it on the mortuary table of analysis for the sake of analysis.

Of course, as has been stressed repeatedly, we are talking about a unique fusion of subjectivity and objectivity. Sartre makes no claims to 'scientific objectivity'. His network of concepts aims as much at evoking as at situating and explaining. Yet, his fused 'subjective' objectivity is infinitely more objective than the pretended 'objectivity' of academic jargon. Knowing only too well that we are always within the parameters of man's fundamental quest, he does not simply 'observe' and 'describe', he *participates* and *moves* at the same time as he *demonstrates*. His way has nothing in common with the pseudo-scientific 'objectivity' of socially insensitive academic jargon that resembles the enzymes of the digestive system which turn everything that comes their way invariably into the same sort of end-product.

Sartre's conceptual framework is radically different. It is more like a sensitive dual prism which collects from all directions the lightwaves of the epoch of which he is an exemplary witness. He breaks up the received impressions into their constituents through the dual prism of his compelling personality only to resynthesize them in *his* totalizing vision that powerfully *re-enters* the world from which it is taken. 'To show and to move at the same time' from the standpoint of the *future*—that is his aim. This implies being simultaneously outside and inside and explains why he needs the combined powers of philosophy, literature, and 'myth'. 'I'd like that the public should see our century, this strange thing, from *outside,* as a witness. And that, at the same time everyone should *participate,* for this century is made by the public'.[124] Sartre takes his full share in making this century, by attacking its fetishes and increasing its self-awareness. It is this character of participating testimony, creative and revealing commitment to a total involvement, which gives his lifework its philosophical depth and its dramatic intensity.

*Chapter 3*
# FROM 'THE LEGEND OF TRUTH' TO A 'TRUE LEGEND':
## Phases of Sartre's development
### 1

BEING simultaneously outside and inside is also the task of a biographer, as Sartre himself clearly demonstrates on more than one occasion (Baudelaire, Mallarmé, Genet, Flaubert). Writing on someone is a specific relationship between two distinct 'singular temporalizations' in which sometimes affinities, sometimes elements of contrast predominate. In the case of Flaubert, it is primarily the contrast that attracts Sartre's attention: 'Flaubert represents for me the exact opposite of my own conception of literature: a total disengagement and a certain idea of form, which is not that which I admire . . . he began to fascinate me precisely because I saw him in every way as the contrary of myself'.[125] On other occasions (for example when writing on Mallarmé and on Genet), major affinities are in the foreground. But whether confrontations or affinities set the tone, the job of revealing exploration cannot be properly done without combining the viewpoints of 'inside' and 'outside': the sympathetic understanding of inner motivations, however sharp the contrasts, and the forward drive of critical transcendence, however close the affinities.

Writing on someone is connecting two socio-historically different 'temporalizations', even when Lenin writes about Marx. Such an enterprise sets out from the premise that the first is meaningful for the second, provided that the process of exploration—which is at the same time also a form of clarifying self-reflection—can mediate to the present those features of the original temporalization which objectively contribute to the solution of given tasks and problems. Reflection on the past can only proceed from the meaning the present gives itself—very much in the spirit of the

66

Sartrean 'projection' towards the future: that is, towards the solution of the existing tasks—but the very act of reflection, in virtue of establishing determinate relationships with the past, inevitably also determines its own orientation. Thus reflection and critical exploration become self-reflection and critical self-definition. The meaning of the present is used as a key to unlock the meaning of the past leading to the present, which in its turn unlocks formerly unidentified dimensions of the present leading to the future not in the form of rigid mechanical determinations but as anticipations of aims linked to a set of inner motivations. Thus we are involved in a dialectic movement which leads from the present to the past and from the past to the future. In this movement the past is not somewhere *there,* in its remote finality and 'closure', but right *here,* 'open' and situated between the present and the future, paradoxical as it may sound to those who think in terms of the 'intellectual order' of mechanical chronology. For the fact is that the present can only have one mediation between itself and the future: not the infinitesimal empty moment that separates it from what lies ahead, but the great wealth and intensity of a past brought to life in the expounded time of searching reflection and critical self-examination.

History is thus not simply unalterable but inexhaustible. This is what gives sense to being concerned with the past, and determines the need for constant reinterpretations. Nothing is more absurd than the notion of 'definitive history', a 'definitive treatment' of this or that period, or a 'definitive biography', etc., which, by implication, anticipate a stage when, given the abundant accumulation of definitive chunks, there will be no more need for a constant re-examination of history. In the event of such 'definitiveness', it would not be only the historian who puts himself out of business but man himself who can ignore or routinize his past only at the price of decapitating his own future.

However, there is no danger that such notions might prevail except perhaps in some areas of institutionalized irrelevance. To be sure, the industry of routinized popular history and biography must promise its readers (who are denied the chance of making history beyond the point of abdication through the ballot box) the thrill of authentic voyeurism, providing them with the consolation of 'definitive' treatments and allegedly great 'secret revelations'. If one's participation is confined to looking in on history through the keyhole, the spectacle had better be seen as 'definitive', so as to give one the illusion of observing history in its finality and massive permanence. But this is of little consequence. For man's relation to the past is no privileged domain of positivistically disoriented specialists but an existential dimension inseparable from the dilemmas and challenges of the present. Evaluation of past events and figures, in so far as it arises from the needs of a determinate relationship, has to be as definitive as possible in terms of the *given* relationship which necessarily means that the more definitive it is as a *specific* articulation of linked socio-historical temporalizations, the less definitive it can be in its *universality*. Or, to put it more precisely, its universality must manifest itself through a determinate socio-historical temporarlity. Only the skeleton of pure chronology can have some sort of 'mute universality' and neutral validity—in that it extends over all periods—which is indistinguishable from sheer immediacy and flat particularity. For the data of 'pure chronology' must first be *selected* and arranged in a *structured* order, from a determinate standpoint before they can acquire any meaning whatsoever.

Thus meaning, at any level and in all contexts, is not simply *found* in the subject of one's enquiry (as some sociological and other 'scientific' myth-makers presume, condemning themselves to tottering at the level of generality of a local telephone directory without its self-evident function), but *unfolded* from it through the meaning of the searching temporality. Saying with Sartre that 'the important thing is not what one *is* but what one *does*' is one side of a vital interrelationship. The other was spelled out by

Goethe when he insisted that 'to be able to *do* something one must already *be* something'.[126] It is this being in a situation at a determinate juncture in history, rooted in specific social forces with their interests, needs and orientation, which constitutes the necessary principle of selection. Without that how could one simply 'reproduce' the meaning of Sartre's work, short of reprinting his eight or nine million words, together with an account of a few million related facts and events? Such an enterprise would amount to doing absolutely nothing, even if it were possible. What makes Isaac Deutscher's biographies lasting works is not that they contain everything in a 'definitive' form (how could they?), but that they offer a meaningful selection of data, *relevant* to his own quest and to the orientation of his contemporaries. Thus, the most important single factor in the constitututution of meaning is the underlying passion that animates the search itself.

All this does not mean, of course, that objectivity in history is negated. On the contrary, a precise definition of its nature and limits rescues historical objectivity from the fate of extreme relativism which it suffers through the self-contradictory aspirations of positivism and 'scientism'. They start from the presumed objectivity of 'completeness', ignoring the arbitrariness of the choice of the enquiry itself, whereby the proper relationship between research and researcher is completely overturned. It is not the researcher who looks for data; on the contrary, the availability of abundant data produces the reified researcher of institutionalized routine. And, of course, the self-justifying ideology of such procedure takes the form of ruling out the need for justification of any research whatsoever, no matter how trivial and irrelevant it might be. Anything goes that can be 'researched', nailed to a display board in a form through which the dead 'objectivity' of dusty data is linked to an impersonally 'objective' pseudo-subject. Are we not reassured by the originator of this practice himself that all human facts and events are 'equidistant from God' (Ranke)? He

spends his life 'fighting' historical relativism, only to end up
producing the most exasperated form of it. This is supremely
ironical. For the methodology of unstructured 'completeness' liquidates not only historical objectivity but itself
as well. It turns the 'equidistant' data into *tokens* of equally
meaningful or meaningless equivalence, thus nihilating any
need for completeness: its original aim and *raison d'être*.
And having succeeded in nihilating its own ground, it turns
the activity of producing equidistant equivalences into a
form of self-consuming superfluity.

In truth, the only God relevant to human history is made
in the image of living three-dimensional man, and therefore
the data of this history are decidedly not equidistant from
him. Some are more meaningful than others, and some are
more meaningful to one epoch than to another. Objectivity
in history is not that of a nail, let alone of a stone, for 'man is
not a thinking nail', as Sartre often reminds us. Historical
objectivity is dynamic and changing, as is *life* not in and by
itself—for that would be still reducible to a set of more or less
simplified natural laws—but as it evolves, on a natural basis
radically modified by work and self-reflection, in the *social
sphere*. The objectivity of the search itself is determined by
the conditions of a given temporality which, of course,
include anticipations and assessments of future trends of
development. Nonetheless, in its dynamic objectivity, every
search is subject to criteria of evaluation both as regards its
social determinants (including their limitations) and the
nature (realistic or otherwise) of its anticipations.

Similarly, in the past itself we are concerned with linking
temporalizations, and not with some arbitrary projection
backwards on to an empty screen. For while the past is
inexhaustible, it is certainly not characterless. It cannot be
just moulded, whichever way one pleases, in accordance
with arbitrary whim and caprice: the weight and inner logic
of its evidence sets objective limits to possible reinterpretations. The past is inexhaustible not in and by itself
but in virtue of the fact that it is objectively linked to the

future which is never completely made. As man makes his own history, on the basis of temporal and structural determinations—preserving and transcending them— certain characteristics of the past come to the fore which were not visible before. They were not visible not because people were blind or shortsighted (though, of course, there is an abundance of such instances too) but because they did not exist in the same form before the objective articulation of determinate *relationships*. The ground has certain features before the house is built on it, which, in certain conditions (of which the house itself is an integral part), are painfully evidenced as subsidence by the cracks in the wall. The future does not invent or create the characteristics of the past but articulates them in the course of its own self-realization. This produces the need for constant reinterpretations, setting at the same time well defined objective limits as to which way and how far they can go.

In the course of such reinterpretations—in so far as they correspond to a genuine movement in the social sphere that generates them, rather than being mechanically turned out by the routine of a reified industry of culture—the previous ones are inevitably *aufgehoben* (not 'refuted') in the sense that a more advanced stage can unfold a greater complexity of meaning out of the subject of its linking search. Lukács's assessment of Goethe gives a deeper insight into the great German writer than Hegel's reflections on him, irrespective of the comparative stature of the two philosophers. Nor does his evaluation lay claims to definitiveness. The characteristic feature of a Marxist line of approach is not some attempt to go beyond the sphere of its own transcendability—a petrified absurdity—but precisely its awareness of the temporal determinations of its own quest, not only that of its subject. By leaving the lines of research open, instead of vainly trying to close them, and by reflecting on its own inner motivations and temporal determinations, such an approach, no doubt, radically rejects the illusions of definitiveness and complete finality. At the same time, by acknowledging and exemplifying the dynamism of historical objectivity, it can not only bring to life with greater effectiveness the subject of its search, but also prepare the ground for further interpretations and revaluations, rooted in new existential predicaments which it thus also helps to bring to the fore. No one can realistically aim at more than this linking search which is simultaneously 'outside' and 'inside'—a preserving transcendence of the past which is also a form of determinate temporality and self-transcendence. This is, precisely, what gives such search its *raison d'être*.

2

Another myth that needs dispelling concerns the alleged phenomenon of 'ruptures' and 'radical breaks' in historical and intellectual development. The dialectical interchange of life and work, epoch and writer, make such an idea as an explanatory hypothesis a definite non-starter. The writer, according to Sartre, goes on writing even when he has lost his illusions about the nature and impact of literature, and thus of his own work, for 'he has invested everything in his occupation'.[127] Even if there was nothing else beside this 'ideological interest',[128] it should be enough to caution one about the dialectic of continuity and discontinuity, for it points to something deeper, namely to the fact that 'you have a past that you can't repudiate. Even if you try to, you can never repudiate it completely because it is as much part of you as your skeleton . . . in the long run you have not changed much, since you can never discard the whole of your childhood'.[129] And the man who speaks in such terms, in 1970, is none other than Sartre, who is supposed to have radically repudiated his own past.

Considering the relationship of the writer and his epoch, the problem to be explained is twofold: individuality and 'autonomy' on one hand, and social determinations on the other. This is how Sartre formulates the issue:

> I would like the reader to feel the presence of Flaubert the whole time; my ideal would be that the reader simultaneously feels, comprehends and knows the personality of Flaubert, totally as an individual and yet totally as an expression of his time.'[130]

And in more generalized terms:

> I believe that a man can always make something out of what is made of him. This is the limit I would today accord to freedom: the small movement which makes of a totally conditioned social being someone who does not render back completely what his conditioning has given him. . . . The individual interiorizes his social determinations: he interiorizes the relations of production, the family of his childhood, the historical past, the contemporary institutions, and then he re-exteriorizes these in acts and options which necessarily refer us back to them.[131]

Thus the constituents of an individual's development may be summed up as follows:

1. the formation of his personality and thought in his youth and the interiorization of the institutions he experiences (family, class, etc.);
2. the continued determinations of his social environment, with all its changes, and their interiorizations by the individual;
3. the self-definition of the individual in his social setting through work (e.g. writing), and the response of his social environment to it;
4. the interiorization of his own work and of its social consequences by the individual concerned (of his 'ideological interest' as an intellectual, for instance);
5. a possible re-exteriorization of a critique of the last interiorization as a negation of the social bases of the type of work in question (e.g. the negation of the role of the 'traditional intellectual').

It is clear that while the first four constituents are characteristic of the development of individuals in general, the fifth represents a form of critical self-awareness which is inseparable from a radical critique of society. Furthermore, since that critique appeals to the perspective of a distant future as the necessary condition of its realization, the negation may remain theoretical only (like Bergson's 'liberté intérieure'), coupled with an actual reaffirmation, even if not necessarily re-interiorization, of the mode of existence of the criticized 'traditional intellectual', not as an ideal but as an insuperable reality for the individual concerned, thus reasserting the power of continuity over the expectation of a break. We can see this clearly in Sartre's answer to the question: 'How do you see the new mission of the intellectual?', which begins with the suggestion that 'He must first of all *suppress himself as an intellectual*', and ends with this confession: 'I decided to finish the book [on Flaubert], but as long as I go on working on it, *I remain at the level of the traditional intellectual*'.[132]

Evidently, in a writer's development the crucial factor is how he responds to the conflicts and changes of the social world in which he is situated. This can be differentiated into two basic elements: his own constitution (structure of thought, character, tastes, personality), and the relative degree of dynamism with which the social forces of his epoch confront one another, drawing him in one way or another into their confrontations. To describe the interchanges between a writer and his epoch in terms of 'ruptures' is at best extremely naive on both counts, for neither socio-historical, nor individual development is characterized by 'breaks' alone, but by a complex configuration of changes and continuities. In some epochs (such as the French Revolution) discontinuities are in the foreground, and in others (such as the period between 1871 and 1905) continuities predominate. But there are always changes beneath the surface of continuities, and some basic continuities persist, no matter how radical the breaks in certain regions (the Russian revolution and the conditions of agricultural production for decades thereafter, for instance).

A society is made of multiple layers of coexisting social instruments and practices, each with its own specific rhythm of temporality: a fact that carries far-reaching implications for social development as a whole. This is a major problem which must be treated in its proper setting, namely in the framework of a theory of social transformation and transition. What matters in the present context is that even in the same sphere (material production, for instance) practices going back almost as far as the Stone Age may more or less happily coexist with activities requiring the most advanced forms of technology. This is by no means confined to societies like India where primitive subsistence agriculture is, ironically, complemented by the technology of nuclear arms production. We can find similar instances in our own societies (although the relative weight of the more ancient social practices is, of course, very different in the economic life of our society as a whole). For a Stradivarius on the assembly line is a contradiction in terms. The best chisels for sculptors, are made today by an old blacksmith in London who works with tools and techniques of thousands of years ago, but nonetheless he is able to put to shame the most advanced Japanese, German and American computerized chisel production techniques, by tempering steel in such a way that it optimally combines the qualities of hardness and resilience which together constitute the most desirable chisel. Now if we try to think of all the social spheres combined, with their manifold varieties, different degrees of complexity, phases of 'uneven development' (Marx), and differences in what might be called structural inertia, as well as their reciprocal interactions, conflicts, clashes, and even antagonistic contradictions under determinate historical conditions, it is obvious that the reduction of this breath-taking complexity to the voluntaristic (e.g. Stalinist) simplification of instant 'ruptures' resulting in a 'radical break' with the past, whereafter all problems are caused by the 'enemy', can only produce painful social hernias which might take ages to cure.

*Mutatis mutandis,* the same considerations apply to the development of the individual. For one thing, his need for and ability to change does not necessarily coincide with the dynamism (or, for that matter, social stagnation) of his epoch, and conflicts may be generated from both directions. (This is what produces the individual who is 'out of phase' with his time.) Furthermore, certain dimensions of his complex being are *structurally* less readily amenable to change than others. Thus taste, for instance: in some cultures eating chillies constitutes supreme delight, in others a form of torture. The problem to be explained is not only the stubborn persistence of the acquired taste in the individual even when he is transferred into a sharply different culture, but also the fact that the two extremes are constituted on the shared basis of the original experience of sucking the mother's milk. Both problems are explicable only by some specific configuration of continuity and discontinuity, with the relative predominance of one or the other. Incomparably more so when we take into account the whole complexity of a 'singular individuality'. The way in which the various dimensions combine into a coherent whole (and when they do not, we have the problems of a dislocated personality), despite the structural differences and tensions between the respective temporal rhythms (for, thankfully, a man does not age in one piece, with uniformity, otherwise he would age with the self-accelerating speed of a steel ball rushing down a steep incline) can only be comprehended through the dialectic of continuity and discontinuity.

The structure of an individual's thought is constituted at a relatively early age, and all its subsequent modifications, however great or small, can only be explained as alterations of the original structure, even if the distance covered is as great as from milk to chillies. But it cannot be explained simply as the structure's 'rupture'—which, in and by itself, is nothing and thus explains absolutely nothing: 'rupture' is meaningful only as a well defined interaction of determinate forces—or as the invention of a brand new structure, again either out of nothing, or through a mechanical transference of the determinations of an age on to the mysterious *tabula rasa* (another name for nothing) of a rupturally emptied 'individuality' (which is a contradiction in terms). The lifework of an intellectual exhibits many layers of structural transformations, which are intelligible only as increasingly. more complex superseding preservations (or preserving supersessions) of the original structure.

But to refer to the dialectic of continuity and discontinuity is not enough. To say that history, both individual and collective, manifests itself through continuities and changes would acquire the status of a truism, were it not that determinate 'ideological interests' turn it into a hotly debated theoretical proposition. In considering a writer like Sartre the interesting problem is not the unity of continuity and change in his development but its specific form or configuration. Generally speaking, we can think of this problem in terms of a spectrum within which continuities or discontinuities predominate more or less extensively and to varying degrees of intensity (compare in this respect Modigliani and Picasso, or Kodály and Bartók, for instance). Nor should one be deceived by changes which are precisely manifestations of a deeper underlying continuity. For an individual's intellectual development is made up of many aspects, some of which are far more weighty than others in determining the articulation of the overall structure. When Sartre exclaims that 'on n'est pas plus sauvé par la politique que par la littérature' (one isn't any more saved through politics than through literature),[133] he gives away the key to understanding that the sharply contrasting forms of his *praxis* are different forms of expression of the fundamental underlying continuity: his passionate quest for the 'absolute' of a non-religious 'salvation'.

The salient feature of Sartre's development is the ultimate predominance of continuity through a multiplicity of transformations. His life activity assumes an extremely paradoxical form. For it is not simply dominated by continuities but, on the contrary, appears to be punctuated by incomprehensible discontinuities, described variously as 'radical conversion', lapse into 'ultra-bolshevism', 'radical break with the past', and so on. It is both the paradoxical form of the continuity and the heterogeneous tensions which determine its relative transformations, which together define the specificity of Sartre's intellectual development.

### 3

If we want to follow particular phases of this development, we have to proceed with great caution. For movements in real life are much more subtle than what might be captured through periodizations which, of necessity, freeze any live movement. Changes occur not only between works—let alone between periods or phases—but inside particular works; moreover, continuities are not broken off at points of transition but persist sometimes throughout the whole of a lifework.

· Nevertheless, the relationship between a writer and his epoch cannot be properly understood without fully taking into account the impact of historical events and social transformations even if one must make all the necessary allowances for existing overlaps on the one hand, and the constant 'capillary changes' which are primarily determined by the inner logic of the chosen subject on the other.

Keeping in mind these qualifications, we may define the principal phases of Sartre's development as follows:

1. The Years of Innocence: 1923-1940.
2. The Years of Abstract Heroism: 1941-1945.
3. Search for Politics in the Key of Morality: 1946-1950.
4. Search for Morality in the Key of Politics: 1951-1956.
5. Search for the Dialectic of History: 1957-1962.
6. The Discovery of the Singular Universal: 1963 onwards.

Let us have a brief look at each of these phases.

### 1. *The Years of Innocence: 1923-1940.*

The year 1923 stands for the publication of a short story[134] and of three fragments of a lost novel,[135] followed after a four-year break by the essay on 'The theory of state in modern French thought' referred to above. None of these works has other than purely documentary interest, for they are truly 'pen exercises', rather than original works. The first of Sartre's writings to give a hint of what is to come are his letter contributing to the student enquiry (see above, p. 30) and the *The Legend of Truth,* both written in 1929 but the latter published only in 1931. 'L'Art cinématographique' (c. above, pp. 53-54) is in the same category in that all three exhibit traits of originality against a background of borrowed wisdom, but are still far from indicating a viable road ahead.

The situation changes with *The Transcendence of the Ego,* written in 1934 (published in 1936) and three other major essays on problems of philosophical psychology: *Esquisse d'une théorie des émotions, L'Imagination* (both 1935-36) and *L'Imaginaire: Psychologie phénoménologique de l'imagination,* written between 1935 and 1940, when it was published.[136] According to Simone de Beauvoir, the grand project on philosophical psychology (of which *The Transcendence of the Ego* and *Sketch for a Theory of the Emotions* constitute a small part) is abandoned by Sartre because he considers it 'little more than an exercise'.[137] In truth they are a great deal more than that. While Sartre later sharply revises some of the most extreme statements made about freedom on the basis of the philosophical psychology expressed in these works, he retains their conceptual framework not only in *Being and Nothingness* but throughout his subsequent development. (See, for instance, 'Itinerary of a thought', 1969, which explains his project on Flaubert with the categories of *L'Imaginaire.*[138])

To these works we have to add not only the important essay on temporality in Faulkner (above pp. 56-60) but also his fine short stories[139] and a most remarkable novel, *La Nausée* (Nausea). The general trend is clear. After the first years (1923-28) which produce nothing more than 'exercises', out of the gropings of *The Legend of Truth* some philosophical and literary works emerge which define

Sartre's quest as the exploration of individual experience at the level of a great existential intensity. The social and political dimensions are almost completely absent, or appear only on the horizon, painted with the colours of resignation and 'Melancholia' (the original title of *Nausea*), signalling the triumph of reification and alienation. This absence of the social and political dimensions, before the 'fall' of commitment, give a marked unity to Sartre's first phase of development as the years of sinfully self-oriented innocence.

## 2. *The Years of Abstract Heroism: 1941-1945*

The war brings commitment of a certain kind.

> What the drama of the war gave me [explains Sartre], as it did everyone who participated in it, was the experience of heroism. Not my own, of course—all I did was a few errands. But the militant in the Resistance who was caught and tortured became a myth for us. Such militants existed, of course, but they represented a sort of personal myth as well. Would we be able to hold out against torture too? The problem then was solely that of physical endurance—it was not the ruses of history or the paths of alienation. A man is tortured: what will he do? He either speaks or refuses to speak. This is what I mean by the experience of heroism, which is a false experience. After the war came the true experience, that of society. But I think it was necessary for me to pass via the myth of heroism.[140]

This experience of heroism is abstract not only because Sartre has to contemplate it from the sideline but also because the whole complexity of the epoch—for even a period of historical emergency has its 'ruses' and 'paths of alienation', however different they may be from those of the postwar world—is reduced to a moral dilemma, in accordance with the horizon of a problematic subjectivity and very tentatively self-transcending individuality. The main philosophical work of this phase is *Being and Nothingness*(1943), which announces the possibilities of such transcendence in the extremely abstract categories of 'phenomenological ontology', structured around subjectivity. Sartre's three early plays—*Bariona* (1941), *Flies* (1943), and *Huis Clos* (1943)—fit well into this intellectual framework, and so does *Roads to Freedom* (its first two volumes written in 1941-44 and published in 1945), apart from the aesthetic considerations discussed above; 1945 is also the year of writing two important programmatic essays: 'A propos de l'existentialisme: Mise au point'[141] and *L'Existentialisme est un humanisme*[142]—in which the tone is more positive but the conceptual framework remains the same, despite the new 'experience of society'. The work in which the problematic features of Sartre's abstract heroism break to the fore, without however resulting in an aesthetically or conceptually viable alternative, is *Morts sans sépulture*[143] his 'failed play' (cf. p. 64).

And yet, when we notice the distinguishing characteristics of this phase, we should also be aware of some important continuities. We should notice not only the fact that the 'ontological structure of individual praxes' remains the framework of orientation of Sartre's later writings on morality, including 'Determination and freedom' (1966), but also the structural affinities with the *Critique of Dialectical Reason*, where the contrast is supposed to be the sharpest, for implicitly in *Being and Nothingness*, and explicitly in *Huis Clos*, 'hell is the other'. Now one of the central themes of the *Critique* is what Sartre calls 'the practico-inert': the reign of the other and of his instruments and institutions. And we are confronted with the same gripping definition: *'hell is the practico-inert'*.

## 3. Search for Politics in the Key of Morality: 1946-1950.

If the first phase is characterized by the predominance of self-oriented subjectivity, and the second by the assertion of an abstract moral heroism (freedom as inherent in the ontological structure of being), the third phase is under the sign of the pursuit of a morally committed politics while retaining the sovereignty of the individual. It follows naturally from the earlier phases of which the third represents an extension towards real socio-historical problems, without paying much, if any, attention to institutional realities which are necessary conditions of any possible solution of those problems. Even *Les Mains sales* and *L'Engrenage* (both from 1948) which directly confront some major political issues, do this in the form of *moral dilemmas* that apparently are not amenable to a solution.

Sartre's reflections on commitment in literature are articulated with great intensity and coherence in *Baudelaire* (1946), 'Forgers of myths: the young playwrights of France' (1946), 'The writer's responsibility' (1947) and, above all, *What is literature?* (1947). His articles on politics are full of imperatives, even in their titles: 'Jeunes d'Europe, unissez-vous! Faites vous-mêmes votre destin'; 'Il nous faut la paix pour refaire le monde'; 'Il faut que nous menions cette lutte en commun', etc. He defines the fundamental task of the RDR (Rassemblement Démocratique Révolutionnaire)—a shortlived political movement with which he is associated for a while—as the unification of 'revolutionary demands with the idea of freedom',[145] but he has nothing to say on how to achieve it, except by unrealistically appealing directly to the consciousness of individuals, irrespective of their political affiliations.

The RDR soon collapses, but Sartre's conception of politics as a moral imperative persists for some time. He sees the essence of the Yugoslav experience as 'subjectivity . . . not as a formal ideal but as an effective reality'. And in an introduction to Roger Stéphane's *Portrait of the Adventurer* (1950) he sings the eulogy of Lawrence of Arabia for 'living to the limit an impossible condition', an 'unbearable tension' of antinomies and contradictions.[146] And this is how he defines morality too: it is 'for us simultaneously inevitable and impossible'.[147] Should one be surprised therefore to learn that in the same period he abandons not only volume IV of *Roads to Freedom*, but his *Morale* as well, after 2,000 pages of struggle with its 'insurmountable impossibility'.[148]

4. *Search for Morality in the Key of Politics: 1951-1956.*
   The frustrations of the previous phase—the exasperations

of the Cold War period and Sartre's feeling of impotence to make an impact in a positive direction by means of his moral-political appeals to the concerned individual—bring a major soul-searching. Its outstanding results are *Saint Genet* (1950-52) and, above all, *Le Diable et le Bon Dieu* (*Lucifer and the Lord,* 1951), a magnificent play—perhaps his greatest single work: a drama we might call Sartre's *Guernica.*

The objectivity of history is discovered obliquely, under the threat of nuclear self-annihilation: 'In order to prevent the world from following *its own course,* they threaten with the suppression of history through the liquidation of the historical agent'.[149] Sartre throws himself into feverish political activity, in order to help prevent such ultimate disaster. He becomes a prominent figure in the World Peace Movement, writing articles, and making numerous public speeches on the subject of world peace; and on the plane of internal politics he is a passionate advocate of a new Popular Front.[150]

There are still moments when he maintains the illusions on the political power of independent individuals,[151] but he is trying to establish a close relationship with the French Communist Party. Two major publications mark this trend: *The Communists and Peace* (1952-54), and *L'Affaire Henri Martin* (1953), apart from the play *Nekrassov* (1955) and the film scenario *The Witches of Salem* (1956). And in the field of literary studies his passionate interest is with those who consciously commit themselves; he makes this clear in an interview: 'Mallarmé and Genet—they are both conscious of their commitment . . . [Mallarmé] is our greatest poet. A wild, impassioned man. . . . His was an all-embracing commitment—social as much as poetic'.[152]

Sartre's political radicalization brings also his clamorous break with Camus, and then, not so clamorous but with equal finality, with his much closer friend and collaborator, Merleau-Ponty. He is accused of abdication, which is very far from the truth. In reality, he is trying to influence the

Party from the outside (as witnessed by an important critical article, 'Le reformisme et les fétiches'[153]) while insisting that in France the only viable force of mediation of working-class politics is the Communist Party.

As he later realizes, after the shock of the Hungarian upheaval in October 1956, he is trying to do the impossible. His characterizations of the Party are often straightforward projections of his conception of morality which needs tangible historical agencies for its realization. In the end his effort to unify his moral ideals with political reality, despite his willingness to make some concessions, founders and a new crisis sets in. And just as he characterized our moral predicament earlier as ruled by 'insurmountable impossibility' and simultaneous 'inevitability and impossibility', he later sums up the dilemmas and antinomies of our political predicament in the same terms: 'Collaboration with the CP is both *necessary* and *impossible*'.[154] Thus Politics in the Key of Morality, and Morality in the Key of Politics—however different their emphases in determinate historical situations—come structurally to the same thing: the assertion and reassertion of fundamental antinomies.

## 5. Search for the dialectic of history: 1957-1963

The disappointment of his political expectations passionately denounced in the book-length essay, 'Le fantome de Staline',[155] raises the questions 'why did it all happen?' and 'what are the hopes for the future?', calling for a searching investigation of the structures and determinations of history vis-à-vis the possibilities of individual praxis. This means going back to the foundations, in order

> to provide a philosophical foundation for realism. This in my opinion is possible today, and I have tried to do it all my life. In other words, how can one give man both his autonomy and his reality among real objects, avoiding idealism without lapsing into a mechanistic materialism. I posed the problem in this way because I was ignorant of dialectical materialism although I should add that this later allowed me to assign certain limits to it—to validate the historical dialectic while rejecting a dialectic of nature, in the sense

of a natural process which produces and resolves man into an ensemble of physical laws.[156]

This 'foundation and validation' is a monumental enterprise of which *Critique of Dialectical Reason*, massive as it is, constitutes only a small part. Indeed, in an interview by Madeleine Chapsal in 1959, he optimistically announces: 'The first volume will be published within a month, and the second within a year'.[157] However, the second volume is abandoned after early chapters, and the project is altogether displaced a few years later by a close investigation of 'singular individuality' through the life and work of Flaubert.

Naturally, Sartre's contacts with politics are not broken off, but they assume a very different form. This is the time of the Algerian war, and he is fully involved, as an individual, in the fight against the danger of fascism, against torture, the OAS, and so on. Similarly, the victory of the Cuban revolution is greeted by him with great enthusiasm, and he continues to defend it against all kinds of attack. But he is a loner supporting worthy causes rather than a member or associate of a political movement.[158]

Critical self-examination—in the essays on Brecht, Gorz's *Traitor,* Nizan, and 'Merleau-Ponty vivant' (1961)—takes the form of a severe indictment of his whole generation, together with its 'sclerotic' institutions. The overall picture is rather sombre (likewise in his *Critique*), and *Altona* (1959)—one of his most powerful plays—fits organically into it, with its examination of historical determinations in relation to human responsibility. History is questioned with a hopeful eye towards the future, but no reassurance seems to be forthcoming—at least not for the time being.

## 6. *Discovery of the Singular Universal: 1963 onwards*

The publication of *Words* (1963) signals a form of peace, expressed with serenity also in the lines we have seen on salvation in literature and in politics. It goes without saying, Sartre takes a keen interest in the world of politics, especially in the 'Third World', from writing an introduction to a collection of Lumumba's essays to presiding over the deliberations of the Russell Tribunal. And he defends Régis Debray—in danger of execution in Bolivia—with the same passion with which he condemns the Russian intervention in Prague. There is even a moment of great positive enthusiasm—May 1968 in Paris—when his best dreams about 'imagination in power' seem to come true in his own homeland. All the same, politically he remains an isolated figure even when for reasons of solidarity he accepts the nominal directorship of the persecuted paper, *La Cause du Peuple*.

Realizing that the 'concrete universal' is possible only in a society which is made of the same stuff, he accepts the limitations of the intellectual—in *Words*, in the essays on 'L'universel singulier', in 'A plea for intellectuals', for example—while questioning the conditions of his existence. By far the most important project in this respect is *The Idiot of the Family* (vols I and II, 1971, vol. III, 1972)—an immense work of which nearly 3,000 dense pages are already printed, though it still seems to be very far from the end.

Sartre's *Critique* was supposed to be continued in the following way:

> The difference between the first and second volume is this: the first is an abstract work where I show the possibilities of exchange, degradation, the pratico-inert, series, collectives, recurrence and so on. It is concerned only with the theorectical possibilities of their combinations. The project of the second volume is history itself . . . my aim will be to prove that there is a dialectical intelligibility of the singular. For ours is a singular history. . . . What I will seek to show is the dialectical intelligibility of that which is not universalizable. [159]

It is extremely difficult to imagine how one can comprehend 'history itself' through these categories, since the problem of history is precisely how to universalize the singular without suppressing its specificities. By contrast, howevever, it is very easy to see the natural transition from history to biography, namely from this Sartrean conception of history to the project on Flaubert. For the intelligibility of the non-universalizable singular calls for lived experience as the basis of its comprehension. And the reconstruction of the personage through *l'imaginaire* necessarily involved in it, gives us a 'True legend', at the highest level of complexity. Some of the fundamental structures of history itself thus remain hidden away in the second volume of the *Critique* that never comes, for they do not seem to fit into the framework of Sartre's quest. But, by compensation, the existential dimensions of 'singular universality' are brought to life, with great richness and penetration.

4

As we can see from this necessarily sketchy account, the particular phases of Sartre's development are not simply the result of external determinations, but of a complex interaction between the *internal* determinations of his structure of thought, and the social and political events of his epoch. The fatal immobilism of pre-war years; the immense human drama and suffering of the Second World War; the cold war inaugurated by Churchill's Fulton speech after the short interval of serene rejoicing over the shared victory over Fascism; the menace of a nuclear devastation in the aftermath of the establishment of NATO, soon followed by the outbreak of the Korean war; the explosion of the inner contradictions of the Stalinist system; and the new dynamism of the 'Third World' gathering its own momentum (with Algeria, Cuba, Vietnam, etc.)—each coincides, roughly, with a phase in Sartre's development for which it provides a broad historical and political framework. But the *way* in which Sartre proceeds, and the *distance* he is able to travel, is determined by the innermost nature of his vision itself, as we could clearly perceive in his transitions from self-oriented subjectivity ultimately leading, through the intermediary forms of active (one might even say activist) moral and political commitment, to the problematic individuality of the 'singular universal'.

On the surface, changes not only are in evidence, but they assume the striking form of apparently radical breaks: every phase is *abandoned* in its turn, with conscious public declarations by Sartre as to the 'why?' of the clamorous discontinuities. But if we look closer, we realize that the succession of striking changes unfolds a fundamental *continuity*. Trying to understand Sartre through his breaks—which on the whole are confined to the political level—is like explaining the nature of the tides by the prevalent wind currents. Just as the tide is understood through the force of the moon, and not by the power of the wind even if hurricane strong, Sartre's development is explained by the stubborn continuity of his fundamental quest. If the 'breaks' were the determining feature, how could one account for the lasting validity of the works produced in the preceding phases? The fact is, however, that Sartre's advances do not 'invalidate' his earlier results but essentially preserve them, both in his world of literature and in his philosophical thought. He is a man who perceives the contradictions of the world around him in the form of dilemmas, antinomies and paradoxes. His praise of the 'adventurer' is not a temporary lapse but an expression of his inner tensions which remain a permanent dimension of his lifework. He is the man who 'keeps together the unbearable tension' of the perceived contradictions as insuperable antinomies. For the unresolved tension—through all its transformations—drives him forward and produces the lasting validity of his major works: *Nausea, L'Imaginaire, Being and Nothingness, Flies, Huis Clos, Les Mains Sales, Lucifer and the Lord, Saint Genet, Altona, Critique of Dialectical Reason*, and *The Idiot of the Family*.[160]

In 1945 he declares: 'Mathieu's childhood . . . doesn't matter',[161]—that is, in *his* vision of the world, which means that however much it matters in real life ruled by 'Bad Faith', it *ought not* to matter. In 1959, through the play *Altona,* he shows how the past conditions the present, commenting on the sad reality whereby 'the characters are all the time commanded and held back by the past, as they are by the others. It is because of the past—of their own and of all the others'—that they act in a certain way. *As in real life*.'[162] The contrast is as striking as it is misleading. For again he appeals to the 'viewpoint of the future', and urges men to look at themselves 'from outside', in order to be able to notice that it *ought not* to be like that at all. As he tries to demonstrate also in 'Determination and freedom' six years later, there is absolutely nothing in the 'ontological structure of being' to make them behave like that. If they do, it is because of social and political determinations and their 'interiorizations' by individuals—but they *ought not* to. Witness and participant, he warns us that 'we shall be judged'[163] by the future, our future. Thus we *ought to act* in accordance with the 'ontological structure' of our being (in relation to which Mathieu's or anyone else's past really 'does not matter'), and not the way we actually do. The most striking continuity lies beneath the surface of an apparent break.

The moon that determines the movements of Sartre's tidal waves is his radical quest for unfolding the fundamental dimensions of being, in a world of distracting compromises and temptations, offering lines of easy resistance which lead towards disaster through unfounded self-reassurance and the promise of comfort. This is not his way, and ought not to be ours, he tells us, pursuing the task of persuasion with tireless passion.

'*The marvellous unity of this life is its intransigence in the quest for the absolute*', writes Sartre about his great friend, Giacometti.[164] There can be no better way of summing up the movement and the direction of his own lifework. Such a quest for the absolute is not something mysterious and transcendental. On the contrary, it is very precise and tangible. It means a radical definition of a man's fundamental project in a sense which necessarily implies going *to the limit*, whatever the limit may appear to be to the individual in question at any particular time in the course of his development.

Sartre's heroes—Mallarmé, Genet, Nizan, Fućik, Giacometti, Hikmet, and in fiction Julien Sorel—are men who explore their predicament to the limit. Similarly, his anti-heroes—among them Baudelaire and Flaubert—are those who refuse to do so, thus condemning themselves to the consequences of their fundamental choice: an escape into the imaginary and the acceptance of alienation. 'What interests me about Flaubert is that he *refused to go to the limit*',[165] writes Sartre, clearly indicating the moral sense of his painfully long involvement in the subject. It is 'going to the limit' he himself opts for, and champions with single-minded determination and intransigence, insisting that *the* question is: 'what have you made of your life?'[166] Success is measured by one's ability to establish 'the *real connection* with others, with oneself and with death'[167] as opposed to 'the reassuring, dreary world of the inauthentic'[168] in which men are trapped by 'a moiling of flabby, many-tentacled *evasions*'.[169]

Whatever one may think of Sartre's achievements, no one can accuse him of evasions. Probing the limits, irrespective of the consequences, this is the fundamental defining characteristic of his lifework. His road, from self-oriented subjectivity to the problematic individuality of 'the singular universal', leads over territories full of explosive dilemmas which he depicts in the most paradoxical form. 'There is a morality of politics—a difficult subject, and never clearly treated—and when politics must betray its morality, to choose morality is to betray politics. Now find your way out of that one! Particularly when the politics has taken as its goal bringing about the reign of the human'.[170] Much of Sartre's lifework is spent on identifying such dilemmas and paradoxes, even if he cannot offer solutions to them. For, again, the innermost nature of these dilemmas and paradoxes is that facing the limits is the vital condition of their identification and possible solution. It is Sartre's passionate search for the limits which determines the fundamental continuity of his lifework through all its transformations.

# PART TWO

# Search For Freedom

*'To come into the world as a freedom, confronting Others is to come into the world as alienable. If to will oneself free is to choose to be in this world confronting Others, then the one who wills himself such must also will the passion of his freedom.'*
*'Whether in fury, hate, pride, shame, disheartened refusal or joyous demand, it is necessary for me to choose to be what I am.'* [162]

## Chapter 4
# SEARCH FOR THE INDIVIDUAL:
# THE EARLY WORKS

### 1

DISCUSSING the intellectual development of his generation, Sartre writes in *The Problem of Method:*

> We plunged blindly down the dangerous path of a pluralist realism concerned with man and things in their 'concrete' existence. Yet we remained within the compass of 'dominating ideas'. . . . For a long time we confused the total and the individual. Pluralism, which had served us so well against M. Brunschwicg's idealism, prevented us from understanding the *dialectical totalization*. It pleased us to decry essences and artificially isolated types rather than to reconstitute the synthetic movement of a truth that had 'become'.[171]

Such self-descriptions, with which Sartre's work abounds, must be taken with a pinch of salt. We must constantly keep in mind that in Sartre's declarations we are confronted with such a fusion of subjectivity and objectivity whereby the meaning of the statement is always *self-assertion,* even when its apparent form is *self-criticism.* Sartre's compelling subjectivity cannot admit being in the wrong in the present tense—only retrospectively. Furthermore, the function of his retrospective self-criticisms (which are as a rule spelled out with the pronoun 'we', rather than 'I') is precisely to *assert* the transcendence of the criticized position, in place of *demonstrating* it. This is exactly what happens in the passage on the alleged early confusion of the total and the individual and on the claimed supersession of this position in *The Problem of Method* and in the *Critique of Dialectical Reason.*

We shall return to this particular problem in a moment. Now the point to stress is that the identification by a thinker of a problematic aspect of his own work does not automatically mean that he has found a solution to it. Nor does it mean that the retrospective self-criticism is necessarily valid and is to be accepted at face value. In both instances we are presented with assertions in need of substantiation and evidence before we can come to a conclusion one way or another. One's awareness of a problem may provide the *possibility* of a solution, but should not be confused with the solution itself which has to be established on objective grounds rather than on the sole basis of critical self-assertions, however genuinely *felt* they might be.

This is particularly important in assessing Sartre's development. For one of the salient features of his lifework is that he cannot allow his case to rest simply on the evidence of the *works* he produces but must provide also what he considers to be their only legitimate *interpretations*. This is not simply because he is a 'controversial' writer. Rather, being 'controversial' is itself a necessary consequence of the structuring and organizing principle of his work—of its 'compelling subjectivity'. So much so that beyond a certain point it is impossible to separate work from self-interpretation.

To be sure, Sartre's personal interventions in discussions about his own works—ever since the publication of *Nausea*—are quite unparalleled. He gives an endless number of interviews which he completely dominates. He answers his critics in the most outspoken fashion not only in interviews but in other forms as well, from short articles to book-length essays and from lectures to open letters. Furthermore, his views on his various concerns and on the meaning of his numerous works are faithfully reproduced in Simone de Beauvoires's five long autobiographical volumes. Such an amount of overpowering self-reflection is quite extraordinary by any standard.

But all this is very far from being the whole extent of Sartre's self-interpretations. We have to complement the picture not only with his autobiographical *Words* and

*Self-Portrait* (1975) but also with many of his essays, such as those on Giacometti, N. Sarraute, Camus, Nizan, Merleau-Ponty, in which his personal reflections predominate, whatever the immediate subject matter. And we have to add to them some of his plays (e.g. *Lucifer and the Lord*) and two major biographical works (on Genet and on Flaubert) in which self-interpretations are very much in the foreground. Indeed the vast majority of his lifework is more or less directly concerned with self-examination.

The nature of Sartre's quest is such that 'probing the limits' means two things: first, an uncompromising assessment and reassessment of his own *internal* limits—of the 'authenticity' or non-authenticity of his own choices and decisions; and second, the assertion of his subjectivity, his constantly scrutinized self, in the world around him, with the aim of highlighting the fundamental difference between the 'ontological structure of being' and the historically given situation. (The problem of 'interiorization' is concerned with the intersection of the two.) Self-examination thus constitutes the vehicle of assessing the problems of an epoch, and the concern with the problems of the age, as articulated through the categories of responsibility and authenticity, constitutes the nodal points of renewed self-examination.

This is why whatever may happen to be the subject of Sartre's enquiry, he is always completely absorbed in it. The frequent self-references of his analyses are not simply formal characteristics of presentation and style: they are inseparable from the conception of the subject matter itself. Consequently it is very difficult (and rather problematical) to divorce a Sartrean proposition from its existential context—the 'when?' and 'why?' of its conception—and assess its validity entirely on its own. Sartre not only *agrees* with his own generalizations: he is *one* with them. (His self-references are often meant as *authentications*[172] of this existential dimension of his assertions.) In other words, he is fully and passionately *committed* to the position he happens to hold at any given time. No wonder, therefore, that he cannot concede a point except retrospectively, when the point at issue has ceased to be an integral part of his overall theoretical framework.

It is because of such intense existential involvement in the problems at stake that Sartre must assume a belligerent posture vis-à-vis his critics, and not because of some mysterious 'temperament' that might be considered the underlying psychological cause of his aggressive self-assertions. (In any event, a man's temperament is controllable, if there is a good enough reason and Sartre would be the first to argue this, in the spirit of his early works on philosophical psychology.) The passionate defence of his position is as vital to the realization of his project as its original formulation. And since the subjective element is such an integral part of the whole enterprise, *up to a point* he can rightfully claim for himself a privileged status in explaining the meaning of his own works, in that a completely objective reading of works of this kind is by definition inadequate. No doubt there is something suspicious about the recurrant formula with which he rejects criticism from both left (be it the French CP[173] or Lukács,[174]) and right (e.g. Camus[175]) by declaring that the critics have not read his works, not to mention his dismissal of Guérin's self-explanation with the summary statement that 'he doesn't understand anything of his own book',[176] as we have seen above. All the same, the partial truth in such accusations is that Sartre's own reading of the works in question is different from the interpretations he contests. In other words, he insists on the importance of the *angle* (the subjective element) in the articulation of theories which has a bearing on the question of validity in a much more positive sense than is generally acknowledged.

However, having said that, we cannot ignore the problematical aspects. A lifework that requires the author's frequent intervention on his own behalf reveals its vulnerability in that he will not be eternally there to supply every age with self-interpretations which are constantly reformulated so as to be in tune with the changing socio-historical circumstances. Ultimately his work, just as anyone else's, must rest on the evidence the work itself displays, in relation to which self-interpretations are necessarily marginal. A compelling personality may succeed in imposing his self-image on his contemporaries—at least on some of them—but future generations will make up their own mind about him without such interventions.

Paradoxically, in the long-drawn-out process of historical validation the author's assertive self-interpretations may prove to be counter-productive in that they may give support to artificial polarizations and sidetrack the orientation of critical assessment from the whole of the lifework to some of its partial aspects. For while it is vitally important to keep in mind the author's passionate involvement in *specific* problems and concerns—from the angle of which he interprets himself as much as anything else—in order to be able to understand the *particular* points and phases of his development, self-interpretations are of a very limited value in assessing the *totality* of his development precisely because they are always deeply rooted in specific situations and concerns. Thus we are again confronted with the dilemma of 'individualization' and 'universalization': the same thing that is a great asset at one level turns out to be a potentially major drawback at another.

To account for the whole of a lifework, one has to integrate the totality of particular points and phases in a dynamic movement without suppressing the existential vitality of the individual elements. Any attempt at *directly* universalizing a particular phase—which is always con-stituted out of more or less conflicting elements—will only result in an historical *projection* of a specific part over the whole, and at the same time in the liquidation of the dynamic tension inherent in it. For any particular phase represents *ipso facto* also a specific level of attainment and point of rest which, if generalized, inevitably freezes the movement (which led to it and will go beyond it) and sharply distorts the overall picture.

By contrast, the only properly historical mode of proceeding is to use the *movement iself* as the *principle of selection* applied to all specific points and phases. Accordingly, those elements will be highlighted at any particular point in an author's development which represent the *links* of the overall movement and thus display the fundamental *trend* of his development. Thus universalization will emerge as the *overall structure*—a dynamic and not a static structure—of which the individual elements have changing relative weights. For what *dominates* a specific point or phase may occupy a very *subordinate* position at another, and vice versa; and it is the *overall pattern*—the dynamic whole—which ultimately and objectively determines the respective structural correlations, maybe assigning a much greater relative weight to an element of embryonic strength than to the temporarily dominant but transitory elements whose importance diminishes as the pattern of overall development unfolds.

It is thus easy to see that the author's self-interpretations, in so far as they are expressions of whatever may happen to be his dominant preoccupations at a particular point in time, need not (one might indeed argue, cannot) faithfully reflect the overall movement with all its intricacies and delicate balances which have to be assessed from a certain distance, but not from the distance of the newly acquired and championed position that itself must be integrated and made subject to a critical examination in the overall framework. And since the intensity of an author's passionate involvement in a new phase is what is in question here, we must be particularly careful about the self-interpretations of an author—Jean-Paul Sartre—who consciously carries the principle of existential involvement and commitment to its utmost limits. A hasty acceptance of his self-explanations at their face value (it does not matter whether approvingly or with a negative attitude towards the claimed changes), which seems to charactierize too many writings on Sartre, tends to bog down discussion on rather peripheral aspects of his work (e.g. the notoriety of his allegedly 'radical conversion'), diverting attention from its structuring principles and basic dimensions. This is why we have to treat them with particular care.

2

This takes us back to our original question: should we subscribe to Sartre's strictures about the alleged confusion of the total and the individual, the failure to understand the problem of dialectical totalization in his early work, coupled with the claim of a radical advance in this respect in his *Critique* and in the works related to the *Critique*? We have to postpone for a while any attempt at a more detailed answer to the second half of the question, apart from reiterating that Sartre's conception of dialectical totalization leads to an impasse in the second part of the *Critique* and to the transmutation of its quest for 'making history intelligible' into a form of fictional biography. Let us see now how things are in the early works.

There can be no doubt about it, the search for the individual is the central preoccupation of these works. This is inherent in the problematic which aims at laying the foundations of a phenomenological psychology, setting out from the 'irreducible fact'[177] of consciousness. However, it would be quite wrong to suggest that the problem of totality is ignored. On the contrary, it occupies a very important place in every one of the early works. And there are no signs of the total being confused with the individual. If anything, the lines of demarcation are too sharply drawn, rather than being blurred. What is highly problematical about Sartre's early analyses of totality is of an altogether different character, as we shall see in a moment.

We find already in Sartre's first important philosophical study, *The Transcendence of the Ego,* a theory of consciousness articulated in relation to the problem of totality. In a critical reference to Husserl's view of the 'transcendental I' as the condition of unity and identity of consciousness Sartre writes:

> The individuality of consciousness evidently stems from the nature of consciousness. Consciousness (like Spinoza's substance) can be limited only by itself. Thus it constitutes a *synthetic and individual totality* entirely isolated from *totalities of the same type*, and the I can evidently be only an expression (rather than a condition) of this incommunicability and inwardness of consciousness. Consequently we may reply without hesitation: the phenomenological conception of consciousness renders the unifying and individualizing role of the I totally useless. It is consciousness, on the contrary, which makes possible the unity and the personality of my I. The transcendental I, therefore, has no *raison d'être*'.[178]

This point is further developed in the section on 'The constitution of the ego as the pole of actions, states, and qualities':

> . . . the intuition of the ego is a constantly gulling mirage, for it simultaneously yields everything and yields nothing. How could it be otherwise, moreover, since the ego is not the *real totality* of consciousness (such a totality would be a contradiction, like any infinite unity enacted), but the ideal unity of all states and actions? Being ideal, naturally, this unity can embrace an infinity of states. But one can well understand that what is given to the concrete, full intuition is only this unity in so far as it incorporates the present state. By virtue of this concrete nucleus a more or less sizeable quantity of empty intentions (by right, an infinity of them) are directed towards the past and towards the future, and aim at the states and actions not presently given. Those who have some acquaintance with phenomenology will understand without difficulty that the ego may be at the same time an *ideal unity* of states, the majority of which are absent, and a *concrete totality* wholly giving itself to intuition: this signifies merely that the ego is a noematic rather than a noetic unity. A tree or a chair exist no differently. Naturally, the empty intentions can always be fulfilled, and any state or action whatsoever can always reappear to consciousness as produced or having been produced by the ego.[179]

Thus we are presented with a whole cluster of concepts—
'individual totality' and 'totalities of the same type', 'real
totality', 'ideal unity' (or ideal totality), and 'concrete
totality'—in terms of which the relationship between
consciousness and the world is spelled out. And Sartre is by
no means content to remain within the sphere of subjective
experience. On the contrary, his central aim is ontological.
Not only in the sense that he claims to have produced in his
conception of the ego 'the only possible refutation of
solipsism'.[180] rectifying Husserl's failures in this respect,[181]
but also in so far as he aims at undermining what
he calls 'metaphysical materialism'[182] by opening the
phenomenological bracket in the spirit of a philosophical
'realism'.[183]

Sartre's interest in phenomenology is, from the beginning,
existential-ontological. He wants to grasp the 'existents' in
their facticity, as opposed to the various kinds of metaphysical presuppositions or prejudgments which seem to
dominate not only philosophical theories but also their
applications in psychology and elsewhere, and his
enthusiasm[184] for the potentialities of phenomenology is the
direct expression of such concerns. However, he must soon
realize also the limitations of Husserlian phenomenology as
regards his own programme:

> Phenomenological descriptions can discover, for instance, that the
> very structure of the transcendental consciousness implies that this
> consciousness is constitutive of a world. But it is evident that they
> will not teach us that consciousness must be constitutive of such a
> world, that is *exactly* the one where we are, with its earth, its
> animals, its men and the story of these men. We are here in the
> presence of a primary and *irreducible fact* which presents itself as a
> *contingent* and irrational specification of the noematic essence of
> the world. And many phenomenologists will call 'metaphysics' the
> investigation whose aim it is to uncover this *contingent existent in
> its entirety*.[185]

Thus the concern with totality is further concretized as
facing the *world* as it is, as it *exactly* happens to be in its

contingency and facticity, with a view to 'uncover this
contingent existent in its *entirety*'. This contingent world of
the 'existents' is the world of things and the world of men
which we can uncover in its complex totality. Even the
'famous "subjective" responses: hatred, love, dread,
sympathy . . . are nothing but modes of uncovering the
world'.[186] In the spirit of his own interpretation of
phenomenology which already treats Husserl's 'bracket' as
opened, Sartre hails the German philosopher as someone
who 'restored to us the world of the artists and
prophets . . . he cleared the ground for a new treatise of the
passions. . .'; from now on the cult of interiority (Bergson,
Proust) is completely untenable: 'everything is outside,
everything, including ourselves: outside, in the world,
together with others. It is not in I don't know what kind of
retreat that we discover ourselves but on the highway, in the
city, in the middle of the crowd: *thing among things, man
among men.*'[187]

The 'new treatise of the passions' for which Husserl is
supposed to have cleared the ground is, of course, Sartre's
*Being and Nothingness* in which we learn that 'Existential
psychoanalysis is going to reveal to man the real goal of his
pursuit, which is being as a synthetic *fusion of the in-itself
with the for-itself*; existential psychoanalysis is going *to
acquaint man with his passion.*'[188] In truth, it is not Husserl
who clears the ground for this conception—except in an
indirect sense, by providing the field for Sartre's corrective
reflections—but Sartre himself, in his early works, and to a
large extent also in *Being and Nothingness*. As we know,
volume two of the latter, which should have carried out in
detail the programme announced in the last quotation, has
never been written—at least not in the originally intended
form. But of course many of Sartre's subsequent writings—
not only the abandoned *Morale* but also *Saint Genet,* as well
as numerous shorter essays, and above all *The Idiot of the
Family*—take up the problematic of making man acquainted
with his passion, and try to carry it nearer to a conclusion.

Thus the Sartrean quest for the absolute—the elucidation of the real goal of man's pursuit, which implies the refutation of various misconceptions—has to set out from the analysis of passion and emotion as we encounter it in the world of contingent existents: in the goal-directed life-activity of living individuals. The question: what makes man drive on through success and failure, achievement and disaster? cannot be answered in abstraction, at the generic plane of some mystifying universality (like 'World Spirit'), but must find its supporting evidence in the various manifestations of human passion as ways in which living individuals take cognizance of the world in which they are situated and try to cope with the problems and challenges of their situation.

The early works, while clearing the ground, articulate the main tenets of Sartre's philosophy. The critique of Husserl proceeds on two lines:

1. the establishment of a genuine need for phenomenological reduction (Husserl's *epoché*) in terms of Sartrean existential categories, as spelled out in *The Transcendence of the Ego*;

2. an examination of what Sartre considers to be inadequate in Husserl's account of the forms and modalities of consciousness, which lead Sartre to specify an ontological framework in which a solution might be envisaged to all that remained elusive to Husserl.

On the first point, Sartre's judgement is very severe. He quotes with approval Fink's study on Husserl[189] which insists that the 'natural attitude of mind'—which gives rise to scientific theories—is perfectly coherent in itself, and therefore there is no reason whatsoever for exercising a phenomenological reduction. Sartre goes on:

> There [in the natural attitude] one will find none of those contradictions which, according to Plato, lead the philosopher to effect a philosophical conversion. Thus, the *epoché* appears in the phenomenology of Husserl as a *miracle*. Husserl himself, in *Cartesianische Meditationen* [Section I.], made an extremely vague allusion to certain *psychological motives* which would lead to

undertaking reduction. But these motives hardly seem sufficient. Moreover, reduction seems capable of being performed only at the end of lengthy study. It appears, then, as a knowledgeable operation, which confers on it a sort of gratuitousness. On the other hand, if 'the natural attitude' appears wholly as an effort made by consciousness to escape from itself by projecting itself into the me and becoming absorbed there, and if this effort is never completely rewarded, and if a simple act of reflection suffices in order for conscious spontaneity to tear itself abruptly away from the I and be given as independent, then the *epoché* is no longer a miracle, an intellectual method, an erudite procedure: it is an *anxiety* which is imposed on us and which we cannot avoid: it is both a pure event of transcendental origin and an ever possible accident of *our daily life*.[190]

Even if Sartre's conclusion is rather unexpected, the thrust of his argument is abundantly clear. Having successfully liberated himself from the shackles of academic philosophy (Brunschvicg, etc.), Sartre is determined not to get involved in some other kind of academic operation which might turn out to be merely an intellectual method, a complicated erudite methodological procedure preserved for the few. He is looking for a method which has an existential basis in everyday life and is thus open to all. This conception, which directly links the *epoché* to anxiety and dread, establishes through the same link also the vital relationship with the existential categories of *freedom,* thus indicating the possibility of self-liberation through 'purifying reflection'—of which Sartre speaks in *Emotions,* a closely related work[191]—as the tangibly relevant function of the whole philosphical enterprise he is engaged in. Thus, in the course of the Sartrean analysis, a rather abstract problem of phenomenological methodology is transmuted into a major pillar of existential ontology.

The second point of criticism mentioned above concerns the forms and modalities of consciousness as characterized by Husserl. Sartre takes as his point of reference a Dürer engraving which we can perceive at will as a 'thing-object' or as an 'image-object', and he makes the following obser-vations:

Such hyletic ambivalence is possible only in a small number of privileged cases (paintings, photographs, copies, etc.). Even if the alternatives were available, one would still have to explain *why* my consciousness intends some matter as image rather than as perception. . . . the distinction between mental images and perceptions cannot derive from intentionality alone. A difference in intention is necessary but not sufficient. The matter must also be different. . . . [Husserl's solution, though insightful, is 'quite incomplete'.] . . . We know now that we must start afresh, setting aside all the phenomenological literature, and attempting above all to attain an intuitive vision of the intentional structure of the image. . . . We should also compare, image-consciousness and sign-consciousness, in order to free psychology once and for all from the egregious error of making images into signs and signs into images. Finally and above all the *hyle* peculiar to images should be examined. It might be that on the way we would have to leave the realm of eidetic psychology and resorting to experimentation and inductive procedures. But eidetic description is the starting point. The way is open for a phenomenological psychology. [192]

Thus the question 'why?' concerning the formation of an image rather than of a perception, again leads towards the articulation of an existential ontology. For the possibility of a 'phenomenological psychology' as envisaged by Sartre (as being synonymous with 'existential psychology', in contrast to the strictly phenomenological 'eidetic psychology') has for its precondition a radical departure from 'all the phenomenological literature' in that its programme necessarily implies the opening of the phenomenological bracket.

This we find clearly indicated, in a more generalized form, in a key passage of *L'Imaginaire*:

We shall give the name of '*situations*' to the different immediate ways of apprehending the *real* as a world. We can therefore say that the essential prerequisite that enables consciousness to imagine is that it be '*situated in the world*' or more briefly, that it 'be-in-the-world'. It is the situation-in-the-world, grasped as a concrete and individual reality of consciousness, which is the motivation for the construction of any unreal object whatever and the nature of that unreal object is *circumscribed* by this motivation. Thus the situation of consciousness does not need to appear as a pure and abstract condition of possibility for all imagination but as the concrete and *exact* motivation for the appearance of a certain particular imagination. . . . Thus, although as a result of producing the unreal, consciousness can appear momentarily delivered from 'being-in-the-world', it just is this 'being-in-the-world' which is the *necessary condition* for the imagination.[193] . . .

We may therefore conclude that imagination is not an empirical and superadded power of consciousness, it is the *whole* of consciousness as it realizes its *freedom*: . . . as consciousness is always 'in situation' because it is always free, it always and at each moment has the concrete possibility of producing the unreal. These are the various motivations which decide at each moment whether consciousness will only be realized or whether it will imagine. The unreal is produced *outside world* by a consciousness which stays in the world and it is because he is *transcendentally free* that man can imagine.[194]

As we can see, the reality of the world is asserted through the category of 'situation' which assumes a central role in Sartre's lifework. (Significantly, his essays on a variety of subjects are collected in ten volumes—so far—of *Situations,* and one of the most important areas of his activity, drama, is defined by Sartre as the 'theatre of situations'.) Indeed, the category of situation, linked to the surpassing function of the human reality, constitutes the philosophical foundation of Sartre's idea of *commitment* which is thus not something arbitrary, subjective, and voluntaristic, but inherent in the ontological structure of being as conceived by this existential philosopher. Of course, at this stage 'situation' is not spelled out yet as 'commitment', but remains an abstract philosophical principle. Nevertheless, the formulation of this principle is the necessary pre-condition for the articulation of Sartre's vision as 'commitment' during the war, as well as of the organic insertion of 'commitment' into his philosophical system as a whole.

We should also notice that the phenomenological bracket is opened by Sartre in the only possible way accessible to him, given his vital existential concerns. As a solution to Husserl's problem of 'motivations', the specific character of a determinate mode of consciousness—in this case: imagination—is explained by the specificity of the situation itself. But the '*whole* of consciousness' which finds itself *in situation* is, of course, the consciousness of a living human individual. This is why the relationship is described in terms of the '*concrete* and *exact* motivations' of 'a certain *particular* imagination' as opposed to the '*pure* and *abstract* condition of possibility for *all* imagination'. Thus 'consciousness in situation' is related to the whole of the world in which it is situated at a given temporal juncture. Its total character—which makes Sartre speak of the *whole* of consciousness—is therefore necessarily that of an *individual totality* (isolated from 'totalities of the same kind', as we have seen before) confronting the whole world.

All this does not mean that the total and the individual are confused, since the dialectical totalization of individual totalities as situated in the real world is a perfectly legitimate concern—and indeed it remains Sartre's characteristic way of proceeding up to the present time. What it certainly does mean is that Sartre sets out from individual existential determinations—concrete life-situations and the projects corresponding to them—in his search for an ultimate overall synthesis. He builds his ontological structures on the foundation of that 'synthetic and individual totality' which is for him the existential reality, and he asserts the primacy of individual praxes in all his works. This is why he has to reject with undisguised hostility what he calls—in his earliest as much as in his latest works—'metaphysical materialism' which would introduce the 'individual totality' on the historical stage at a much later point of development than Sartre's conception for which it constitutes the primary premise and the absolute point of departure.

But it is meant only as the point of departure, not as the overall synthesis itself. In Sartre's conception we are presented with a *movement*: one that has the internal logic of totalization in which the parts constitute an organic whole, or at least point to the whole:

> We said, in our Introduction, that the significance of a fact of
> consciousness came to this: that it always pointed to the *whole*

human-reality which was making itself emotional, attentive, perceptive, willing, etc. The study of the emotions has indeed verified this principle: an emotion refers to what it signifies. And what it signifies is indeed, in effect, the *totality* of the relations of the *human reality* to the *world*. The onset of emotion is a *complete* modification of the 'being-in-the-world' according to the very peculiar laws of magic.[195]

Thus the lines of demarcation are firmly drawn, and the overall framework of reference is 'the totality of the relations of the human reality to the world'. Sartre is, therefore, less than just towards his early works when he summarily characterizes them as works in which the total is confused with the individual. And he is more than generous towards the later works in claiming the solution of the problem of totalization, while in fact on this point his position is characterized by minor changes and a fundamental continuity throughout his lifework.

3

Let us now examine the problematic aspects of the young Sartre's conception of totality and see what happens to them in the course of his later development.

The first point to note is that the *methodological dualism* of phenomenology is transmuted by Sartre into an *ontological law*:

That exists spontaneously which determines its own existence. In other words, to exist spontaneously is to exist for oneself and through oneself [exister *pour soi* et *par soi*]. One reality alone deserves to be called 'spontaneous': consciousness. To exist and to be conscious of existing are one and the same for consciousness. Otherwise stated, the supreme *ontological law* of consciousness is as follows: for a consciousness the only way of existing is to be conscious that it exists. It is therefore evident that consciousness can determine itself to exist, but that it cannot act on anything but itself. A sensory content may be the *occasion* for our forming a consciousness, but we cannot act by means of consciousness on the sensory content, dragging it from nowhere (or from the unconscious), or sending it back. If images are consciousness, they are pure spontaneities. Consciousness of itself, self-transparency, and existing only to the extent that it knows itself, an image therefore cannot be a sensory content. It is perfectly futile to represent it as 'rationalized', as 'permeated by thought'. There is *no middle ground*: either it is *wholly thought*, and one thinks by means of the image, or it is *sensory content* and one would think on the occasion of an image. In the latter case, the image will be *independent* of consciousness, appearing to consciousness according to laws peculiar to an image which is not consciousness. Such an image, which must be awaited, deciphered, and observed, is simply a thing. Any inert and opaque content takes its place, by the necessity inherent in its type of existence, among objects, that is to say, in the external world. *That there are only two types of existence, as thing in the world and as consciousness, is an ontological law.* [196]

We have the greatest sympathy for Sartre's implicit aim: the critique of *reified consciousness* as manifest in mechanistically determinist theories, including the 'unconscious' of psychoanalysis [197] inasmuch as it falls into this category. It is in the same context that Sartre elaborates his concept of 'bad faith' (*mauvaise foi*) [198] as the dialectical alternative to the theories he criticizes. There can be no doubt about it, both his critique of crude psychological determinism, [199] and his concept of bad faith represent major and lasting achievements in Sartre's philosophy. At the same time, the social dimension is missing in both respects, thus greatly reducing the effectiveness of his explanations. The critique of reified consciousness remains necessarily partial so long as its terms of reference are confined to the theories themselves, without asking the question about the social foundations of those theories which reproduce, in however 'sophisticated' a manner, the structure of practical reification in a reified theoretical form. [200] For reification does not arise out of the structure of consciousness itself (if it did, we could do nothing about it) but appears as a result of a complex totality of social processes of which the consciousness of the individuals constitutes an integral part. Similarly, the concept of bad faith must be integrated into a general theory of ideology of which even in Sartre's later works there are only some fragments. In the absence of such integration, 'bad faith' is called upon to explain too much, with the result of getting the focus of its explanatory specificity blurred.

The efficacy of Sartre's critique of reified consciousness is, moreover, vitiated by the extreme dualism of his approach. The active character of consciousness is established on the basis of the tautology that the existence of consciousness is one and the same thing as the consciousness of its existence—in other words, that consciousness is conscious and self-consciousness is conscious of itself—which is then declared to be 'the supreme ontological law of consciousness'. This 'ontological law' is in turn used to rule out *a priori* the 'middle ground', and thus all possibility of *mediation* is foreclosed. As a result, we are presented with the ultimate 'ontological law' according to which there are *two types of existence*: the 'thing in the world', and consciousness. The whole argument is built on this dualistic assumption without which it cannot be sustained. As it stands, its critique can only apply to some *inconsistent dualism* which might wish both to retain its dualistic principles and to make use of the notion of a 'middle ground' as a bastard third type of existence; this is why Sartre insists that there can be *only* two types. But what if we entertain as an alternative the *monistic* framework of explanation? What if we seek in the dialectic of the one and the many—the one and only type of existence and its manifold mediations and transitions—the answer to the problems at stake? Clearly, in that case the argument that rests on the categorical assertion of extreme dualistic assumptions evaporates in thin air. Sartre, however, never makes a serious attempt at facing the monistic alternative, for such a confrontation would compel him to try to justify his own assumptions. He prefers to thunder, instead, against 'metaphysical materialism' and 'the dialectic of nature', while simply reaffirming the categorical validity of his own premises as the necessary basis of all discussion on the subject. And thus, starting out from the positions of methodological dualism—the programme of a phenomenological reduction of experience up to its 'irreducible' elements within consciousness—we end up with the ontology of a *radically fractured totality* from which *mediation* is exiled, with the antinomies necessarily inherent in this fracture. As we have seen above, Sartre censured Husserl on account of the 'miracle' of the *epoché*. Now, as a result of his own dualistic 'ontological law' which produces his radically fractured totality, we are presented with a *mystery* in place of the miracle: the bewildering ability of consciousness to use the sensory world as the vague 'occasion'—for heaven forbid to think in terms of dialectical *determinations*—of its own *spontaneous self-generation*.

The second point to mention is the *negative* determination of totality. This solution appears in the course of Sartre's application of some Heideggerian principles (with significant modifications) to the analysis of the imaginary:

> All creation of the imaginary would be completely impossible to a consciousness whose nature it would be precisely to be 'in-the-midst-of-the-world'. . . . For a consciousness to be able to imagine it must be able to *escape* from the world by its very nature, it must be able by *its own* efforts to *withdraw* from the world. In a word *it must be free*. Thus the thesis of unreality has yielded us the possibility of negation as its condition. Now, the latter is possible only by the *'negation' of the world as a whole,* and this negation has revealed itself to us as being the reverse of the very freedom of consciousness. . . . But, reciprocally, the possibility of *constructing a whole* is given as the primary structure of the act of taking perspective. It is therefore enough to be able to posit reality as a *synthetic whole* in order to posit oneself as *free from it* and this going-beyond is freedom itself since it could not happen if consciousness were not free. Thus *to posit the world as a world or to 'negate' it is one and the same thing.* In this sense Heidegger can say that *nothingness is the constitutive structure of the existent.*[201]
>
> The imaginary thus represents at each moment the implicit meaning of the real. . . . this specific position of the imaginary will be accompanied by a collapsing of the world which is no more than the *negated foundation of the unreal.*[202]

This position should not be mistaken for some advocacy of

arbitrariness. Indeed, Sartre makes explicit his firm opposition to such views. This is how he clarifies his relation to Heidegger's idea of surpassing which establishes nothingness as the constitutive structure of the existent:

> But this surpassing cannot be brought about by any means whatever, and the freedom of consciousness must not be confused with the arbitrary. For an image is not purely and simply the world-negated, it is always the world negated from a certain point of view, namely, the one that permits the positing of the absence or the non-existence of the object presented 'as an image'. The arbitrary position of the real as a world will not of itself cause the appearance of the centaur as an unreal object. For the centaur to emerge as unreal the world must be grasped as a world-where-the-centaur-is-not, and this can only happen if consciousness is led by different motivations to grasp the world as being *exactly* the sort in which the centaur has no place.[203]

Similarly, he makes some important qualifications on the relationship between imagination and freedom as well as between nothingness and the world of existence:

> . . . the imagination, which has become a psychological and empirical function, is the necessary condition for the freedom of empirical man in the midst of the world. For, if *the negating function belonging to consciousness*—which Heidegger calls surpassing—is what makes the act of imagination possible, it must be added on the other hand that this function can manifest itself only in an *imaginative act*. There can be no intuition of nothingness just because nothingness is nothing and because all consciousness intuitive or not is consciousness of something. *Nothingness* can present itself only as an *infra-structure of something*. The experience of nothingness is not, strictly speaking, a direct one, it is an experience which is in principle given 'with' and 'in'. The analyses of Bergson are pertinent in this connection: any attempt to *directly* conceive death or the nothingness of existence is by nature bound to fail. The gliding of the world into the bosom of nothingness and the emergence of human reality in this very nothingness can happen only through the position of something which is nothingness in relation to the world and in relation to which the world is nothing. By this we evidently define the structure of the imagination. It is the appearance of the imaginary before consciousness which permits the grasping of the process of turning the world into nothingness as

its essential condition and as its primary structure. . . . The imaginary is in every case the 'something' concrete towards which the existent is surpassed.[204]

Thus, Sartre's intention is perfectly clear. On the one hand he wants to assert the *complete freedom* of consciousness and its vital negating function. On the other hand, he is very much concerned with showing that consciousness, despite its freedom—or rather because of it, since 'consciousness is always "in situation" because it is always free', and the other way round, as we have seen above—cannot possibly construct another world than *exactly* the one in which we happen to live. Of course, this is a most uneasy solution that constantly oscillates between the extreme poles of total indeterminacy and its diametrical opposite: the massive contingency, facticity, 'absurdity'[205] and absolute givenness of the 'things in the world', with all their iron determinations. The very moment the freedom of consciousness is affirmed in its categorical form, it is already negated, in an equally categorical form, by the absolute contingency of the real as it exactly happens to be—thus the feeling of absurdity. Equally, the moment the real is asserted as exactly given, it is already negated and 'surpassed', for the function of consciousness is the 'surpassing of the real in order to make a world of it'.[206] Nevertheless, no matter how paradoxical this conception is, the existential motivation behind it is the affirmation of great concern: the *full* acknowledgement of the objectivity of the real in its exact givenness (in opposition to any attempt at directly inflating 'nothingness' into a pseudo-objective myth), and the equally full and passionate rejection of its iron determinations in the name of 'surpassing' through the existential projects of the human world.

But to return to the negative determination of totality, 'constructing a whole' (or 'positing the world as a world') and negating it comes to 'one and the same thing'. This view assigns to nothingness and negation the key role, as 'the constitutive structure of the existent'. The consequence of such a definition is that totality (the real as a world) is identifiable only through its 'collapse', that is when the world appears as nothing more than 'the negated foundation of the unreal'. Thus the world is not the *foundation* of the unreal (the imaginary)—for that would still preserve the reality of the real when it is elevated to the status of totality—but only its *negated* foundation. This means that when the imaginary constructs the real as a whole through its negating function, what it brings about is not totality as real but merely a complete 'nihilation' which assumes the form of an unarticulated *imaginary totality* that necessarily loses its totality in direct proportion to its reconstitution as the real. We are thus presented with another, even if this time inexplicit, 'ontological law', one which postulates an *inverse ratio* in the relationship between the total and the real. The problem is, therefore, not the confusion of the total and the individual but the existential nihilation of the former through the identification of 'totalization' and 'néantisation'.

In such a conceptual framework there can be no room for negation *within* the sphere of objective reality itself: negation must always come from the outside. For 'that which is denied must be imagined. In fact, *the object of a negation cannot be real* because it would be affirming what is being denied—but neither can it be a complete nothing, since it is something that is being denied. So the object of a negation must be posited as imaginary.'[207] Thus the 'dialectic of nature'—indeed any non-Sartrean kind of 'realist' ontology—must be *a priori* ruled out by this conception. In truth, not because of the alleged logical contradiction, for Sartre is the last person to worry about *formal* logical contradictions. (There is nothing wrong with that. One of the most crucial dialectical categories: *Aufhebung*—superseding-preservation and preserving-supersession—is precisely a fusion of positivity and negativity. It is exactly the kind of 'surpassing affirmation' which Sartre strangely wants to exclude here as a violation of logic.) The real reason is the overall ontological construct which *precedes* the logical argument rather than being derived from it, notwithstanding Sartre's presentation of the issues. As a matter of fact, Sartre must disregard any possible counter-argument to his own—for example, the simultaneously positive-affirmative and negative-surpassing character of *Aufhebung*—because such counter-arguments would undermine his ontological assumptions.

As we have seen above, in the passage on the 'supreme ontological law of consciousness', Sartre declares that 'consciousness can determine itself to exist' because its nature is to be free (by definition). However, the price he has to pay for such a definition—and he does so with great consistency—is to admit that this free consciousness 'cannot act on anything but itself'. Consequently, in order to be able to fulfil its negating function, consciousness must first *homogenize* the object of its negation with itself. This can take place only in the form of a peculiarly Sartrean double negation which, unlike Hegel or Marx, does not reproduce reality at a higher level but constantly reestablishes the fragmentation of reality. The first negation is universal or generic in that it must *comprehensively* (or categorically) nihilate the reality character of the real in order to be able to 'act' upon it once the real (transmuted into the 'negated foundation of the unreal') is subsumed under the sphere of nihilatingly totalizing consciousness. (As we can see, 'totalization' is the necessary function of this nihilating homogenization.) And the second negation is partial or specific in that *something* is being denied by imagination on the ground of the previous universal negation. And since the specificity of the second negation cannot arise without affecting universality (the imaginary totality) itself, as produced through the first negation, we are thrown back into a real completely severed from totality: the world of fragmentation and isolation, compartmentalization and 'serialization', privatization and deadly confrontation—in one world, the desolate world of *reification*. No wonder, therefore, that the existential picture of this world is painted with the most sombre colours: 'When the imaginary is not posited as a fact, the surpassing and the nullifying of the existent are swallowed up in the existent; . . . *the person is crushed* in the world, run through by the real, he is *closest to the thing*.'[208]

This takes us to the *third* major point which concerns the world of objects and their utilizability. In *Nausea* the problem appears in a most graphic form as the main theme of the novel:

> I am no longer free, I can no longer do what I want. Objects ought not to touch, since they are not alive. You use them, you put them back in place, you live among them: they are useful, nothing more. But they touch me, it's unbearable. I am afraid of entering in contact with them, just as if they were living animals.
>
> Now I see; I remember better what I felt the other day on the sea-shore when I was holding that pebble. It was a sort of sweet disgust. How unpleasant it was! And it came from the pebble, I'm sure of that, it passed from the pebble into my hands. Yes, that's it, that's exactly it: a sort of nausea in the hands.[209]

From here Sartre's hero goes on to say, as the theme unfolds, first, that Nausea is not inside him but, on the contrary, he is the one who is 'inside it',[210] and then, that Nausea is himself.[211] Such a transition, on the surface of it, seems to correspond to the stages whereby (1) man comes into contact with the world of objects and simply utilizes them (absence of nausea); (2) he perceives the threatening character of objects (the pebble, the nausea in the hand); (3) he is surrounded and engulfed by the world of objects (he is inside nausea); and (4) he is himself reified (he is one with nausea, he is 'it'). However, things are rather more complicated than that in Sartre's vision. For the point of total takeover—an unexpected, strange experience of wholeness—suddenly transmutes everything by some 'magic' into fullness and life and into overflowing plenitude. Significantly, at this point Sartre's hero has his revelation about the nature of existence. This is how he describes it:

> It took my breath away. Never, until these last few days, had I

suspected what it meant to 'exist'. . . . usually existence hides itself. It is there, around us, in us, it is us, you can't say a couple of words without speaking of it, but finally you can't touch it. . . . And then, all of a sudden, there it was, as clear as day; existence had *suddenly* unveiled itself. It had lost its harmless appearance as an abstract category: it was the very stuff of things, that root was steeped in existence. Or rather the root, the park gates, the bench, the sparse grass on the lawn, all that had vanished; the *diversity* of things, their *individuality,* was only an *appearance,* a veneer. This veneer had melted, leaving soft, *monstrous masses,* in disorder— naked, with a frightening, obscene nakedness.[212]

Such a wholeness from which the veneer of diversity and individuality has been removed, cannot be grasped, according to Roquentin-Sartre, in terms of human measures which we apply to the world of utilizable objects. Thus the reflection about the 'superfluity' of all existents leads to the identification of the 'absolute' and the 'absurd', 'nausea' and 'existence', 'existence' (nausea) and 'contingency' (nausea)—all explained as dimensions of the World . . . that huge absurd being':

I realized that there was no half-way house between non-existence and this rapturous abundance. . . . Superfluous: that was the only connexion I could establish between those trees, those gates, those pebbles. It was in vain that I tried to count the chestnut trees, to situate them in relation to the Velleda, to *compare* their height with the height of the plane trees: each of them escaped from the relationship in which I tried to enclose it, isolated itself, overflowed. I was aware of the *arbitrary* nature of these relationships, which I insisted on maintaining in order to delay the *collapse of the human world of measures,* of quantities, of bearings; they no longer had any grip on things. . . .

The word Absurdity is now born beneath my pen; . . . I had found the key to Existence, the key to my nausea, to my own life. . . . over there, I touched the thing. But here I should like to establish the *absolute* character of this *absurdity.* . . . I, a little while ago, experienced the absolute: the absolute or the absurd. . . . *Absurd; irreducible;* nothing—not even profound, secret aberration of Nature—could explain that. . . . the world of explanations and reasons is not that of existence. . . .

Yes, I had already scrutinized, with that same *anxiety,* unnameable objects, . . . I had already felt their cold, *inert*

*qualities escape,* slip between my fingers. . . . And the pebble, that
wretched pebble, the origin of this whole business: it was not . . . I
couldn't remember exactly what *it refused* to be. But I had not
forgotten *its passive resistance.* . . .

The essential thing is contingency. I mean that, by definition,
existence is not necessity. To exist is simply to be there; what exists
appears, lets itself be encountered, but *you can never deduce it.*
There are people, I believe, who have understood that. Only they
have tried to overcome this contingency by inventing a necessary,
causal being. But no necessary being can explain existence:
contingency is not an illusion, an appearance which can be
dissipated; it is *absolute* and consequently perfect *gratuitousness.*
Everything is gratuitous, that park, this town, and myself. When
you realize that, *it turns your stomach over* and everything starts
floating about, . . . that is the nausea; . . .

I was the root of the chestnut tree. Or rather I was all
consciousness of its existence. Still detached from—since I was
conscious of it—and yet lost in it, nothing but it. An *uneasy
consciousness* and yet one which let itself hang with all its weight
over that piece of inert wood. . . . Existence is not something
which allows itself to be thought of from a distance; it has to *invade
you suddenly,* pounce upon you, weigh heavily on your heart like a
*huge motionless animal*—or else there is *nothing* left at
all. . . . That idea of transition was another invention of man. An
idea which was too clear. . . . Admittedly a movement was
something different from a tree. But it was still *an absolute. A
thing.* . . . Everything was full, everything was active, there was no
unaccented beat, everything, even the most imperceptible move-
nent, was made of existence. . . . Existence everywhere, to
infinity, superfluous, always and everywhere; . . . my very flesh
was throbbing and opening, abandoning itself to the *universal*
burgeoning, it was repulsive. . . .

There were fools who talked to you about *willpower* and the
*struggle for life.* . . . Impossible to see things that way. Weak-
nesses, frailties, yes.[213] . . . [The trees] did not want to exist, only
they could not help it; . . . Tired and old, they went on existing,
unwillingly and ungraciously, simply because they were *too weak to
die,* because death could come to them only from the outside:
melodies alone can proudly carry their own death within them like
an *internal necessity;* only they don't exist. *Every existent is born
without reason, prolongs itself out of weakness and dies by
chance.* . . .

Did I dream it up, that huge presence? . . . It went up as high as
the sky, it flowed away everywhere, it filled everything with

gelatinous subsidence and I could see it going deeper and deeper, far beyond the limits of the park and the houses at Bouville, I was no longer at Bouville or anywhere, I was floating. I was not surprised, I knew perfectly well that it was the World, the *World in all its nakedness which was suddenly revealing itself*, and I choked with fury at that *huge absurd being*. You couldn't even wonder where it all came from, or *how it was that a world should exist rather than nothing.*[214]

As we can see, the depiction of Roquentin's experience in the park graphically unfolds the main tenets of Sartre's existential philosophy. The world of objects—as differentiated, determinate, utilizable, countable, comparable, etc.—turns out to be the world of appearance and 'veneer', and, through anxiety, the absolute unveils itself as undifferentiated wholeness, huge and overpowering presence, absurd and gratuitous contingency, all-pervasive existence, the World as irreducible, naked, 'huge absurd being'. Here we are given the Husserlian 'direct intuition of essence' in its existentialist version, with the phenomenological bracket wide open. Its driving force (or 'motivation') is passion and emotion which force the absolute to 'reveal itself'. This enterprise is characterized at the plane of experience as anguish, nausea, powerless fury, etc. Man is driven on by passion which shows itself as the primary structure of his existential reality.

Naturally, *Nausea* is trying to convey the existential message in a fictional form, utilizing the means of graphic depiction, metaphorical suggestion, and dramatic presentation. The evocative aim requires that the philosophical ideas be wedded to vivid imagery and cannot simply follow a course of their own. Thus the various conceptual elements become fused into one another sometimes as a direct result of the imagery itself, while a strictly conceptual development of the same ideas would require a sharper definition and a more clearly differentiated expression. Nevertheless, all the constituents of the young Sartre's general conception are present in *Nausea,* in a specific form, and the world of objects—in relation to the problem of 'utilizability'—is depicted in fundamentally the same way as in his rather more abstract works on philosophical psychology written in the same period.

We can see this very clearly in his *Sketch for a Theory of the Emotions*, though of course here the lines of demarcation are more firmly drawn. This is how Sartre characterizes in this work the fundamental contrast between the world as the 'totality of utensils' and the world as a 'non-utilizable whole':

> Consciousness can 'be-in-the-world' in two different ways. The world may appear before it as an organized complex of utilizable things, such that, if one wants to produce a predetermined effect, one must act upon the determinate elements of that complex. As one does so, each "utensil" refers one to other utensils and to the *totality of utensils*; there is no *absolute action,* no *radical* change that one can introduce immediately into this world. We have to modify one *particular* utensil, and this by means of another which refers in its turn to yet another, and so on to *infinity*. But the world may also confront us as one *non-utilizable whole*; that is, as only modifiable without intermediation and by *great masses*. In that case, the categories of the world act *immediately* upon the consciousness, they are present to it at no distance (for example, the face that frightens us through the window acts upon us without any means; there is no need for the window to open, for a man to leap into the room or to walk across the floor). And, conversely, the consciousness tries to combat these dangers or to modify these objects at no distance and *without means,* by some *absolute, massive* modification of the world. This aspect of the world is an entirely coherent one; this is *the magical world*.[215]

Here we are confronted with another hopeless dichotomy. The world in which we have to act by means of 'utensils'—the world of countable things and comparable objects, predetermined instruments and goal-oriented institutions, teleological targets and individual actions, determinate powers and specific transformations—is an infinitely fragmented world which cannot be pictured as *a whole* from the point of view of the individual who is trying to act upon it because doing so would involve us in yet another logical contradiction: that of putting an end to infinity, or controlling and transforming infinity through a particular, infinitesimal part of it. The Sartrean construction is so fatefully dichotomous that we are either confined to the infinitesimal fraction so as to resign ourselves to the idea of action as an infinite series of small mediations of utensils by utensils by utensils by . . . to infinity, or we directly confront totality as undifferentiated wholeness and non-utilizable whole (the 'huge absurd being' we have encountered in *Nausea*) and 'act' upon it 'at no distance and without means', producing some 'absolute, massive modification' through the *magic* of emotion. Even to envisage taking hold of totality in order to affect it radically in a non-magical way would mean contemplating a dreadful self-contradiction.

Obviously, one would be an extremely simple-minded neo-positivist cheerfully to accept the predicament of fractional mediations in the name of a 'social engineering': the labour of a demented Sisyphus who disregards the odds of infinity against him and predicates a successful outcome to his own efforts. Sartre has nothing in common with such an attitude. His picture of the predicament of man in the world of utensils is very far from being a cheerful one. On the contrary, for him 'the Universe remains dark' (1964), as we have seen above.[216] And it would be vain to expect the removal of the gloom through the other side of the dichotomy. For the 'massive modification of the world' occurs only in what Sartre explicitly calls '*the magical world*'.

But, of course, this could not be otherwise, thanks to the Sartrean characterization of the world of utilizable things. His representation of the 'totality of utensils' as an infinite series of partial mediations is a self-defeating (but in relation to the acting individual coherent) misrepresentation in that it is depicted as an *unstructured totality*. The vague talks about the 'organized complex' of utilizable things (as earlier about the 'occasion' of the self-generation of consciousness, in place of its dialectical determination through mediated reciprocities and interactions), does not help in the least to solve this problem. For an 'organized complex' which is assigned the form of an infinite series is not organized at all in any proper sense of the term. It is more like a contradiction in terms—an organized whole which is not a totality—than a genuine structure. Indeed, *seriality* as such is not an 'ontological structure of being' but the *mere postulate* of an inherently problematical structure: the 'countable' arrangement of unstructured things in an infinite ('open') series, at the formal-conceptual level; and a mystifying *phenomenal manifestation* of an underlying structure (the structure of reification and commodity fetish) in the sphere of social reality.

Sartre's picture of the world as unstructured totality on closer inspection turns out to be the product of a *double dichotomy*: (1) the diametrical opposition between the 'thing in the world' (the world of things and objects) and consciousness, and (2) the antagonistic existential opposition between man (consciousness) and 'the other'. It goes without saying, radical change through action is conceivable only if the world is a *structured totality* in which some constituents have a greater strategic function than others; and the strategic importance of any particular factor ('utensil', 'institution', 'means') is in direct proportion to its ability to control the *structure as a whole*. (As we can see, this is not a question of mere 'countability', but of a *qualitative* location—key, strategically vital, etc.—of the factor in question within the overall structure.) If we try to bring about a radical change in our society by first addressing, say, a local tea-party of fox-hunters' wives, urging them to use their good offices with their husbands, and then we move on to the next particular 'utensil' and to the next thereafter, and so on, in the chain of the established 'organized complex', we are indeed going to get lost forever in the maze of our self-imposed infinite series.

Fortunately, however, there are other ways of producing radical changes in the social world. The necessary preconditions of major social change are (1) the iden-

tification and utilization of the historically given contradictions, forces and institutions, and (2) the adequacy of
the subject of the action to the task. If, however, the subject
is conceived as an isolated individual, he is bound to remain
a prisoner of the infinite series. For social reality is a
structured totality only in relation to a subject who is himself
a complex whole: the *social* individual integrated (through
his class or, in a classless society, in some other form) into
the community to which he happens to belong. In the eyes of
the isolated individual the social totality must, of course,
appear as the mysterious aggregate of particular steps which
he cannot conceivably control beyond an extremely limited
point, if that. Thus this isolated individual who is
opposed—in the spirit of the Sartrean double dichotomy—
not only to the world of objects but also to the human beings
of the given social world characterized as 'the other', cannot
do other than admit the powerlessness of his own actions in
the 'world of utilizable things' and embark on the curious
strategies of the 'magical world'. This is where the
Heideggerian heritage weighs heaviest on Sartre's shoulders. The undialectical conception of the world as an
unstructured totality, and the closely interrelated characterization of the subject of human action as an isolated
individual, are transmuted into ahistorical 'existential
structures', and the social world is subsumed under the
world of magic: the world of the emotion.

> . . . during an emotion, the consciousness abases itself and abruptly
> transmutes the *determinist world* in which we live, into a *magical
> world*. But, conversely, sometimes it is this world that reveals itself
> to consciousness as magical just where we expect it to be
> deterministic. It must not, indeed, be supposed that magic is an
> ephemeral quality that we impose upon the world according to our
> humour. There is an *existential structure* of the world which is
> magical. . . . the category of 'magic' governs the interpsychic
> relations between men in society and, more precisely, *our
> perception of others*. The magical, as Alain says, is 'the mind
> crawling among things'; that is, an *irrational synthesis of*

*spontaneity and passivity.* It is an *inert activity,* a consciousness rendered passive. But it is precisely in that form that we appear *to others,* and this, not because of our position in relation to them, nor in consequence of our passions, but *by essential necessity.* Indeed, consciousness can only be a transcendent object by undergoing the modification of passivity. . . . It follows that *man is always a sorcerer to man and the social world is primarily magical.*[217]

Emotion may be called a *sudden fall of consciousness into magic*; or, if you will, emotion arises when *the world of the utilizable vanishes abruptly* and the world of magic appears in its place. We must not, therefore, see in emotion a passing disorder of the organism and the mind which enters and upsets them from outside. On the contrary, it is the return of consciousness in the magical attitude, one of the great attitudes which are essential to it, with *the appearance of the correlative world—the magical world.* Emotion is not an accident, it is a mode of our conscious existence, one of the ways in which consciousness understands (in Heidegger's sense of *Verstehen*) its Being-in-the-World.[218]

While some parts of these quotations are most illuminating about the nature of the emotion itself, the utilization of emotion as the key to understanding the social world (as magic) is problematical in the extreme. For man may be 'a sorcerer to man'—but do we not all know that sorcerers are an 'invention' of man, in the Sartrean sense of the term? And if men behave *as if* they were sorcerers, it is not because of some essential ontological necessity issuing from a permanent existential structure that forever manifests itself as an unavoidable irrational synthesis of spontaneity and passivity, but because of determinate—and at least in principle removable—socio-historical conditions. To embark on the task of removing these conditions by *restructuring* the social world in which we happen to live, in accordance with genuine human ends and in opposition to the self-propelling power of 'magically' reified institutions, is precisely what confers meaning on the human enterprise at the present stage of history. And no 'magic' is going to help in that.

It is not necessary to go on any longer; for some additional aspects of this complex of problems which we might wish to examine are only corollaries of the basic tenets seen so far. As the examples quoted above have shown, in Sartre's early philosophy totality is: (1) dualistically *fractured*; (2) *negatively determined*; and (3) *unstructured* both as 'totality of utensils' arranged in an infinite series, and as social totality called 'the magical world'. Naturally, in Sartre's later works there are some changes also in these respects, and their extent and precise nature will be discussed in some detail in the chapters that follow. Now we must confine ourselves to indicating briefly the general trend of Sartre's later development as directly related to the present context.

On the first point we find that in some of his later works Sartre becomes aware of the *need* for mediation, and at least the *postulate* of such mediation repeatedly appears in the *Critique* and elsewhere. However, the dualistic structure of his thought tends to reassert itself, no matter how hard he tries to overcome the fracture in *particular* contexts. He puts forward *one side* of the dualistic opposition, to function as mediation, which it cannot conceivably do. Thus, in place of genuine structural mediations we get declarations such as *'irreducible particularity* is one way of *living universality'*[219] *'the child becomes this or that because he *lives* the *universal* as *particular'*[220] whereby 'lived' and 'living' (which belong to the particular) become the pseudo-mediations between universality and particularity. This solution provides a blanket justification for the systematic *avoidance* of the true problem of mediation, namely: how is it possible to live the universal as particular? A question to which the answer can only be: 'through specific mediations' (which, of course, calls for the precise identification of these specificities) and not 'through living it'—Sartre's answer—which is begging the question. And, of course, begging the question not as a result of some 'confusion' (a favourite 'explanation' in neo-positivist philosophy which itself begs the question by explaining alleged confusion by alleging confusion) but out of the internal necessity of a philosophy which simultaneously wants to *retain* unchanged its dualistic presuppositions (the structural framework of its reasoning)—e.g. 'What we call freedom is the *irreducibility* of the *cultural* order to the *natural* order'[221]—and 'mediate' them by declaring that 'irreducibility' is mediation itself.

Second, negative determination remains all-pervasive in Sartre's philosophy, wherever we look. Three illustrations should suffice here, concerning (1) reality in general; (2) particular individuals; and (3) a complex social whole like the city. According to Sartre, the fundamental dimension of human reality, possibility, articulates itself as 'the presence of the future as that which is lacking, and that which, by its very *absence*, reveals reality'.[222] In the second respect we learn that 'Every man is defined negatively by the *sum total of possibles* which are *impossible* for him; that is, by a future more or less *blocked off*'.[223] And in the third context we read that 'a city is a material and social organization which derives its *reality* from the *ubiquity of its absence*'.[224] Again, Sartre tries to introduce historical qualifications, and again the original structure tends to reassert itself. We can see this dilemma in the way he approaches history. He is critical of marxism for its alleged failure to study the structures of history—the object of Sartre's enquiry in the *Critique*—'for themselves'.[225] Paradoxically, however, his ontological analysis of these structures under the aspect of the 'theoretical possibilities of their combinations',[226] tends to negate the historicity of history by defining it as a fundamental existential structure: 'If History escapes me, this is not because I do not make it; it is because the *other* is making it as well.'[227] Thus, if history escapes me it is not because the 'other' is *whatever he is like* (i.e., antagonistically opposed to 'me', for determinate socio-historical reasons), but because he is 'the other' (i.e., because of the existential ontological structure of 'otherness'). Consequently, either the other ceases to make history and leaves that job to me, or history will continue to escape me. And again, either the other ceases to be the other, or history will remain the way we know it from the past, namely beyond conscious human control. And since such possibilities are at best confined to transitory moments—like the obliteration of the antagonism between the 'I' and 'the other' in the structurally unstable 'fused group'—'the other' continues to cast its immense dark shadow on history, thanks to Sartre's negative determination of the existential ontological structures.

And finally, the problem of unstructured totality. It is in this respect that the changes are most obvious in Sartre's later philosophy. He gets involved in an intensive study of historical temporalization as manifest through exchange, the 'pratico-inert', series, collectives, recurrence, etc., although primarily from the point of view of the 'theoretical possibilities of their combinations', as we have seen a moment ago. At times he even remarks on the historical specificity of the conditions under which the infinite series dominates, but with a tendency to take back—or at least greatly to weaken—through the next step in his line of reasoning the historical specification. We can see this very clearly in the following quotation:

> It is necessary to take up the study of collectives again from the beginning and to demonstrate that these objects, far from being characterized by the direct unity of a consensus, represent perspectives of flight. This is because, *upon the basis of given conditions,* the direct relations between persons depend upon particular relations, and these on still others, *and so on in succession,* because there is an objective constraint in concrete relations. It is not the presence of the others but their *absence* which establishes this constraint; it is not their union but their separation. For us the reality of the collective objects rests on recurrence. It demonstrates that the *totalization is never achieved* and that the totality exists *at best* only in the form of a detotalized totality.[228]

Furthermore the early double dichotomy reappears, in that history as such is depicted as the sphere of irreconcilable antagonism in which man is opposed to 'the other' and 'existence'—in its particularity and irreducibility—to knowledge. (Also: we are confronted with a 'struggle of *thought* against its *social instruments*'[229]—as if thought itself were not a social instrument.) And even references to magic are retained, as late as 1973 ('relations between people . . . are complicated by some *magic*'), together with the famous sentence from the early work on *Emotions*: '*man is a sorcerer for man*'[230] repeated word for word. No wonder that for Sartre the resolution of the antagonism depicted in his existential-ontological account of history cannot be the *realization* of history (in Marx's words, 'true history' that follows mankind's antagonistic 'pre-history') but only the problematical postulate of its *dissolution*: 'History will have only one meaning, when it will tend to be *dissolved* in the *concrete men* who will make it in common'.[231] Thus, since the various insitutional etc. forms of our 'detotalized' social totality are characterized as 'realities, whose being is directly proportional to the *non-being of humanity*',[232] the ideal of human self-realization must appear as the *direct* experience of universality by concrete man whose pre-condition is the progressive dissolution of all those differentiations and mediations through which history articulates itself.

4

The methodological principles of a philosophy are insep-arable from the basic propositions through which any comprehensive orientation of thought towards reality can be defined. Naturally, for analytical purposes, methodological rules may have to be treated separately. But they are not intelligible in themselves, nor are they capable of providing justification for themselves. To try to explain methodolog-ical principles and rules by themselves can only result in the infite regress of meta-meta— . . . meta-methodology or in circularity, or a combination of the two (as in some neo-positivistic 'analytic philosophy' which exhausts itself in the production of a self-consuming methodology for the sake of methodology by obsessively sharpening its carving knife until the blade completely disappears in the steel-dust of self-perfection and the philosopher is left holding the bare handle). The problems of method arising out of the task at hand, and the philosophical comprehension of experience prescribes its own—explicit or latent—method. Any particular set of methodological rules presents itself as a specific way of sifting and selecting from among all the available data, with a view of constructing a coherent whole. Specifying how to proceed, what to include or exclude, how to define the relationship between philosophical knowledge and the totality of available (including scientific and everyday) knowledge, how to relate philosophical activity to the totality of human praxis, and so on,—all this would be meaningless if it could not be justified by the nature of the philosophical enterprise itself as developed throughout history. (Why on earth should one pay the slightest attention to the rules of a particular philosophical method unless one wanted to participate in the further development of this collective human enterprise?) Furthermore, the rules of a particular method would be arbitrary if they could not be justified by the results as compared to those obtainable through the adoption of alternative methods. Phenomenological reduction, for instance, is totally pointless without the explicit or implicit critical references to the alleged deficiences of the 'natural attitude', and thus to the whole complex of controversial issues—in epistemology and ontology—which gave rise to the elaboration of the phenomenological method in the first two decades of the twentieth century.

The methodological rules and principles are constituted in the course of the articulation of a given philosophy as a whole. This is why they cannot be simply transferred from one setting to another without all the necessary modifications which homogenize the rules of method and the thematic principles of the philosophy in question. Ontological shifts call for significant methodological changes even in philosophies which explicitly profess to abide by the same rules. Husserl, Heidegger, Sartre, Merleau-Ponty are all phenomenologists in a sense. However, the way they all apply and modify the, rules of phenomenology varies considerably from one philosopher to the other but even in the development of each.[233] This is not the place to pursue these problems systematically. Limitations of space demand that we confine ourselves to a brief discussion of the dialectical interrelationship between method and *Weltanschauung* (world view) as manifest in Sartre's own writings.

Already at the time of his earliest encounter with Husserl, Sartre's enthusiasm for phenomenology is tempered by concerns which are eminently his own. When Raymond Aron, in the spring of 1933, draws his attention to Husserl's philosophy, he is already looking for some method through which he might be able to express *his own* views on existence and contingency in a more coherent form. He welcomes the discovery to the extent to which it can be subordinated to his own conception and integrated into his own quest. This is the most telling part of Simone de Beauvoir's account of the incident. For while leafing through Levinas's book on Husserl which he picks up on the Boulevard Saint-Michel soon after the talk with Aron, Sartre's 'heart missed a beat when he found references to contingency: *Had someone cut the ground from under his feet, then?* As he read on he reassured himself that this was not so. Contingency seemed not to play any very important part in Husserl's system'.[234] Thus, Sartre has very firm ideas right from the beginning on what he wants the phenomenological method for: the coherent formulation of his own existential-ontological concerns. His commitment to the latter precedes by several years his encounter with phenomenology, but they fill his mind in a rather chaotic form. Now that he has made his discovery, he is determined to use phenomenology so as to give shape, order and discipline to his strongly felt views. From such intention it also follows that in so far as the new method is not suited to the task he has in mind, it will have to be modified as required. For he sees clearly, right from the outset, that—through his own problematic of contingency—he introduces something significantly new into Husserlian phenomenology. No wonder, then, that Sartre's very first serious reflection on this method, in 1934, takes the form of a radical reassessment of its principal tenets, from the 'transcendental ego' to the *epoché*, and from the question of 'motivations' to the characteristically Sartrean way of opening the phenomenological bracket.

Of course, the relationship between method and ontology should not be conceived on the model of one-sided determinations but as a form of dialectical reciprocity. This means that once the Sartrean version of phenomenology is constituted, on the basis of his major ontological principles, the methodological framework tends to circumscribe the limits within which reality is experienced and evaluated. Thus, for instance, when in *The Problem of Method* Sartre expresses his total agreement with the marxist Lefèbvre's method, he reads the latter's words characteristically in his own key. For these are the exact terms of Lefèbvre's analysis: '(a) *Descriptive*. Observation but with a scrutiny guided by experience and by a general theory. (*b*) *Analytico-regressive*. Analysis of reality. Attempt to date it precisely. (*c*) *Historical-genetic*. Attempt to rediscover the present, but elucidated, understood, explained.'[235] And this is how Sartre interprets it:

> We have nothing to add to this passage, so clear and so rich, except that we believe that this method, with its phase of *phenomenolog-ical description* and its *double* movement of *regression* followed by *progress,* is valid—with the modifications which its objects may impose upon it—in all the domains of anthropology. Further, it is this method which we shall apply, as we shall see later, to *significations,* to *individuals* themselves, and to the *concrete* relations among individuals. This method alone can be heuristic: it alone at once defines the *originality* of the fact and makes comparisons possible.[236]

As we can see, Sartre's primary interest is in 'significations' (elsewhere he calls it 'hierarchized significations'[237]), individuals, concreteness, and 'originality' (uniqueness) to be connected with universality through comparisons, in the service of a *heuristic*. In one word, his concern is to find a method best suited to explain a *particular individual* (Flaubert, for example) in most comprehensive way. Anthropological knowledge, as Sartre sees it, is mobilized towards this end. By contrast, Lefèbvre's enquiry is concerned with a rural community and, through studying it, with the definition of the methods appropriate to the field of rural sociology. Accordingly, for him the *descriptive* phase is just what it says, namely, taking inventory of the data as encountered in the given rural community, within the framework of a general theory of society. Which means that there can be no 'pure description', since evaluation is an integral part of the enterprise at all phases, in virtue of the general theory brought to bear upon the data of description. Significantly, however, Sartre translates 'descriptive' into *phenomenological description*—which is a radically different enterprise both in that it claims to be 'pure description' and that its aim is the identification of 'essences'.

The second phase for Lefèbvre is 'analytico-regressive'. For he wants to *date* (his italics) with precision the various historical layers that coexist in the given structure; that is, he wants to identify the heterogeneity of the elements—with all their contrasts—that make up the structure. In other words, this phase is concerned with the elucidation of a cross-section of the structure, whereas the third phase concentrates on the 'historical-genetic' comprehension and elucidation of the dynamic whole of the present. Characteristically, again, this complementarity of the 'analytico-regressive' (or 'structural-analytic') and the 'historical-genetic' dimensions is translated by Sartre as the 'double movement of regression followed by progress', while in fact the term 'progress' does not appear in Lefèbvre's classification. In any case, it is not clear why the historical-genetic phase should be called 'progressive', since Lefèbvre's point was not meant to establish a *temporal* sequence but to stress the two forms in which history and structure are treated in the study: history as subordinate to structure (the analytico-regressive dating of the various elements of the structure), and structure as subordinate to history (the historical-genetic comprehension of the present).

If we want to understand the reasons why Sartre decodes for himself and translates for us Lefèbvre's terms the way he does, we have to go back a long way into the past, right to the early constitution of his methodological principles as spelled out in the *Sketch for a Theory of the Emotions*. In this we find the following key passage:

> The various disciplines of phenomenological psychology are regressive although the ultimate term of their regression is, for them, purely ideal: those of *pure phenomenology,* on the contrary, are *progressive*. It may, no doubt, be asked why, under these conditions, one should choose to employ the two disciplines simultaneously; pure phenomenology might seem to suffice. But, if phenomenology can prove that emotion is realization of the *essence* of the human-reality in so far as the latter is affectivity, it will be impossible for it to show that the human-reality must necessarily manifest itself in such emotions as it does. That there are such and such emotions and not others—this is, beyond all doubt, evidence of the *factitious character of human existence*. It is this *factitiousness that necessitates* a regular *recourse to the empirical*; and which, in all probability, will forever prevent the *psychological regression* and the *phenomenological progression* from complete convergence.[238]

Here we have Sartre's original methodological principles which continue to structure, notwithstanding some important changes, also his much later reflections on the 'progressive-regressive method': *psychological regression* (or 'recourse to the empirical'), and *phenomenological progression* orientated towards the 'essence of the human-reality'. The reason why Sartre must envisage a *double movement* is itself twofold: on the one hand, the 'purity' of pure phenomenology which means that the *facticity* (or 'factitiousness') of the human existence must *escape* it by definition; and on the other hand, the facticity of human existence (that is to say, its 'such-and-such' character; its nature *exactly* as we experience it) calls for disciplines to which facticity is accessible if one wants to understand and elucidate the object of the enquiry. How to integrate the two, remains somewhat of a mystery, given the radical dualism of Sartrean ontology and its correspondingly dualistic methodological rules. The double movement is bound to remain a constant 'to-and-fro', an oscillatory movement of reciprocal reflection from one pole towards the other, and so on. Sartre himself admits this by saying that psychological regression and phenomenological progression are destined *forever* not to converge, although strangely enough he adds, 'in all probability'—a qualification contradicted by the necessity inherent in his own depiction of the irreconcileable opposition between existential facticity and pure phenomenological essence.

This dilemma is clearly visible also in another youthful work, *L'Imagination,* in which the earlier seen opposition between facticity and essence is complemented by that between *particularity* ('individual fact', 'examples') and *universality.*

> Phenomenology is a description of the structure of transcendental consciousness based on intuition of the essences of these structures. This description takes place, of course, on the level of reflection . . . which aims at the discovery of essences. That is to say, it begins by taking its stand from the outset on the *terrain of the universal.* Though proceeding in terms of *examples,* little importance is attached to whether the *individual fact* which serves as underpinning for the essence is *real* or *imaginary.* Should the 'exemplifying' datum be *pure fiction,* the very fact that it was imaginable means that it embodied the sought-for essence, for *the essence is the very condition of its possibility.*[239]

Thus, we are confronted with the dichotomies of facticity versus essence ('the essences of the structures of transcendental consciousness'), actuality versus possibility, and

existential particularity versus phenomenological universality. We get essences, possibilities and universality at
one pole, and facticity, actuality and particularity at the
other. And since mediation (the 'middle ground', the 'third
type of existence', etc.) has been *a priori* ruled out, as we
have seen above, integration is hardly conceivable. In its
place we find the suggestion of a somewhat mysterious
*dissolution* of the two poles (and of the problem at stake)
through the oscillatory double movement of reciprocal
reflection (in later terminology: 'cross-referencing',
'va-et-vient'), just as the antagonism of history is supposed
to disappear through the *dissolution* of history. This is why
even in its much later formulation

> the existentialist method . . . wants to remain heuristic. It will have
> no other method than a continuous cross-reference; it will
> progressively determine a biography (for example) by examining
> the period, and the period by studying the biography. Far from
> seeking immediately to *integrate* one into the other, it will *hold them
> separate* until the reciprocal involvement *comes to pass of itself* and
> puts a temporary *end to the research.*'[240]

5

Another major preoccupation in Sartre's philosophy is his
attempt to provide a 'foundation' to marxism through his
own existential phenomenology. It would again be quite
wrong to see this only in the Sartre of *The Problem of
Method* and its aftermath. For in point of fact the origins of
this orientation go back in his work at least as far as *The
Transcendence of the Ego,* although his early attitude to
marxism shows greater reservations than in the late 1950s.
We have to bear in mind two important considerations in this
respect. First, that Sartre as a student learns about a
mechanical kind of marxism both from those hostile to it (his
professors) and those (like Politzer) who champion its cause.
And second, that there is a long-standing philosophical
tradition—Simmel and Max Weber are among its

founders—which concedes to marxism, after many years of *Totschweigen* (execution by silence), the value of being of partial interest (as a supplier of interesting historical hypotheses) while insisting that it is devoid of a proper philosophical and methodological foundation. Accordingly, even the young Lukács entertains for a number of years the idea of producing the missing philosophical-methodological foundation, and Heidegger moves in the same intellectual orbit as far as the problematic of 'founding' is concerned, although, understandably (in the years of German dis-integration following the 1914-18 war rendered only more painful by the success of the Russian revolution) his 'fundamental ontology' is meant as a foundation not *for* marxism but *against* it, transferring the problems of alienation and reification from the socio-historical sphere (the world dominated by capital) to the plane of existential-ontological temporality as manifest through the 'human condition' in history as such.[241]

As we have seen in connection with 'Temporality in Faulkner', the young Sartre is very far from simply adopting the Heideggerian approach. His political sympathies are on the side of the working class, even if he is unable to identify himself with it as a militant, unlike his friend Nizan. If Sartre is apathetic, it is because he is highly sceptical about the possibility of a successful socialist revolution, and not because he is hostile towards the aims of such a revolution, which he predicates as an abstract imperative. His quest, at this stage of his development, is orientated towards defining the field of action of the individual, and therefore any conception of determinations—be it psychoanalysis or marxism—which does not set out from the individual's conscious (though in different ways conscious) self-determination, must be considered extremely prob-lematical.

Obviously, if the value of marxism is assessed in a framework whose centre of reference is the existentialist individual and his consciousness (with the aim of ascribing responsibility even to 'unreflective' consciousness[242]), even a dialectical conception of marxism must appear mechanical. In this sense, it is quite secondary how subtle Politzer and other marxists of Sartre's youth might or might not be. (In other words, this point is relevant at best only as one limited factor in explaining the formation of Sartre's ideas, but not the persistence of his views on marxism.) For any form of marxism evaluated from the standpoint of an existential-individual ontology must appear in need of 'founding'. In such a framework, marxism cannot be more than a fertile (maybe even: the best) 'historical hypothesis' whose *possibility*, however, must be established on the foundations of a phenomenological-existential methodology. That history is made under determinate socio-economic conditions, indicating certain laws at work, all this may be very plausible—but how is it *possible* in relation to consciousness and its 'project'? So long as this foundation is not defined in terms of the individual and his existential project, the historical conditions and laws must appear as *external mechanisms* that precede the individual, and the philosophy which concentrates on them as a *mechanical* philosophy, whatever its merits at the level of 'historical hypotheses' that, by definition, must be established on the ground of a 'fundamental ontology' (existential anthropology) and therefore cannot found themselves. Thus, insofar as the 'historical hypotheses' of marxism cannot be subsumed under the existential conception of ontology (anthropology), marxism must be 'validated', 'complemented', 'corrected', etc.—in short it must be superseded by the existentialist quest. This is why Sartre maintains an ambivalent attitude towards it even in works in which his explicit aim is to announce the 'dissolution' of existentialism within marxism, as we shall see in a moment.

But to return to the early works, this is how this problem appears in *The Transcendence of the Ego*:

> It has always seemed to me that a *working hypothesis* as fruitful as *historical materialism* never needed for a foundation the absurdity

which is *metaphysical materialism*. In fact, it is not necessary that the object precede the subject for spiritual pseudo-values to vanish and for ethics to find its bases in reality. It is enough that the me be contemporaneous with the World, and that the subject-object duality, which is purely logical, definitely disappear from philosophical preoccupations. The World has not created the me; the me has not created the World. These are two objects for absolute, impersonal consciousness, and it is by virtue of this consciousness that they are connected. This absolute consciousness, when it is purified of the I, no longer has anything of the subject. It is no longer a collection of representations. It is quite simply a first condition and an *absolute source of existence*. And the relation of interdependence established by this absolute consciousness betweel the me and the World is sufficient for the me to appear as 'endangered' before the world, for the me (indirectly and through the intermediary of states) to draw the whole of its content from the World. No more is needed in the way of a *philosophical foundation* for an *ethics* and a *politics* which are *absolutely positive*.[243]

As Sartre's subsequent development shows, things are a great deal more complicated than our quotation suggests, for notwithstanding the adoption of the proposed philosophical foundation for an 'absolutely positive ethics and politics', both remain an elusive goal in his lifework. And this is by no means a surprising development. To declare that the subject—object duality is 'purely logical', in conjunction with the ultimate postulate of a subjectless 'absolute, impersonal consciousness': the 'absolute source of existence', is not sufficient to make the underlying problem disappear. In any case, such consciousness is very far from conforming to Sartre's characterization of not having 'anything of the subject'. Although it is contrasted with the strictly individual consciousness, it represents in Sartre's philosophy that *conflation* of the individual and the collective subject which we have seen above, in connection with his essay on Faulkner. The phenomenological concept of intentionality enables Sartre to tie the two poles together, so that he can describe consciousness in general, despite calling it 'impersonal', in terms indistinguishable from the characteristics of an individual consciousness: '*Consciousness is frightened* by its own spontaneity because *it senses* this spontaneity as beyond freedom';[244] indeed, in this framework even the ego can be described as intended by consciousness 'to mask from consciousness its very spontaneity'.[245] In other words, consciousness is said to produce its 'egological structure' in order to deceive itself.

At this point we can see that the philosophical function of the Sartrean solution is 'not so much theoretical as practical'[246]—in the sense that it points to a *latent* moral philosophy, though of course not to an 'absolutely positive' one:

> Everything happens, therefore, as if consciousness constituted the ego as a *false representation* of itself, as if consciousness *hypnotized itself* before this ego which it has constituted, absorbing itself in the ego as if to make the *ego its guardian* and its law. It is thanks to the ego, indeed, that a distinction can be made between the *possible and the real*, between *appearance and being*, between the *willed and the undergone*.
>
> But it can happen that consciousness suddenly produces itself on the pure reflective level. Perhaps not without the ego, yet as escaping from the ego on all sides, as dominating the ego and maintaining the ego outside the consciousness by a continued creation. On this level, there is *no distinction between the possible and the real*, since the *appearance is the absolute*. There are *no more barriers*, no more limits, nothing to hide consciousness from itself. Then consciousness, noting what could be called the fatality of its spontaneity, is *suddenly anguished*: it is this *dread*, absolute and without remedy, this *fear of itself*, which seems to us constitutive of *pure consciousness*.[247]

The concept of 'barriers' is the key to understanding this whole set of relations, as indeed also the analysis of temporality in Faulkner culminated in the passionate exclamation: 'a *barred* future is still a future'. Collision with barriers is an indubitable fact of the 'human-reality'. In this respect the existential question, according to Sartre, is twofold: (1) how to account for the barriers we meet: and (2) how to deal with them? Since any deterministic conception of the world has been *a priori* rejected, and consciousness described both as the human-reality itself[248] and as the absolute source of existence, consciousness as such must be responsible for producing its own barriers. It sets up the ego as 'its guardian and its law', and thus it produces the distinctions between the possible and the real, between appearance and being, between the willed and the undergone, etc.—distinctions which all rebound against it. Thus the 'reality principle' appears (through differentiating between the possible and the real) and takes charge of our daily life. The result is a mode of existence that can be described only with the negative categories of Sartre's latent moral philosophy. The picture of such existence is truly desolate and well deserves Sartre's passionate condemnation. All seems to be lost until, suddenly and paradoxically, the barriers themselves come to the rescue: 'All ways are *barred* and nevertheless we must act. So then we try to change the world; that is, to live it as though the relations between things and their potentialities were not governed by deterministic processes but by magic. But, be it well understood, this is no playful matter: we are *cornered*, and we fling ourselves into this *new attitude* with all the force at our command.'[249]

The new attitude appears as the effective negation of the previous mode of existence: consciousness 'lives the new world it has thereby constituted—lives it directly, *commits itself* to it, and *suffers* from the qualities that the concomitant behaviour has assigned to it. This means that, all ways out being *barred,* the consciousness *leaps* into the magical world of emotions. . . .'[250] However, this negation is bound to remain a problematic solution. Not only because—in accordance with the underlying *spontaneity*—the 'new attitude' cannot be induced but simply arises on its own whenever it does happen to arise ('it can happen . . .', 'suddenly. . .', etc.), but also because the new state is ruled by *fatality*. 'The fatality of its [consciousness'] spontaneity' is described as 'consciousness dropping asleep'[251] because 'consciousness is *caught* in its own snare. Precisely because it is living in the new aspect of the world by believing in it, the consciousness is *captured* by its own belief, exactly as it is in dreams and hysteria. The consciousness of the emotion is *captive,* but by this it must not be understood to be fettered by anything whatever *outside* itself. It is *captive to itself. . . .* Thus, when consciousness is living the magical world into which it has precipitated itself, it tends to *perpetuate* that world.[252]

Hence Sartre's fascination with the imagery of man who is simultaneously the *victim* and the *executioner* responsible for his own undoing.[253]

Thus the 'vertiginous freedom' and 'infinite overflow' of consciousness does not bring liberation and fulfilment to man. Consciousness succeeds in extricating itself from the contradictions of one of its fundamental 'attitudes' only to get trapped by the fatality of the other. Man seems to be locked into a world of antinomies: a predicament which imposes on him, as the only authentic mode of existence, the imperative of ceaseless negation. This is why the 'adventurer' is Sartre's hero who recognizes 'the vanity of action and its necessity', based on the 'absolute existence of man and the absolute impossibility of such existence'—a hero who finds fulfilment only in the 'infinitesimal moment that separates life from death'.[254] Sartre's latent moral philosophy thus unfolds as the categorical negation of this antinomous world; or, to put it another way, the categorical negativity of his thought makes itself intelligible as a latent moral philosophy that never comes to a point of rest. In his vision man ought to negate the conditions of existence, and the more so the harder he is tossed between the horns of the existential antinomies. It is the moral intensity of this negating passion which refuses to admit any set of determinations prior to the self-determination of consciousness, so that the latter shall assume total responsibility for the human-reality it constitutes.

Significantly enough, in this conception of philosophy the epistemological-ontological and the moral categories are inextricably intertwined. So much so, that epistemological-ontological objections to phenomenology are answered by moral assertions:

> The theorists of the extreme Left have sometimes reproached phenomenology for being an idealism and for drowning reality in the stream of ideas. But if idealism is the philosophy without *evil* of Brunschvicg, if it is a philosophy in which the effort of spiritual assimilation never meets *external resistances,* in which *suffering, hunger,* and *war* are diluted in a slow process of the unification of ideas, nothing is more unjust than to call phenomenologists 'idealists'. On the contrary, for centuries we have not felt in philosophy so *realistic* a current. The phenomenologists have plunged man back into the world; they have given full measure to *man's agonies* and *sufferings,* and also to his rebellions.[255]

We can witness here the shift from epistemology to moral philosophy as idealism is defined in terms of a failure to face up to *evil* dominating our world in the shape of suffering, hunger and war; and similarly, 'realism' is defined as a passionate moral concern about 'man's agonies and sufferings'. It is secondary, whether or not the phenomenologically bracketed and 'reduced' hunger retains much resemblance to real hunger: in any case, in Sartre's philosophy the doors of the phenomenological bracket are wide open. What is of a paramount importance for understanding the structure of his philosophy is the fact that right from its early constitution his epistemological-ontological categories are permeated by the intense moral passion which has its primacy in his thought as deeply as the principle of 'the primacy of practical reason' predominates in the Kantian system.

This means that we are confronted with a structural integration of moral and ontological and other categories, and not just with lateral connections and associations. Sartre articulates his epistemological-ontological categories in order to sustain his own conception of morality. He takes notice of what he calls 'metaphysical materialism' only to the extent to which the presumed ethical corollaries of such a conception of philosophy clash with his own moral concerns. He does not examine and refute the basic propositions of this philosophy at the level at which they are formulated but simply insists that one does not need 'the absurdity which is metaphysical materialism . . . for spiritual *pseudo-values* to vanish and for *ethics* to find its bases in reality'. And the reason why he cannot contemplate a philosophical foundation different from his own (in which consciousness is the 'first condition and the absolute source of existence') is, again, not epistemological-ontological but *moral*. For if the object preceded and determined the subject, it would be impossible to ascribe to the subject that categorical, absolute, total responsibility which Sartre wants to ascribe to it.[256]

Naturally, in this conception, because of the inextricable structural integration and fusion of the epistemological-ontological and the moral categories, 'ontology' must be identified with *anthropology*. For nothing is admissible prior to the 'human reality' which becomes the absolute foundation of everything. Fundamental ontology and *existential anthropology* thus become synonymous:

> . . . it is precisely for the human reality that to exist is always to assume its being; that is, to be *responsible* for it instead of receiving it from outside, as a *pebble* does. And since 'the human reality' is essentially its own *possibility,* this existent can itself *'choose'* what it will be, achieve itself—or lose itself. . . .
>
> Thus the human reality which is *myself* assumes its own being by understanding it. This understanding is mine. I am, then, first of all, a being who more or less obscurely understands his reality as a man, which means that *I make myself a man* by understanding myself as such. I can therefore *question myself* and, on the basis of that interrogation, carry out an analysis of the 'human reality' which will serve as the *basis for an anthropology.*[257]

The structural integration and fusion of the categories works, of course, both ways. Not only are the anthropological-ontological categories permeated by existential morality but also, the other way round, the categories of Sartrean ethics are fully intelligible only in their anthropological-ontological context. 'Responsibility', 'freedom', 'possibility', 'choice' and so on are not quite what they would mean in a specific ethical proposition. At times even Sartre feels that he must put them in inverted commas, as the term 'choose' in the last quotation—since the subject is denied by Sartre the status of a subject (which in fact amounts to a characteristically Sartrean conflation of the individual and the collective subject, as we have seen above). This is why Sartre's moral philosophy must remain a *latent* one, resisting all his efforts which aim at articulating it as a relatively autonomous system of morality. And this is why any concept of ontology that fails to identify itself with existential anthropology must be rejected by Sartre even when his openly professed and genuinely believed aim is the integration (or 'dissolution') of existentialist 'ideology' within marxism.

Sartre's ambivalent attitude to marxism mentioned above has its roots in the incompatibility between existentialist anthropology and marxian ontology. Not that he himself conceptualizes the problem in this form. On the contrary, given his political-moral solidarity with the perspectives of a socialist transformation of society, he is anxious to stress his complete agreement with Marx. All the same, the ambivalence transpires through the shift in his arguments, as well as through his final summing up of the prospects of integrating existentialism and marxism. He gives three different explanations for his critical attitude:

1.   His criticisms are meant for Engels.[258]
2.   He is critical of contemporary 'mechanical marxism'.[259]
3.   His critical qualifications are intended 'to assign certain limits to dialectical materialism—to validate the historical dialectic while rejecting the dialectic of nature'.[260]

In the third explanation we are remarkably close to the original formula which praised historical materialism as a fruitful working hypothesis (now he validates the hypothesis) and rejected the 'absurdity which is metaphysical materialism' (now he limits dialectical materialism by rejecting the idea of a dialectic of nature, worried that it would 'reduce man'[261] to a simple product of physical laws, which exactly corresponds to the early complaint against 'metaphysical materialism').

As to Sartre's final summing up of the prospects of integrating existentialism and marxism, we can see very clearly that those who lamented the alleged liquidiation of existentialism and talked about Sartre being 'swallowed up by marxism'[262] had no real ground for such views. For Sartre's own words speak loud for themselves, and they speak very differently:

> Thus the autonomy of existential studies results necessarily from the negative qualities of Marxists (and not from Marxism itself). So long as the doctrine does not recognize its anemia, so long as it founds its Knowledge upon a *dogmatic metaphysics* (a dialectic of Nature) instead of seeking its support in the comprehension of the *living man,* so long as it rejects as irrational those ideologies which wish, as Marx did, to separate being from Knowledge, and, in *anthropology,* to found the knowing of man on *human existence,* existentialism will follow its own path of study. This means that it will attempt to clarify the givens of Marxist Knowledge by indirect knowing (that is, as we have seen, by words which regressively denote existential structures), and to engender within the framework of Marxism a veritable comprehensive knowing which will rediscover man in the social world and which will follow him in his *praxis*—or, if you prefer, in the *project* which throws him toward the social possibles in terms of a defined situation. Existentialism will appear therefore as a fragment of the system, which has fallen outside of Knowledge. From the day that Marxist thought will have taken on the *human dimension* (that is, the *existential project*) as the *foundation of anthropological Knowledge,* existentialism will no longer have any reason for being. Absorbed, surpassed and conserved by the totalizing movement of philosophy, it will cease to be a particular inquiry and will become the *foundation of all inquiry.* The comments which we have made in the course of the present essay are directed—to the modest limit of our capabilities—toward hastening the moment of that *dissolution.*[263]

Thus, in place of a 'radical conversion' leading to a

'liquidation' of existentialism we find a statement which firmly reasserts not only Sartre's opposition to 'dogmatic metaphysics' but also his lifelong programme of founding marxism on an existential anthropology. And the last word, 'dissolution', could not be more distant from what it suggests to careless reading. For the message is spelled out with precision in the preceding sentence. Existentialism will be 'dissolved' only when it becomes *the foundation of all inquiry,* that is the universally accepted premise of all future philosophy.

In any case, even if Sartre is willing to read Marx in his own key, their views on the relationship between ontology and anthropology are far from being identical. For as far back as 1844 Marx emphasized that

> man's feelings, passions, etc., are not *merely anthropological* phenomena . . . but *truly ontological* affirmations of essential being (of *nature*). . . . Only through developed industry i.e. through the medium of private property—does the *ontological essence* of human passion come to be both in its totality and in its humanity; the science of man is therefore itself a product of man's establishment of himself by practical activity.[264]

Thus, for Marx, ontology and anthropology are not synonymous; the former is the unquestionable foundation of the latter and in that sense 'precedes' it. Consequently, the problem is not simply 'materiality' namely 'the fact that *the point of departure is man as animal organism* which sets out from needs and creates material ensembles',[265] but precisely the objective ontological conditions under which such developments can take place. This is what makes Marx insist on the ontological principle inherent in the development of modern technology which consists in 'resolving each process into its constituent movements, *without any regard to their possible execution by the hand of man'.*[266] Whether or not one should apply the term 'dialectic of nature' (and if so with what qualifications) to the study of such conditions, need not worry us here. What matters is that they are clearly not 'anthropological'—they concern nature's fundamental laws of motion and the prerequisites of human development in accordance with and in response to such objective natural laws—but constitute the ultimate points of reference of ontology into which a dialectical conception of anthropology must be integrated as a part in the whole. Since, however, the integration of existentialism and marxism envisaged by Sartre is diametrically opposed to this, his programme of 'founding' marxism remains as far from its realization today as in 1934.

6

Sartre's early works are written in a period of great contradictions which threateningly foreshadow the possibility of a 'cataclysm' never seen before. For perceptive men who are willing to bear witness, the gravity of the predicament is evident not only in the great world economic crisis of 1929-33, but also in the 'solutions' that follow that crisis, from the rise of fascism to the chronic depression and unemployment that characterizes the life of all the liberal capitalist countries throughout the 1930s, alleviated only at the tragic price of 're-vitalizing' the economy, at the outbreak of the Second World War, in the service of war material production which sets its devastating pattern for the production of prosperity also after the war. Looking back on this period in 'Situation of the writer in 1947', Sartre describes its formative power in graphic terms:

> From 1930 on, the world depression, the coming of Nazism, and the events in China opened our eyes. It seemed as if the ground were going to fall from under us, and suddenly, for us too, the great historical juggling began. The first years of the great world Peace suddenly had to be regarded as the years between wars. Each sign of compromise which we had greeted had to be seen as a threat. Each day we had lived revealed its true face; we had abandoned ourselves to it trustingly and it was leading us to a new war with secret rapidity, with a rigour hidden beneath its nonchalant airs. And our life as an individual which had seemed to depend upon our efforts,

our virtues, and our faults, on our good and bad luck, on the good and bad will of a very small number of people, seemed governed down to its minutest details by obscure and collective forces, and its most private circumstances seemed to reflect the state of the whole world. All at once we felt ourselves abruptly situated. The detachment which our predecessors were so fond of practising had become impossible. There was a collective adventure which was taking form in the future and which would be our adventure. . . . The secret of our gestures and our most intimate designs lay ahead of us in the catastrophe to which our names would be attached. History flowed in upon us; in everything we touched, in the air we breathed, in the page we read, in the one we wrote; in love itself we discovered, like a taste of history, so to speak, a bitter and ambiguous mixture of the absolute and the transitory.[267]

The experience of history can be bewildering if it is reflected in consciousness as a form of historical relativism. Similarly, the perception of the collective forces which dominate a historical situation can be paralyzing if the individual is unable to define his own margin of action in relation to them. Sartre is extremely anxious to steer clear of both dangers. With respect to the first, the overriding interest of his quest is to find *'the absolute at the heart of relativity itself'* so as to be able to oppose it to *'moral relativism'*.[268] And with regard to the power of the collective forces, his aim is to demonstrate the 'possibilities'—and the responsibility—of the individual to face up to 'man's agonies and sufferings' in this world of collective adventure which he cannot really escape, no matter how hard he might try to through the strategies of 'bad faith'.

In his search for the integral, though not sovereign, individual Sartre wants to demonstrate that the man of his quest is totally free (responsible) and yet totally situated in a contingent world. How is this possible? Is such a view compatible with the prevailing conceptions of man? Sartre's answer is an emphatic no, and he sets out to prove the validity of his own idea of man: this is in fact the most central theme of all his early works. We have already seen his objections to marxism. In addition, let us briefly refer to two other principal lines of approach from among those he criticizes: positivism and psychoanalysis.

In the positivistic cult of the 'facts', Sartre identifies a basic structural defect: the absence of a proper concept of man—which means that we get an aimless, almost totally blind accumulation of facts and no real theory. Thus: 'If, later on, there ought to be a definitive concept of man—which itself is doubtful—this concept is to be envisaged only as the crowning concept of a complete science, which means that it is postponed to infinity.'[269] The whole is disregarded and fragments usurp its place. And since the specificity of the human (man as a 'synthetic totality') does not guide the enquiry itself, hopes that it might emerge from the maze of fragmentary, mechanistic determinations, must be considered completely gratuitous.

Sartre's attitude to psychoanalysis is equally negative, although—in contrast to his views on the varieties of positivism—he acknowledges that its problems are novel and important and therefore must be accounted for in his own terms. The reason why he must reject the psychoanalytic theories is the same that lies behind the criticisms he voices in other directions: the radical inadmissibility of determinations prior or external to the self-determinations of consciousness. This is why the critique of psychoanalysis remains central with him, no matter how hard he tries—in an intellectual climate highly favourable to psychoanalytic explanations—to give the maximum credit to Freud himself for focusing attention on an area of great importance. He sees clearly that what he is calling into question is 'the *principle itself* of psychoanalytic explanation', for in psychoanalysis 'what is signified is entirely cut off from the signifying'.[270] To this approach he opposes his own dialectic conception of the relationship between signifying, signified, and signification:

> If, then, it [consciousness] has a signification, it must contain this within itself as a structure of consciousness. This does not mean that the signification must be perfectly explicit. There are many

possible degrees of condensation and of clarity. It only means that we should not interrogate the consciousness from outside, as one would study the remains of the fire or the encampment, but from within; that we should look onto it for the signification. The consciousness, if the *cogito* is to be possible, is itself the fact, and signification and what is signified . . . if symbolization is constitutive it is legitimate to see an immanent bond of comprehension between the symbolization and the symbol. Only, we must agree upon this, that consciousness constitutes itself by symbolization. In that case there is nothing behind it, and the relation between symbol, symbolized and symbolization is an intrastructural bond of consciousness. But if we go on to say that the consciousness is symbolizing under the *causal compulsion* of a transcendent fact—which is the repressed desire—we are falling back upon the theory previously indicated, which treats the relation of the signified to the signifying as a causal relation. The profound contradiction in all psychoanalysis is that it presents at the same time a bond of *causality* and a bond of *understanding* between the phenomena that it studies. These two types of relationship are incompatible.[271]

Significantly enough, the same line of reasoning is followed by Sartre in an interview more than three decades later, culminating in the rejection of the 'mythology of the unconscious' constituting 'a set of rigorous mechanistic determinations . . . a causality . . . a mechanism'.[272] And no wonder. For too much would have to go if Sartre decided to significantly modify his views on these points. The fact is that he does not just reject the psychoanalytic principle of explanation for certain facts and problems but provides his own rival explanation. As we learn from Simone de Beauvoir's memoirs, the main concepts of his alternative to psychoanalysis were spelled out already in the early 1930s when:

> Sartre worked out the notion of *mauvaise foi* [bad faith] which, according to him, embraced all those phenomena which other people attributed to the *unconscious mind*. We set ourselves to expose this dishonesty in all its manifestations: semantic quibbling, false recollections, fugues, compensation fantasies, sublimations, and the rest. We rejoiced every time we unearthed a new loophole, another type of deception.[273]

A great deal more is built on such foundations later on, and *mauvaise foi* remains one of the central concepts in the whole of Sartre's lifework, articulated in all its details in *Being and Nothingness* and used in many subsequent works. And the function envisaged by Sartre for his own 'existential psychoanalysis' is radically different from that of traditional psychoanalysis. Again, it is important to bear in mind the role of morality in Sartrean philosophy as a whole in order to be able to understand and appreciate the function he assigns to existential psychoanalysis: 'the various tasks of the for-itself can be made the object of an existential psychoanalysis, for they all aim at producing the missing synthesis of consciousness and being in the form of *value* or *self-cause*. Thus *existential psychoanalysis is moral description,* for it releases to us the *ethical meaning* of various human projects.'[274] Clearly, no variety of Freudian theory could fulfil such functions. This is why traditional psychoanalysis and 'existential psychoanalysis' remain worlds apart, and Sartre has to embark on the arduous task of writing a 'new treatise of the passions' relying entirely on his own resources, taking for his centre of reference the 'factitious' predicament of the existential individual.

Socially, Sartre's early works are conceived between two poles of negativity: the passionate condemnation of his own class and of the bourgeois order of society that goes with it on the one hand, and the rejection of the idea of identifying himself with the struggle of the working class on the other. Simone de Beauvoir's recollection of an incident illustrates very well that the negation of the prevailing order by Sartre is not coupled with a positive involvement. Instead, he opts for the position of the self-oriented outsider, however much sympathy he might feel at times for the underdogs from a fairly remote distance. This is how Simone de Beauvoir's account goes:

> The columns of the daily press were full of bankruptcies, scandals, and the suicides of businessmen and international financiers. The world was moving into a state of flux. Sartre often wondered

whether we should not join those who were working for this revolution. I recall one conversation in particular, which took place on the *terrasse* of the big café in Rouen, the Café Victor, that looked out on the *quais*. Even in spheres where we were ideologically well-informed, to come up against some concrete fact still always had an effect on us, and would give rise to copious subsequent discussion. This was what happened on this particular afternoon. A docker, decently dressed in his blue smock, sat down at a table next to ours: the manager ejected him. The incident did not teach us anything, but it illustrated the idea of class segregation with all the naïveté of an Epinal print, and served as the point of departure of a far-reaching discussion. We got to asking ourselves whether it was enough for us to sympathize with the struggle being fought by the working classes: ought we not to join in it? . . . On this particular occasion we decided . . . that though the proletarian struggle was of concern to us, it was even so *not our struggle*; all that could be asked of us was that we should always *speak out on its behalf in any argument.*[275]

Thus, instead of a passionate identification with the struggle for a new society, we find a paternalistic intellectualism, confined to taking part in merely theoretical discussions and arguments. Naturally, this is not just a biographical detail that serves simply to add colour to the background of Sartre's development, but a major factor in the constitution of his philosophical system as a whole. The decision to be *'critical rather than constructive'*[276] is a rather vague way of describing what is at stake here. For in reality it means that the criticism itself—which is devoid of a positive ('constructive') frame of reference—is condemned to be extremely abstract and remote from the tangible social realities.

The young Sartre takes up his stand in the no-man's-land of the self-oriented outsider, which carries far-reaching consequences for the articulation of his philosophy. Since his moral rebellion is voiced in a social vacuum, his criticism can only be manifested in the form of an abstract moral imperative that must remain latent and wedded to the categories of an existential ontology, as we have seen above. Similarly, since the idea of social-political commitment is rejected by Sartre—although the concept of moral commitment is an integral part of his philosophy right from the early 1930s—the existential categories in which his views are spelled out in his original system tend to be *ahistorical* ('for-itself', 'in-itself', 'vertigo of possibility', 'absolute flight', 'monstrous spontaneity'), notwithstanding 'the experience of history' which he describes retrospectively in 1947. And as far as the relations of domination and oppression are concerned (which, again, he condemns in the form of a moral 'ought'), in his early works they are converted into the abstract existential-ontological antagonism between the 'for-itself' and 'the other' at one level, and into the conflicts of 'interpsychic' (and indeed 'intrapsychic') relations at another, thus depriving them of their socio-historical specificity. (Also, alienation and objectification tend to be fused with the help of variants of the category of reification, and such fusion produces the same sort of effects.) Finally, since the standpoint of Sartre's early works is that of the negatively defined, self-oriented outsider who emphatically rejects the orientation of his own class without being able to adopt the perspectives of its polar opposite, the 'subject' of his philosophy cannot be a socio-historically specific and tangible *collective subject* but an existentialist fusion of *particular individuality* (the contingency and facticity of the existential individual) and *abstract universality* (consciousness as such in its 'impersonal spontaneity').

Thus, Sartre's search for the individual in his early works reveals—in the spirit of the Kierkegaardian opposition to Hegel—the absolute as 'the unsurpassable opaqueness of the lived experience',[277] or in other words, as 'the *irreducibility* and the specificity of what is lived'.[278] What this quest produces is not the *individual*—for the real individual cannot be truly grasped except in his socio-historical specificity and universality, as the *social individual*—but *individuality* and *particularity* as such: 'the absolute at the heart of relativity itself', defined as the opaque irreducibility of the lived experience. (This is particularity directly raised to the level of the absolute, which procedure becomes the Sartrean version of 'universalizing the individual' while insisting on irreducibility and non-universalizability.) Here, again, we can see the social determinants of this conception. For later Sartre has to admit that the unsurpassable opaqueness of lived experience—for instance, suffering—vis-à-vis knowledge holds only 'to the degree that knowledge remains *powerless to transform it*';[279] which means that the whole question of 'absolute irreducibility' and 'unsurpassable opaqueness' hinges on *social praxis* itself, of which knowledge and lived experience are integral dimensions and therefore cannot be abstractly-antinomously opposed to one another on the alleged ground of some 'fundamental ontology'.

Many things change significantly in the course of Sartre's later development. The war years shatter the self-erected walls of his social vacuum, and the problem of commitment—not only moral and literary-aesthetic but also social and politic—comes to occupy a central place in his writings in the most varied contexts (from literary analyses to political polemics) and at all levels (from occasional remarks to systematic philosophical treatments). Naturally, the increasing social awareness carries with it a conscious effort to put into relief the political and the historical dimensions of his concerns, which calls for the modification of some fundamental early propositions and categories. Inevitably, though, such an enterprise—however passionately felt in the circumstances of tangible social crises—must be carried out by Sartre in the framework of a philosophy whose structure has been constituted under very different conditions and with rather different preoccupations in mind. Thus he is forced to respond to the challenge of the dramatic socio-historical developments (during the war and after) in terms of his philosophy as originally articulated during the 1930s, while restructuring it to the extent to which this is feasible internally. This of course is not possible without the constant manifestation of major tensions[280] between the original structure and the new demands of which he becomes a passionate champion. That he is unable to resolve these tensions, is inherent in the antinomous structure of his original system. That he is unwilling to resolve them simply by discarding his antinomies is a measure of his stubborn integrity and of the depth of his commitment. The fact that a philosophical solution to the problems he has embraced in his original system is not forthcoming must be considered in conjunction with the other side of the coin. For keeping alive the 'unbearable tension' of his antinomies is the fertile ground on which Sartre dramatically depicts—and by no means only in the medium of the theatre—the world in which we all live, thus creating a work which is manifestly representative of our times.

## Chapter 5

# FREEDOM AND PASSION:
## The World of *Being and Nothingness*
### 1

FUNDAMENTALLY *man is the desire to be'* (565)[281]–states a
cryptic phrase in *Being and Nothingness*. To understand it,
we must realize that in the world of *Being and Nothingness*
all the principal categories hinge on 'being', including 'the
desire to do', which is reduced either to 'having' (576) or to
'being' (581). Furthermore, 'having' itself is turned into
being through 'possession' which is said to be 'a magical
relation; I *am* these objects which I have' (591), for 'In
possession *I am my own foundation* in so far as I exist in an
In-itself'(592). Thus when two years after writing *Being and
Nothingness* Sartre asserts that 'existentialism defines man
through *action*',[282] and that existentialism is 'a morality of
action and of commitment',[283] we witness a significant shift
of emphasis which opens up new possibilities of tangible
social and political involvement in his postwar development.

However, during the war years things remain more
abstract in Sartre's conceptual universe. *Being and
Nothingness* is a monumental synthesis—'An Essay on
Phenomenological Ontology', according to its subtitle—
which sets out from asserting the primacy of subjectivity and
remains anchored to the psychological categories of Sartre's
early work. The abstractness of *Being and Nothingness* is
the consequence of the compression of a great variety of
heterogeneous philosophical problems into the categories
worked out on the basis of Sartre's early inspiration in
philosophical psychology. And when he later calls it *'the
eidetics of bad faith'*, sharply contrasting its approach with
'the empirical study of our fidelities, and of the inhuman
forces which pervert them',[284] he provides a very apt
characterization of the limits of this great work. For the

notorious difficulties of comprehension are not so much a matter of inherent complexity as rather of the forbidding strangeness of the subjective key in which the work is composed, presenting a comprehensive synthesis of 'man and the world' under its subjective aspects, and objectivity—in the spirit of 'phenomenological realism'—appears massively mediated and transmuted into the categories of Sartrean existentialist subjectivity.

*Being and Nothingness* is an ontology conceived from the standpoint of this subjectivity, and 'the experience of society' is brought into play only to the extent to which it can provide—often splendidly graphic—*illustrations* for the highly abstract 'world' (not the empirical world but an ontological construct) in which 'the human reality' (subjectivity or individuality) is situated.

> All this happens as if the For-itself had a *Passion* to lose itself in order that the affirmation 'world' might come to the In-itself. . . . the world and the instrumental-thing, space and quantity, and universal time are all pure hypostasized nothingnesses . . . 'There is' being because I am the negation of being, and worldliness, spatiality, quantity, instrumentality, temporality—all come into being only because I am the negation of being' (217).

All this may sound disturbingly subjective and remotely abstract. Nevertheless, the underlying intent is amply clear: to provide a forcefully coherent elucidation of everything in terms of the being of 'the human reality' and the *passion* which animates it and makes its 'project' intelligible. As we have seen in the preceding chapter, in 1934 Sartre credited Husserl with the great achievement of clearing the ground for a new treatise of the passions. Now he makes it clear why in his view Husserl himself could not embark on the realization of the project of writing the much needed new treatise of the passions. 'Because Husserl has reduced being to a series of meanings, the only connection which he has been able to establish between my being and that of the Other is a connection of *knowledge*. Therefore Husserl cannot escape solipsism any more than Kant could'(235). It goes without saying, to envisage a new treatise of the passions in terms of even the most sophisticated form of solipsism would be absurd.

Asserting the primacy of being must be the point of departure and the necessary ground of analysis on which such a study is feasible. Sartre therefore proposes an approach not just different from but diametrically opposed to Husserl's. Instead of reducing being to meanings (knowledge), he explains knowledge and meanings in terms of being and its project, insisting that being is 'the self-evident irreducible' and therefore any attempt at reducing it to something else, and thus trying to go beyond it, is self-contradictory: 'for obviously it is impossible to advance further than being' and we have reached the absolute limit 'when we have reached the project of being'(565). All that remains then is an elucidation of this project of being—the same thing as 'to acquaint man with his passion'(626)—which in no way implies going beyond being or reducing it to something else. On the contrary, the task of elucidation amounts to the project of advancing towards being as it constitutes itself, and the understanding of the ontological structure of being is not a *theoretical* enterprise but an inherently *practical* one (the task of 'practical reason' in Kantian terminology), involving the elaboration of the—never completed—*Ethics* and *Existential Psychoanalysis*. Sartrean ontology thus culminates in the latter, providing a foundation for them, but it is simultaneously also founded by its own Ethics and Existential Psychoanalysis, in that it cannot conceivably envisage any other foundation. This conceptual structure may be schematically illustrated as on p. 159. Such a conceptual structure may appear to be circular, and in a particular sense certainly it is circular. However, the circularity involved is not some 'conceptual confusion' or defect whose removal might improve Sartre's philosophy. Removing it could be conceived only at the price of

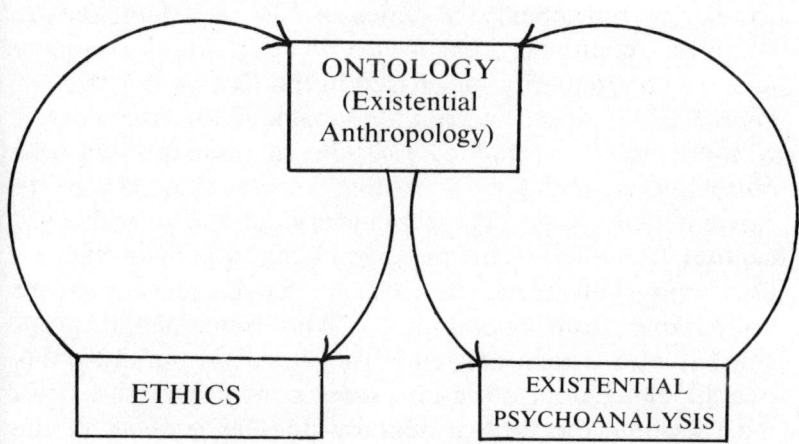

liquidating the essential characteristics of Sartrean existentialism which cannot be reduced to a neat, formally
consistent but platitudinous epistemology, nor indeed a
Husserlian phenomenology envisaged as a 'rigorous science'. Sartre could only pour scorn on all such attempts,
characterizing even Husserl's aim at conceiving philosophy
as a 'rigorous science' (*eine strenge Wissenschaft*) as 'the
idea of a madman genius, but *a mad idea* none the less'.[285]
For in his philosophy we are directly concerned with man
interrogating himself about his own project which he tries to
hide from himself, with all the ambiguities, subterfuges,
strategies of bad faith and circularities involved. This is why
Sartrean 'phenomenological ontology' must be conceived
as an existential anthropology which is fused with practical
moral and psychoanalytical concerns in this 'new treatise of
the passions', and thus 'circularly' it coils back into itself by
founding itself precisely through the selfsame existential
dimensions which it claims to found. Consequently, to try to
eliminate existential anthropology from Sartre's
phenomenological ontology, in order to render it 'formally
consistent', would be tantamount to the futility and
absurdity of trying to square the circle.

In any event, Sartre is not in the least embarrassed by this circularity but openly assumes it, as we shall see in numerous contexts, from *Being and Nothingness* to the 'dialectical circularity' discussed in the *Critique of Dialectical Reason*. Assertions like: 'no dialectic for my relations with the other but rather a *circle*'(363) abound in *Being and Nothingness*, and they constitute an essential part of its existential message. The 'circularity' of the overall conceptual framework and the paralysing stalemate suggestively conveyed through remarks like the one just quoted are inseparable from one another. The fundamental propositions of Sartrean existentialism are determined by this overall conceptual structure, and, conversely, the latter must assume the form it actually does as a result of the innermost nature of the fundamental existentialist propositions. Indeed Sartre would argue that given the absolute character of the *existential circle*—the necessary assumption of 'contingency' and 'facticity', which means that '*we can never get outside the circle*'(363)—the *existentialist circle* is its only adequate philosophical equivalent or approximation.

We shall have to return to these problems on more than one occasion. Now the point to stress is that *Being and Nothingness* is truly intelligible only as a monumental sketch of the strikingly original outlines of the new treatise of the passions, structured around the apparently circular proposition that *freedom is passion and passion is freedom*. Thus in this work we get not simply a 'reconciliation' of freedom and passion, after centuries of philosophical debate which insisted on the primacy of one or the other, at the expense of one or the other, but the passionate assertion of the essential *identity* of the two. Thus freedom is no longer conceived as purely transcendental, leaving the world of appearance and necessity locked into itself while claiming to supersede it transcendentally by postulating a separate world of essences and freedom (the world of the *Ding an sich*—'thing in itself'—of Kant and his followers)—it is the

most fundamental dimension of human existence passionately striving to realize itself. And Sartre violates
traditional philosophy not only as regards the formal
characteristics of his work but even in the mode of
development and style of presentation. Instead of providing
a 'detached, objective description', followed by 'rigorously
sustained proof' (the ideal even of that 'madman genius',
poor Husserl), he passionately asserts and reasserts his
basic proposition concerning freedom and passion in so
many different forms, and the 'existential proof' emerges
through the plausibility of its 'authenticity': another concept
which refers back to freedom in an apparent circularity, by
reasserting in its own way the basic identity of freedom and
passion.

If 'the fundamental project, the person, the free realization of human truth is everywhere in all desires'(567), and
if it is our freedom itself 'which constitutes the limits which it
will subsequently encounter'(482), as Sartre asserts, then all
varieties of psychological determinism are *a priori* ruled out
as being structurally incapable of even perceiving the
problem, not to mention providing a viable solution for its
difficulties. 'Exact and objective psychology' must be
dismissed as a 'solipsism' (229) which treats the other as an
object, denying its subject character in much the same way
as we find in Sartre's famous description of one of the
fundamental strategies of bad faith. The same considerations apply to knowledge in general. 'The point of
view of *pure knowledge* is contradictory; there is only the
point of view of *engaged knowledge.* . . . an engaged
upsurge in a determined point of view which *one is*'(308).
Thus, knowledge is a dimension of being, and 'mistakes' or
'misconceptions' of knowledge must be made intelligible on
the ground of the fundamental ontological structures,
instead of being 'dissolved' through conceptual manipulation: a solipsistic circularity which assumes the
separate existence and absolute legislative power of its
own—'detached', 'objective', 'exact', 'rigorous', 'unam-

biguous', etc.—thought. As against all such approaches, Sartre insists on the necessary practical embeddedness of theoretical viewpoints. In his advocacy of an 'existential psychoanalysis' he does not proceed from a theoretical refutation of psychological determinism (traditional psychoanalysis being only one of the manifold varieties of the latter) but from identifying the practical determinants which are uncritically projected in the theoretical image:

> In each moment of reflection anguish is born as a structure of the reflective consciousness in so far as the latter considers consciousness as an object of reflection; but it still remains possible for me to maintain various types of conduct with respect to my own anguish—in particular patterns of flight. Everything takes place as if our essential and immediate behaviour with respect to anguish is flight. *Psychological determinism*, before being a *theoretical* conception, is first an *attitude of excuse*, or if you prefer, the basis of all attitudes of excuse. It is a reflective conduct with respect to anguish; it asserts that there are within us *antagonistic forces* whose type of existence is comparable to that of *things*. . . . It provides us with a nature productive of ours acts, . . . endowing them with an *inertia* and externality eminently reassuring because they constitute *a permanent game of excuses*. . . . But this determinism, a reflective defence against anguish, is not given as a reflective intuition. It avails nothing against the evidence of freedom; hence it is given as a *faith to take refuge in*, as the ideal end towards which we can flee to escape anguish. . . . Thus we flee from anguish by attempting to apprehend ourselves from without as an *Other* or as a *thing* (40-3).

As we can see, the reified images of psychological determinism are explained in terms of determinate practical attitudes emanating from the ontological structure of being which constitutes Sartre's basic concern in this 'eidetics of bad faith'. Such theoretical reifications of the human reality are both necessary, in so far as they arise out of the anguishing ontological structure, and not out of theory as such, and freely assumed, in that they can be practically opposed by alternative types of attitude and conduct and by their appropriate conceptualizations. And the necessary failure of these deterministic theories of psychological reification, which represent a capitulation to flight and excuses, calls for a radically new treatise of the passions which insists simultaneously on the inescapability of freedom ('man is condemned to be free') and on the necessary situation of this freedom in the contingency of human existence motivated by its ontological passion. (Empirical passion is said to be the symbolic expression of the fundamental ontological passion.) For 'all human existence is a passion, the famous self-interest being only one way *freely chosen* among others to *realize this passion*'(626).

2

In a discourse in which *ambiguity*[286] is consciously assumed and cultivated, rather than being considered a residue of conceptual imperfection which must be removed by means of appropriate analytical procedures, the use of metaphors is not meant simply to enliven the style of presentation. In *Being and Nothingness* metaphors appear with great frequency, and they are inextricably entangled with the philosophical message which cannot be conveyed in any other form. Many years later in an interview Sartre criticizes his own use of metaphors in *Being and Nothingness*, giving as an example the much quoted phrase: 'Man is a useless passion', which received hostile comments not really on account of its literary qualities, but because of its atheistic message according to which 'the passion of man is the reverse of that of Christ, for man loses himself as man in order that God may be born. But the idea of God is contradictory and we lose ourselves in vain. Man is a useless passion'(615). This is how Sartre argues his case in 1965:

> If I forget myself for a moment and use a literary turn of phrase in a philosophical work I always feel slightly that I am pulling a fast one on my reader; it is a breach of trust. I once wrote the

sentence—remembered because of its literary aspect—*L'homme est une passion inutile* (Man is a useless passion). A case of breach of trust. I ought to have put that in strictly philosophical terms. In my *Critique of Dialectical Reason* I do not think I was guilty of breach of trust at all. [287]

To be sure, it is far from being the case that Sartre avoids in his later works the literary practices which he now condemns as 'a breach of trust', even if their extent is more limited in the *Critique of Dialectical Reason* than in *Being and Nothingness*. However, this is not at issue at this point where our concern is to show the role they play in articulating and authenticating the suggestive philosophical message of Sartre's 'eidetics of bad faith'.

In any case, it is hard to accept not only that the example given by Sartre is a breach of trust, but also that the phrase in question could be translated into 'strictly philosophical terms'. For if the literary mode of expression is an essential condition of conveying the philosophical message (not to mention also subjectively authenticating it, which is very much the case with *Being and Nothingness*), then obviously it cannot be considered a breach of trust. One may then still legitimately challenge the problematical character of a particular philosophical discourse which needs the extensive use of metaphors for its articulation. In that case the whole discourse would be called into question, and not just some isolated phrases which could be translated into a less evocative form. But how could one put in 'strictly philosophical terms' the undoubtedly striking phrase: 'Man is a useless passion'? As we have seen already, so much hinges on references to 'passion' as a fundamental ontological characteristic in this 'new treatise of the passions' that any attempt at removing passion from the definition of 'the human reality' would empty it of its central core around which everything else is structured.

Each human reality is at the same time a direct project to metamorphose its own For-itself into an In-itself-For-itself and a project of the appropriation of the world as a totality of being-in-itself, in the form of a fundamental quality. Every human reality *is a passion* in that it projects losing itself so as to found being and by the same stroke to constitute the In-itself which escapes contingency by being its own foundation, the *Ens causa sui*, which religions call God(615).

Take away 'passion' from this discourse and it loses both its suggestive power and its existential meaning. On the other hand, if Sartre's strictures apply to the adjective 'useless' only, and not to 'passion'—which is hard to know, since he gives no indication of how to render the criticized phrase 'in strictly philosophical terms'—then the self-criticism amounts to very little indeed, if anything at all, in that the message of a *necessary failure* (the literal meaning of ontologically frustrated '*useless* passion') is in fact very effectively conveyed by the adjective he uses, without involving any breach of trust at all. Paradoxically, therefore, Sartre's sweeping condemnation of the particular example in rather harsh terms is the expression of his reluctance to be critical of the philosophical discourse of *Being and Nothingness* as a whole, since the continuities of this discourse with his later thought, despite some significant differences, are far too weighty to enable him to embark on a far-reaching critical examination of this work. 'Self-criticism' again appears as a retrospective 'should have been' coupled with a positive *self-assertion* claiming an exemplary solution of the problem in the *Critique of Dialectical Reason*, while in fact not only is the greater part of the categorial framework of *Being and Nothingness* retained (though, of course, complemented by a range of new categories) but even some particular arguments and examples from the early work reappear in new contexts in the later work, requiring a reference to the original context (not provided by Sartre himself) in order to acquire their full significance.[288]

The overpowering use of metaphors in *Being and Nothingness* is not simply a literary way of rendering with

greater evocative power an abstract philosophical proposition. If it had been meant as such, it would have been a
failure; for the characteristic of abstractness remains despite
the graphic imagery, as we have mentioned before. Nor is it
the consequence of an unavoidable dialectical complexity in
terms of which Sartre emphatically defends the long
involved sentences of his *Critique of Dialectical Reason*.
The numerous metaphors of *Being and Nothingness* are not
isolated examples of literary presentation: they constitute a
coherent whole, and as such they are inextricably linked to
the *ambiguities* of the conceptual framework itself. To
understand and appreciate the nature and importance of
these metaphors we must first focus attention on the
underlying ambiguities in light of which the particular images
of Sartre's 'eidetics of bad faith' reveal their necessity in the
constitution of a coherent, powerful and highly specific
philosophical discourse. A few examples should suffice to
illustrate the connections we are concerned with.

After asserting that '*my freedom eats away my freedom*'(480), Sartre goes on to discuss the relationship
between the particular and the 'global':

> . . . it is necessary to consult each man's history in order to get from
> it a particular idea with regard to each individual for-itself. Our
> *particular* projects, aimed at the realization in the world of a
> particular end, are united in the *global* project which we are. But
> precisely because we are *wholly* choice and act, these partial
> projects are not *determined* by the global project. They must
> themselves be choices; and a certain margin of contingency, of
> unpredictability, and of the absurd is allowed to each of them
> although each project as it is projected is the *specification* of the
> global project on the *occasion* of particular elements in the situation
> and so is always understood in relation to the totality of my
> being-in-the-world. . . . freedom is the freedom of choosing but not
> the freedom of not choosing. Not to choose is, in fact, to choose not
> to choose.(480-1)

The elements of this reasoning are most intricate, and they
are made even more complicated by the fact that they are not

always rendered conceptually explicit. Instead, metaphors are brought forward at some key points, and they are fully integrated into the development of the argument so that they can carry part of and thus support the whole of the existential message. It is the need to keep together a number of *antinomous* factors—resisting the temptation of an easy solution by paying just lip service to one side of the antinomy while dogmatically asserting the validity of the other: say 'freedom', at the expense of 'contingency'—which makes the task of putting everything 'in strictly philosophical terms' not merely difficult but wellnigh impossible. If I am 'wholly choice' (wholly freedom), then the particular elements of a situation cannot possibly amount to a *determination*, which would sharply contradict my 'absolute freedom' and the corresponding 'absolute responsibility', but only to an *'occasion'* on which my freedom must freely determine itself. (Must, in that even if it does not, it actually does in the mode of 'choosing not to choose'.) Consequently, that strange hybrid of a conceptual metaphor (or metaphorical concept): the Sartrean 'occasion'[289] is born which keeps perilously balanced on a razor's edge the antinomous requirements of freedom and contingency-facticity, without suppressing either side in favour of the other. Furthermore, since 'the free project is *fundamental*, for it is *my being'*(479), it must have some significant characteristics which, however, cannot possibly amount to a character, nature, or determining determination, since that would, again, undermine my freedom. Similarly, every one of my choices must be freely chosen from an infinite range of possible choices, and at the same time they must be totally unjustifiable in that 'justifiability' would impose itself as a kind of moral *determination* which preempts and destroys my freedom and thus reveals itself as existentially repugnant, no matter how 'moral'. If, therefore, the concept of my 'original', 'initial', 'fundamental' and 'global'[290] project is to be meaningful at all, the global project must have some significant effect on my particular choices without, however, *determining* them in the slightest. Thus another strange concept is brought into play: the *'specification'* of the global project in the form of the particular projects on the *'occasion'* of the particular *'elements'* of my situation, which in no circumstances should be interpreted as a *determination* of my choices either by my global project (my being) or by the (social, political, psychological, and other) forces at work in my situation. *Situation*, too, should not be thought of as a set of objective conditions which determine my project, but rather as the concrete embodiment of my project, and thus as something created by me on the 'occasion' and through the unification of certain 'elements' which I happen to encounter in my contingency and facticity. As in Kant's philosophy, the determinations of the empirical world cannot condition or contradict my freedom which retains, despite all evidence to the contrary, its absolute power. ('Man cannot be sometimes slave and sometimes free; he is *wholly* and *forever free* or he is not free at all'(441)—as Sartre puts it.) But in contrast to Kant's philosophy, freedom can be contradicted by *itself*, and not even just a little, but wholly and absolutely, and still without invalidating in the least the categorical absoluteness of freedom. If this sounds absurd, it does not really matter in a 'strictly philosophical sense'. Sartre takes up the gauntlet and defiantly calls it absurd, with the proviso that this is not because a philosophical thought fails to master its formal rules, but as a matter of the ontological conditions of the human reality:

> Since freedom is a being-without-*support* and without-a-*springboard*, the project to be must be constantly renewed. I choose myself perpetually and can never be merely by virtue of having-been-chosen; otherwise I should fall into the pure and simple existence of the in-itself. The necessity of perpetually choosing myself is one with the pursued-pursuits which I am. But precisely because here we are dealing with a choice, this choice as it is made indicates in general other choices as possibles. The possibility of these other choices is neither made explicit nor posited, but it is *lived in the feeling of unjustifiability*; and it is this

which is expressed by the fact of the *absurdity of my choice* and consequently of my being. Thus *my freedom eats away my freedom*(480).

As we can see, freedom is not limited by something external to it, and yet it is totally nihilated. The absolute validity of freedom is categorically asserted, and yet, the conditions of its realization (negation) in conformity with my contingency and facticity are fully respected, without prejudging in the least whether the particular manifestations of my freedom as unified under my unique global project will be marked by 'authenticity' or by 'bad faith'. The Kantian problematic which insists on the absoluteness of freedom is fully retained, and yet it is totally transformed in that it is no longer confined to a transcendental world. The antinomous elements of the Sartrean conception are held together, even if in a most uneasy way, and the existential concept of freedom ceases to be a sublime transcendental principle. It assumes a tangible shape, indeed a body, and appears voraciously engaged in a very 'un-Socratic' function which should scandalize any self-respecting utilitarian liberal. We catch a glimpse of it: *eating*. And, horror of horrors, '*my freedom eats away my freedom*', for which I can only blame myself. The metaphor—just like the others mentioned before—is neither a literary device for rendering things more vivid, nor is it translatable. It is an essential part of the specific philosophical structure which displays a number of very different levels, including the 'unsaid' and the 'figuratively implied' as well as the 'metaphorically condensed', in addition to the 'strict philosophical terms' of an explicit conceptual progression. To be sure, one may very well question the *fundamental ambiguity* of Sartre's conception of freedom in *Being and Nothingness*, with its *antinomous structure* of categorical assertion and simultaneous negation. What must however, be beyond dispute, is that given the—no matter how problematical—elements of this conception, 'my freedom eats away my freedom' represents an essential constituent as well as a most fitting summing up of it.

The same ambiguity is in evidence in Sartre's depiction of the relationship between the For-itself and the In-itself as 'a *double play* of *unilateral oppositions*' devoid of reciprocity, insisting on the affinity of the For-itself with 'the "ambiguous" realities of Kierkegaard'(94), so as to be able to assert that 'Value is *everywhere* and *nowhere*; at the *heart* of the nihilating "reflection-reflecting", it is *present* and *out of reach*, and it is simply *lived* as the concrete meaning of that *lack* which makes my present being'(95). Given the antinomous conception of the relationship between the For-itself and the In-itself as *unilateral* (rigid, non-dialectical) oppositions, one needs the metaphor of a '*double play*' to bring them together at all. And since we are confronted with a relationship totally devoid of reciprocity, the envisaged synthesis of 'In-itself-For-itself or value' can only be conceived as an '*unrealizable totality*'(94). Thus the fundamental ambiguity is unavoidable in view of the antinomous structure. The impossible synthesis of unilateral oppositions can only exist as an unrealizable totality, and as such it must reside 'everywhere and nowhere': it must be simultaneously 'at hand', immediately present, and totally out of reach. The sense we encounter here is a strictly subjective sense. It amounts to saying that even though Value (the 'In-itself-For-itself') is an unrealizable totality, the fundamental project of 'the human reality' (my being, with all its 'absurdity') is intelligible as a passionate striving for the realization of the unrealizable, impossible synthesis. The sets of metaphorical concepts employed by Sartre do not change the antinomous relations; nor are they meant to. They cannot create the movement of reciprocity leading to synthesis on a ground for which *a priori* antagonism is predicated 'forever'. All they can do and are meant to do is to provide a *subjective authentication* for the striving of my 'human reality' toward the impossible synthesis of an unrealizable totality. In the absence of such an authentication the discourse about 'authenticity' would become totally vacuous and Sartre's 'eidetics of bad faith' would undermine and destroy itself. Thus the metaphors are both necessary and untranslatable. For given the elements of this conception, only a subjective authentication is feasible,[291] which, however, cannot be produced 'in strictly philosophical terms'. At the same time 'the *double play* of unilateral oppositions'—arguably a contradiction in terms 'in strict philosophical terms'—effectively and legitimately provides just the kind of movement which keeps the antinomies together and holds them apart while subjectively authenticating the possibilities of individual choice 'against all odds': very much in the spirit of Sartre's existential discourse as articulated in *Being and Nothingness*.

Similarly, the relationship between the For-itself and being is described as an extreme paradox: 'the For-itself is *immediate presence* to being, and yet at the same time it *slips in* as an *infinite distance* between itself and being'(218). The coincidence of immediate presence and infinite distance cannot be conceptualized 'in strictly philosophical terms'. It must be established through the vivid imagery of the For-itself turned into infinite distance '*slipping in*' between itself and being. This particular conceptual edifice is extremely fragile: it would collapse even under the most delicate touch of a 'strict philosophical' examination. The perilously unstable conceptual elements (the for-itself which *is one with* immediate presence but at the same time *it* slips in between *itself* and being as an infinite distance) are supported by the imagery which does not reconcile the antinomous constituents *conceptually* (that would be perilously unstable conceptual elements (the For-itself which *is one with* immediate presence but at the same time *it* slips in between *itself* and being as an infinite distance) are 'unification' of the elements of another impossible unification: that is, the figurative-evocative synthesis of the antinomous constituents *conceptually* (that would be deliberately kept apart. The paradoxical unification–separation and the fundamental ambiguity corresponding to it again assert themselves as inherently necessary to the existentialist message.

Having designated value as an 'unrealizable totality' in virtue of its being the impossible unification of the In-itself-For-itself—an unrealizable totality which we nevertheless must strive for, as we have seen—the being of value which we must encounter (and indeed we *must* encounter it, otherwise it would be totally devoid of existential plausibility and subjective authentication) can only be ' a *phantom-being* which *surrounds* and *penetrates* the For-itself through and through' (203). (Note even the way in which the expression 'through and through' is superadded in order to intensify the evocative power of the surrounding and penetrating phantom-being.) In an axiological framework like this the realization of the aims we set ourselves is, yet again, depicted as an impossible unification by definition, and it is compared to the predicament of an ass trying to reach a carrot tied, hopelessly beyond his reach, to the shaft of the cart he is pulling:

> Thus we run after a possible which our very running causes to appear, which is nothing but our running itself, and which thereby is by definition *out of reach*. We *run toward ourselves* and we are—due to this very fact—the being which *cannot be reunited with itself*. In one sense the running is void of meaning since the goal is never given but *invented* and projected *proportionately* as we run toward it. In another sense we cannot refuse to it that meaning which it rejects since in spite of everything possibility is the meaning of the For-itself. Thus there is and there is not a meaning in the flight (202-3).

The imagery is very suggestive and its function is the same as before: the simultaneous assertion of immediate vicinity and unreachable distance sustains the impossible unification of the human reality with its being. In the spirit of existentialism, just as my being must be constantly recreated through the perpetual renewal of the project which it is, the goal of my pursuit—since I am 'pursued-pursuits'—can never be given in that its givenness would act as a determinism and undermine my freedom. From this negative determination of the existentialist position vis-à-vis determinism arises the strange imagery of 'running toward ourselves', pursuing the goal of the impossible unification of ourselves with our being, which is by definition 'out of reach'. What else could such a pursuit be if not 'meaningless meaning' and 'meaningful meaninglessness'? And since the goal must forever remain out of reach, 'authenticity' must reside in the *running* itself which '*proportionately invents*' and projects its goal without ever making it. (This is why 'all human activities are *equivalent* . . . and all are doomed to failure. Thus it amounts to the same thing whether one gets drunk alone or is a leader of nations' (627). What counts is the running itself—towards ourselves—which we invent proportionately as we run toward it, namely ourselves.) Again, the discourse would be thoroughly incoherent 'in strictly philosophical terms'. For how does one run toward oneself, strictly speaking? (The image of the ass and the carrot is a very bad example. It does not convey at all Sartre's meaning as it emerges from the lines that immediately follow it. For in the ass's case the goal is in fact given in the carrot, and the ass would not be ass enough to go on 'forever' as a pursued-pursuits-pursuing an unreachable carrot.) In the spirit of Sartre's existentialism, the anti-nomous elements must be firmly kept apart at the discursive level. And yet, this must be accomplished without allowing them to be represented as antagonistic forces within us 'whose type of existence is comparable to that of things' (40). The possibility of an existential mastery over them must be demonstrated, if the existentialist conception of freedom is to mean anything at all. But given the role of contingency and facticity in the same conception, the power of freedom in reaching its unreachable goal of the impossible unification can only be demonstrated in the form of a subjective authentication, which is suggestively accomplished by complementing the discursive level with a metaphorical level in such a way that the two levels are not developed side by side—that would amount to no more than the introduction of conceptually superfluous literary embellishments—but become fully *integrated*. The remarkable 'mass-appeal' of Sartre's existentialism (to the point of becoming a 'cult' which dominated the cafés of the Quartier Latin in Paris in the immediate postwar years), despite the forbidding abstractness and intense ambiguity of its conceptual framework as a whole, is inseparable from this characteristic of a total integration (fusion) of the metaphorical and discursive levels in *Being and Nothingness*.

The last example which we can afford to quote in this limited space concerns the concepts of 'causality', 'motion' and 'time'. In a conceptual framework in which freedom and choice, project and goal, situation and being are defined in the form we have seen, the concepts of 'causality', 'motion' and 'time' must equally be defined in such a way that the existentialist discourse is not disrupted but, on the contrary, intensified. The language of determinism is emphatically rejected, and we get a definition of causality as

> the apprehension of the 'appeared' *before* it appears, as being *already there* in its own nothingness so as to *prepare* its apparition(208).

Similarly,

> Motion has no more of being; it is the *least-being* of a being which can neither arrive nor be abolished nor wholly be. Motion is the *upsurge of the exteriority of indifference* at the very *heart* of the In-itself. This *pure vacillation* of being is a contingent venture of being(213).

And from this point it is only one step to say that

> universal time is revealed as *present vacillation*; already in the past it is no longer anything but an *evanescent line*, like the wake of a *ship which fades away*; in the future it is not at all, for it is unable to be its own project. It is like the steady progression of a *lizard on the wall*. Moreover its being has the *inapprehensible ambiguity of the instant*, for one could not say either that it is or that it is not(213).

The fundamental ambiguity of 'is and is not', of 'everywhere and nowhere', of 'immediate presence and infinite distance', of 'meaning and meaninglessness', and so on, is central to the existentialist message. This ambiguity, in all its particular manifestations, is the existential ambiguity of freedom and contingency: of the absoluteness of freedom and the iron necessity of its embodiment in the concrete situation of the human reality. Keeping the anguishing authenticity of the existentialist discourse diametrically opposed to determinism and its 'bad faith' while acknowledging the full weight of contingency and facticity, means an immensely difficult balancing act on a high wire, with the constant danger of precipitating, split into two, on the side of mechanical determinism with one half, and of 'pure indeterminacy' with the other. To rescue 'causality', 'temporality', and 'motion' from the reified objectivity of mechanical determinism without allowing them to disintegrate in the vacuous discourse of 'indeterminacy' Sartre needs not only the strange imagery of a 'something-nothing' which 'prepares'—not *determines*—'its apparition', but also a whole range of metaphors and images—from 'pure vacillation' and 'present vacillation' to the 'evanescent line of a ship which fades away' and to the 'steady progression of a lizard on the wall'—so that the arduous balancing act can be maintained. The pressures of sustaining the existentialist discourse through this balancing act, which uses the metaphorical level to join together in a most unstable union elements of strict determination and absolutely indeterminacy, produce a manipulation of concepts which may appear sheer sophistry if read in a purely discursive sense, separated from the total context. We have seen the telling description of the various manifestations of the global project as its 'specifications', so as to guard against the possibility of a deterministic reading. Similarly, in our quotation of a moment ago, nothingness is already there before it appears in order to '*prepare* its[292] apparition', leaving the meaning of the term 'prepare' vaguely undefined in function of the balancing requirements. But perhaps the most striking example is to be found in the context of a definition of the relationship between 'past' and 'facticity'. These two terms, insists Sartre, indicate one and the same thing:

> The Past, in fact, like Facticity, is the invulnerable contingency of the In-itself which I have to be without any possibility of not being it. It is the *inevitability* of the *necessity of fact*, not by virtue of *necessity* but by virtue of *fact*. It is the being of fact, which can not *determine* the content of my motivations but which *paralyses* them with its contingency because they can neither suppress it nor change it;(118) . . .

It is a sour consolation that the inevitability which permeates our being in the mode of a necessity of fact does so not by virtue of *necessity* but by virtue of *fact*, and this kind of differentiation, considered 'in strictly philosophical terms', appears to be nothing but hair-splitting sophistry. The same goes for the assertion that this curious necessity of fact which imposes itself as *inevitability* does not *ipso facto* also *determine* our motivations but only *paralyses* them. And yet things appear in a different light if we insert these propositions into Sartre's discourse as a whole, instead of examining them in isolation. For Sartre draws a firm line of demarcation between *motivation* and *determination*, which in turn carries with it the necessity of a radical redefinition of all the interrelated concepts in the same spirit, including 'causality', 'temporality', 'motion', and indeed 'necessity' and 'inevitability' inasmuch as they are admissible into the framework of the existentialist discourse. But since the innermost structure of this discourse is starkly *antinomous,* there remains in it an immense *tension* 'through and through' which tends to split it apart, despite all efforts of conceptual manipulation and metaphorical unification. It is this tension which bursts out into the open as an apparent sophistry in those contexts in which the naked discursiveness still predominates: before, that is, Sartre succeeds in complementing the discursive level of his discourse with the metaphorical level, thus producing the only feasible existentialist unification of the antinomous elements in the form of a subjective authentication.

This is what we can witness in the example just quoted. The existentialist antinomy sternly asserts itself immediately after the somewhat baffling talk about the necessity of fact and the non-determining paralysis of motivations, making them intelligible in strictly discursive terms when Sartre admits that 'Between *past* and *present* there is an *absolute heterogeneity*'(119). But things cannot be left at that, nor are they intended to be, as evidenced by the strange conceptual manipulation of inevitability and free motivation which anticipates—or, rather, postulates—some sort of a synthesis, even if it cannot accomplish its aim. And, of course, a conceptual unification of *absolute heterogeneity* 'in strictly philosophical terms' would be a monstrous contradiction in terms. Yet it must be accomplished somehow for the sake of the existentialist message. Thus we find on the other side of the brutally open conceptual divide—the explicit admission of an 'absolute heterogeneity'—a most remarkable *homogenization* of this heterogeneity, accomplished through the use of a graphic imagery. We witness a 'presentification' of the past (that is, its transformation into some sort of a lived present)—which could not conceivably work on a strictly discursive level—and the assertion of its *'evanescent* value', with an appeal to *memory* as a framework of *subjective authentication*. We are presented with a beautiful description which successfully buries the existentialist antinomy deep below the surface (where it remains until it is bound to erupt again in some other context) and we are left with the *impression* of a unification:

> . . . *memory* presents to us the being which we were, accompanied by a *plenitude of being* which confers on it a sort of *poetry*. That *grief* which we had—although fixed in the past—does not cease to present the meaning of a *For-itself*, and yet it exists *in itself* with the *silent fixity* of the grief of another, the *grief of a statue*.(119)

There is no attempt to pretend that the antinomy of absolute heterogeneity no longer exists. All that happens is that it is made existentially bearable through the poetic power of memory which turns the past into some sort of a present and confers upon it a plenitude of being while also retaining its past character in the silent fixity of a statue. The act of balancing is successfully accomplished without distorting or falsifying its own terms of reference, thanks to the fact that the impossible unification of 'absolute heterogeneity' is confined to the subjective plane. There it produces an existentialist authentication of its categorical rejection of the past as a determinism with an appeal to the experience of lived memory: a procedure which, again, leaves the question entirely open whether we constitute 'the plenitude of being' of our past being 'authentically' or in 'bad faith'. Sartre's existentialism needs no more than an indication (proof would be far too strong a term) of the *possibility* of authenticity vis-à-vis the absolute contingency of the past, and this is precisely—no less, no more—what it succeeds in producing through the full integration of the discursive and metaphorical levels. For given the inherently antinomous structure of Sartre's discourse, (a) the only way it can produce the indication of a *possible authenticity* is the massive use of metaphorical imagery; and (b) even through the most extensive use of such imagery it can only produce the indication of a mere *possibility*, followed by frequent assertions of doom and necessary failure, as we have seen above. Thus the occasional footnotes about 'the *possibility* of an ethics of deliverance' which should follow a somewhat mysterious 'radical conversion'(412) must be taken with a mountain-size pinch of salt. To squeeze a coherent 'ethics of deliverance and salvation' out of the category of mere possibility forebodingly resembles the Sartrean imperative of an impossible unification. If later the author of the *Critique of Dialectical Reason* is less dependent on metaphorical imagery than in *Being and Nothingness*, this is partly because he is less orientated toward abstract possibility than before (in that he gives a more positive hearing to the categories of need, necessity and deter-mination) and partly because he tries to introduce the category of *mediation* into the discourse of antinomous oppositions. However, the examination of the precise character of such changes and of the extent to which they may be considered successful must be left to a later chapter (Volume Two).[293]

In *Being and Nothingness* the antinomous conceptual structure remains in evidence from beginning to end, determining the constant recurrence of ambiguities and metaphors. These three characteristics—antinomies, ambi-guities and metaphors—are thus inextricably linked together as *structural* characteristics of Sartre's existentialist dis-course on freedom and contingency. Since the unstable balance that characterizes the existentialist message must be 'invented' and constantly recreated in the form of a coherent set of concepts, and since the metaphorical level plays an essential part in the production of the unique coherence which emerges through the radical transformation of the deterministic language of everydayness in each and every particular context, we encounter the *ubiquitousness*[294] of the metaphorical imagery as an *ongoing process*. The suggestiveness of this imagery cannot be properly appreci-ated simply in terms of the graphic qualities of the particular images—like the play-acting waiter in the café, quoted everywhere—taken in isolation, but goes much deeper. Its intensity is cumulative and arises partly from the ongoing articulation of a coherent system of interlinked images, constituted not entirely unlike a set of musical variations on some fundamental existentialist theme whereby the par-ticular item is always incomparably richer in conjunction with the set as a whole than by itself. But the intensity goes even beyond the remarkable structural coherence of the metaphorical level as a whole. It is also due to the vitally important function which the metaphorical imagery fulfils, through the intermediary of its particular images and 'concept-metaphors', in the constitution of Sartre's existentialist discourse. In other words, the almost hypnotic intensity of this imagery is just as much *conceptual* as it is *representational*. Thus, when Sartre asserts that he should have written *Being and Nothingness* in a way which would have avoided what he now calls 'a breach of trust', he doesn't realize[295] that he could not have done so. And all the better for that. For had he succeeded in conforming to his retrospective ideal, we would have been deprived of one of the most original and representative philosophical works of our century.

3

The way in which the various existentialist themes are developed in *Being and Nothingness* might be termed 'kaleidoscopic', in the sense that a conceptual framework made of remarkably few elements is articulated in detail through a virtually endless number of particular examples and descriptive specifications. The conceptual framework itself might seem very simple at first sight, in view of the extremely limited number of basic categories. However, a closer look reveals some forbidding complications at all levels. For a start, the constantly recurring categories are arranged as antinomous pairs ('Being–Nothingness', 'In-itself–For-itself', 'Self–Other', 'Freedom–Contingency', 'Possibility–Necessity', 'Authenticity–Bad Faith', and the like), and their interrelationship is conceived in the form of the 'unilateral oppositions of absolute heterogeneity', as we have seen above. A further complication is that the contrast of such unilateral oppositions does not constitute a movement: rather, it represents the picture of a paralysing stalemate and therefore any movement we encounter must be introduced 'from outside', as it were. But, of course, there can be nothing 'outside' the fundamental structural outlines of a synthesising philosophical conception. If a particular philosophical totalization conceives the world as a paralysing stalemate, the movement that can be accommodated within the framework of such a totalization must be a rather problematic one. And indeed the 'kaleidoscopic' development of themes, as we shall see in a moment, has the function of creating this peculiar movement in *Being and Nothingness*. We are presented with an endless succession of ingenuous transformations and permutations, both conceptual and metaphorical, whereby illustrative instances taken from everyday life unfold Sartre's conception of the basic ontological structures.

The pattern of this development is most revealing. For the various instances of everyday life, and the corresponding common-sense use of language, are described, moulded, and manipulated by Sartre—sometimes to the point that he himself has to admit that they are 'forced'[296]—until the full correspondence of the empirical instances to the fundamental ontological structures can be asserted. Thus the 'movement' of kaleidoscopic particularization and exemplification cannot introduce any dynamism into the underlying static structures but invariably culminates in the stark reassertion of an all-pervasive paralysis. The conceptual framework of unilateral oppositions sharply delineates the character of the superadded movement which must disappear abruptly the very moment it helps to bring into relief the essential *identity* of the particular existents with the underlying ontological structures. The movement of particularization is strictly in the service of, and indeed subordinate to, asserting and reiterating the primary message of the overall conception. It is, therefore, a total misconception of the nature of *Being and Nothingness* to speak in terms of high praise about Sartre's descriptive talent while making dismissive remarks about his theoretical conception and philosophical rigour. These two dimensions not only stand or fall together but the overall conception unquestionably constitutes the '*übergreifendes Moment*'[297] in relation to descriptive detail and graphic particularization. Undoubtedly, Sartre's description of Pierre's *absence* from the café is a most impressive piece of writing; but only in terms of the total set of relations as specified by Sartre. Indeed, it is completely pointless, and perhaps even meaningless, without the overall ontological conception in which 'nothingness' and 'lack' assume a determinate, multi-faceted, and most unusual meaning in terms of which Pierre's 'tangible absence' can and must be read.

Sartre's great preference for writing philosophy, which is by no means surprising in view of the incomparable ease with which he produces monumental works of philosophy, is understandable precisely in relation to a talent which embarks on the laborious process of drafting the work from the premises of a most firmly laid down (some might say: rigidly preconceived) overall conception as the dominant feature of the whole enterprise. The synthesis is there right from the beginning in the original intuition of the overall conceptual framework, and the process of writing consists in the detailed articulation of the basic intuition under extremely close control at every stage. The great ease of writing arises from the fact that the overall direction of development is unhesitatingly anticipated from the first moment, and thus the new treatise of the passions 'writes itself', so to speak, much as it is described by Sartre in his *Sketch for a Theory of the Emotions*:

> The words that I am writing . . . are exigent. It is the precise manner in which I grasp them in the course of my creative activity that makes them what they are: they are potentialities that have to be realized. . . . I simply feel the traction they exert; I feel their exigence objectively. I see them realizing themselves and, at the same time, demanding further realization. . . . the exigence of the words that I am tracing is directly present, weighty and felt. They impel and direct my hand. But not as though little demons, alive and active, were driving and guiding it in fact: this is a passive exigence.[298]

The curious concept of a 'passive exigence' becomes meaningful in fact with reference to the overall design. Sartre knows the words 'in advance' as they are about to realize themselves because the overall design firmly guides his hand with its 'passive exigence'. For even if the minute details and particular images obviously cannot be known in advance, the precise *direction* of the development and the specific *character* or *type* of the admissible imagery is peremptorily anticipated in the original intuition of the basic outlines and of the categorial framework of an enterprise which consciously undertakes the elaboration of a new treatise of the passions on a premise asserting the fundamental identity of freedom and passion. This is very different indeed from the situation when Sartre rightly castigates his own 'failed play', *Morts sans sépulture* (Unburied Dead), as a play 'without surprise',[299] in that the destiny of the characters is 'absolutely defined in advance'. Such a procedure may be totally inadmissible in the medium of the drama, but the absence of surprises does not constitute a drawback in the development of a philosophical conception in which the relationship between the parts and the whole is justifiably ruled by *necessity*, even in Sartre's existentialism.[300] And inasmuch as the whole enterprise is conducted in the spirit that even the apparently most insignificant gestures are meaningful manifestations of the human reality in its entirety—hence the definition of the task of philosophy as the *'hermeneutic of existence'*[301] already in the *Sketch for a Theory of the Emotions*—the interpretative approach in relation to the analysis or description of any particular situation is automatically given and unceremoniously imposed on whatever detail or illustrative example Sartre happens to mention, from food to mountain-climbing or ice-skating, leaving no room whatsoever for 'surprises' as to the ontological meaning which the particular instances will be allowed to disclose.[302]

There is something quasi-mechanical in this pattern of closely controlled interpretative development which never tires of reiterating the underlying elementary ontological structures on the occasion of each and every particular instance. The extreme unevenness of *Being and Nothing-*

*ness*—a characterization applicable, *mutatis mutandis*, also to Sartre's other philosophical ventures of equally
or even more massive proportions, from *Saint Genet* to the
*Critique of Dialectical Reason* and to the unfinished trilogy
on Flaubert—is a necessary consequence of this 'kaleidoscopic' pattern of development. For the immensely ingenious
overall structure—the invention of the kaleidoscope itself
which in turn produces an inexhaustible variety of complex
images through the interplay of a few simple elements—may
just as easily yield some splendidly impressive and
suggestive pictures as some tediously repetitive permutations. The following example gives a good idea of what
is involved in the latter:

> The Present could not pass except by becoming the before for a
> For-itself which constitutes itself as the after of that Present. There
> is then only one phenomenon: the upsurge of a new Present which is
> making-past the Present which it was, and the Making-Past of a
> Present involving the appearance of a For-itself for which this
> Present is going to become Past. The phenomenon of temporal
> becoming is a global modification since a Past which would be the
> Past of nothing would no longer be a Past and since a Present must
> be necessarily the Present of this Past. This metamorphosis,
> moreover, affects not only the pure Present; the former Past and
> Future are equally affected. The Past of the Present which has
> undergone the modification of Pastness, becomes the Past of a
> Past—or a Pluperfect. So far as the Pluperfect is concerned, the
> heterogeneity of the Present and the Past is now suddenly
> suppressed since what made the Present distinct as such from the
> Past has now become Past. In the course of the metamorphosis the
> Present remains the Present of this Past, but it becomes the past
> Present of this Past. That means first that this present is
> homogeneous with the series of the Past which extends from it all
> the way back to its birth, second that this present is no longer its
> Past in the form of having to be it but in the mode of having had to be
> it. The connection between Past and Pluperfect is a connection
> which is in the mode of the In-itself, and it appears on the foundation
> of the present For-itself. It is this which holds the series of the Past
> and pluperfects welded into a single block. . . . Future and past
> Present are solidified in the In-itself on the foundation of my
> Present. Thus the Future in the course of the temporal process,

passes to the In-itself without ever losing its character as Future. In so far as it is not achieved by the Present, it becomes simply a given Future. When it is achieved, it is affected with the quality of ideality; but this ideality is ideality in-itself, for it presents itself as a given lack of a given past and not as the lacking which a present For-itself has to be in the mode of not being. When the future is surpassed, it remains forever on the margin of the series of Pasts as a former Future—a former Future of a particular Past becomes Pluperfect, an ideal given Future as co-present to a Present become Past(144-5).

And so it goes on, and on, and on, with bewildering tortuosity and repetitiveness. If there can be in philosophy a real 'breach of trust' in Sartre's sense of 'pulling a fast one on the reader', certainly this is it. We might even think that he is here only pulling the reader's leg, if we did not actually know that Sartre is always very serious about everything he writes. The trouble with passages like this is that they bring into play the mechanism of verbal transformations and content themselves with going round and round in circles. If we ask ourselves at the end of the verbal transformations how far we advanced with the problem, the sobering answer is: not at all. This is so strongly the case here that a mere four lines after our heavy quotation Sartre is led to declare that 'it would almost be correct to reverse our terms in order to find the truth'. And why not? We would still be going round in circles, even if in the other direction. This is in fact what we are compelled to do by Sartre for two more pages, at which point he admits that 'We find ourselves once more it seems, at our point of departure'(147). And since in this particular context Sartre has now exhausted the possibilities of abstract conceptual permutations, backwards and forwards, we are presented with another twist as the solution in the sentence that immediately follows: 'But the truth is that *there is no problem*.' Perhaps so. But if so, what was all the fuss about? And here is the answer: 'If we believe that we have met one [problem], this is because in spite of our efforts to think of the For-itself as really For-itself, we have not been able to prevent ourselves from fixing it in the

In-itself' (147). It is good to know that while we were being taken for a ride Sartre was our sincere companion and shared our predicament. This knowledge, however, does not change the disconcerting fact itself, namely that after our long and tortuous journey of verbal self-indulgence we managed to get exactly nowhere.

And yet in a sense it is fortunate that Sartre did not edit out these passages of inconclusive verbosity. For they help to identify the tensions involved and the reasons why even Sartre's incomparable dexterity of conceptual manipulation and linguistic transformation cannot succeed in advancing the problem. If we re-read carefully our quotation—and we must do so several times in order to be able to acquire some perspective over its captivating maze—we find that it takes us nowhere because it merely reasserts in their naked abstractness the basic conceptual imperatives of Sartre's categorial framework as a whole in the context of temporality, without any attempt at a necessary mediation. We know right from the beginning that the fundamental relationship between the For-itself and the In-itself is conceived in such terms that it has inescapable implications for the various dimensions of temporality, just as much as for everything else. (For instance, the absolute heterogeneity between past and present is the necessary concomitant of this fundamental relationship.) However, such implications must be substantiated through particularization and specification, in accordance with the precise character of the existential context in question, otherwise the philosophical enterprise which aims at demonstrating the essential identity of the empirical manifestations of existence with the underlying ontological structures fails to reach its object, and thus fails to indicate the possibility of an authentic existentialist choice in the spirit of the programmatic 'hermeneutic of existence'. In our quotation, regrettably, we witness the unfolding of such a failure. The original implications are spelled out as abstract imperatives and are reiterated again and again as such. We catch a glimpse of the necessary heterogeneity of past and present, followed by a sudden hint of homogeneity. The latter though, in sharp contrast to our earlier quote which tackled the same problem, is not demonstrated through particularization and subjective authentication. It is merely asserted as an abstract structural requirement ('the heterogeneity of the Present and the Past is now *suddenly suppressed*') and since there is nothing to sustain it, it must be immediately taken back ('the connection between Past and Pluperfect is a connection which is *in the mode of the In-itself*'). Furthermore, since we witness the manifestation of contradicatory imperatives—the preservation of heterogeneity just as much as its suppression—the two are abstractly brought together in yet another unsustained declaration according to which the connection between Past and Pluperfect which is in the mode of the *In-itself* 'appears on the foundation of the present *For-itself*'. And the failure is significantly in evidence also at the metaphorical level. For the metaphor of 'welded into a single block' is not *integrated* into the discourse but—again, in sharp contrast to our earlier quotes—it is merely appended to the tail-end of it as a decorative image which wildly overstates what it asserts, thus revealing just as much the author's strongly felt need for the reconcilation of the antinomous tensions as his inability to bring them together in other than abstractly imperatival form. The same considerations apply to the rest of our long quotation, and therefore they need not detain us any longer. What it all adds up to in the end is that in the example we have just seen we are presented not with an existentialist demonstration of a significant correspondance between the temporal dimensions of existence and some fundamental ontological structures but with the singularly uninstructive restatement of what we knew from the very beginning, namely that the For-itself is radically different from the In-itself, and therefore one should not try to 'fix the For-itself in the In-itself'.

The contrast could not be greater with our next example,

which displays at its best Sartre's legendary power to bring to life as a tangible existential reality even the most abstract philosophical connections. Sartre's analysis sets out from defining play as 'an activity of which man is the first origin, for which man sets the rules, and which has no consequences except according to the rules posited'(580). Play is considered a manifestation of freedom through which man 'escapes his natural nature'(581) in virtue of the fact that he is in complete control over the act, its value and the rules. The empirical instances of play are described by Sartre in terms of their deepest existential meaning:

> . . . the desire to do is here reduced to a certain desire to be. The act is not its own goal for itself; neither does its explicit end represent its goal and its profound meaning; but the function of the act is to make manifest and to present to itself the absolute freedom which is the very being of the person. This particular type of project, which has freedom for its foundation and its goal, deserves a special study. It is radically different from all others in that it aims at a radically different type of being. It would be necessary to explain in full detail its relations with the project of being God, which has appeared to us as the deep-seated structure of human reality. But such a study cannot be made here; it belongs rather to an Eth-ics. . . . Nevertheless the fact remains that the desire to play is fundamentally the desire to be(581).

Thus the ontological concern with the experience of play is pushed in one direction to the point where the ultimate structure of the human reality—the project of being God—brings into the picture *Ethics* as the necessary complementary to the ontological analysis. And as Sartre's graphic particularization and specification of the ontological structures progresses in the other direction, again it reaches a point where it necessarily calls for being complemented by the third constituent of this discourse, *Existential Psychoanalysis*(586), as we shall see in a moment. The intensity and richness of these pages would not arise simply from the particular imagery. Rather, they are inseparable from the fact that the empirical instances are referred to the totality of their dimensions in that all three regions of the existentialist discourse—Ontology, Ethics and Existential Psychoanalysis as reciprocally founding one another—are brought into play around the focus of tangible experiences, which in turn clearly displays the structural coherence of a complex philosophical conception as a whole. Sartre takes as his principal example the experience of skiing.

> That pure In-itself [the field of snow], comparable to the absolute, intelligible plenum of Cartesian extension, fascinates me as the pure appearance of the not-me; what I wish precisely is that this In-itself might be a sort of emanation of myself while still remaining in itself. This is the meaning even of the snowmen and snowballs which children make; . . . To ski means not only to enable me to make rapid movements and to acquire a technical skill, nor is it merely to play by increasing according to my whim the speed or difficulties of the course; it is also to enable me to *possess* this field of snow. . . . The upsurge of the snow is the matter of my act in the same way that the upswing of the hammer is the pure fulfilment of the hammering. At the same time I have chosen a certain point of view in order to apprehend this snowy slope: this point of view is a determined speed, which emanates from me, which I can increase or diminish as I like; through it the field traversed is constituted as a definite object, entirely distinct from what it would be at another speed. . . . It is myself then who give form to the field of snow by the free speed which I give myself. But at the same time I am acting upon my matter. The speed is not limited to imposing a form on a matter given from the outside; it creates its matter. The snow, which sank under my weight when I walked, which melted into water when I tried to pick it up, solidifies suddenly under the action of my speed; it supports me. . . . This is because I hold a special relation of appropriation with the snow: sliding. . . . I realize a synthesis which has depth. I realize that the bed of snow organizes itself in its lowest depths in order to hold me up; the sliding is action at a distance; it assures my mastery over the material without my needing to plunge into that material and engulf myself in it in order to overcome it. To slide is the opposite of taking root. The root is already half assimilated into the earth; it can utilize the earth only by making itself earth;[303] . . . Sliding, on the contrary, realizes a material unity in depth without penetrating farther than the surface; it is like the dreaded master who does not need to insist nor to raise his voice in order to be obeyed. An admirable picture of power. From this comes that famous advice: 'Slide, mortals, don't bear

down!'[304] This does not mean 'Stay on the surface, don't go deeply into things', but on the contrary 'Realize syntheses in depth without compromising yourself.' . . . Thus the sliding appears as identical with a continuous creation. The speed is comparable to consciousness and here symbolizes consciousness(582-4).

Thus the eidetic description of the particular example of skiing culminates in the revelation of a *symbolic* relationship which universalizes its significance. Now we can really understand and appreciate why the particular example has been brought into the existentialist discourse. Equally, in relation to this example, we can understand the fundamental difference between pure phenomenology and Sartrean phenomenological description which is undertaken in the service of 'the hermeneutic of existence'. For the 'essence' which a Husserlian description of skiing would disclose could not have anything to do with the existential-ontological region of being: that would be ruled out by the necessary 'bracketing out' which is an *a priori* methodological prerequisite of its approach. Husserlian disclosure of the essence of skiing could only refer to itself for its meaning, and in no circumstances to some fundamental *ontological passion* which it might existentially '*symbolize*'. By contrast, Sartre makes intelligible the project of skiing as a project of 'realizing syntheses in depth', embracing the totality of relations of the human reality in their full intensity. Thanks to this approach, the everyday experience of skiing recedes from our horizon by billions of light years: the conception of a symbolic meaning makes the commonplace experience simply incommensurable with its existentialist counterpart. Now the 'hermeneutic of existence' puts in front of us something totally different: the snow as 'impenetrable and out of reach', representing the 'synthesis of self and not-self'(585) in a specific mode of possessive appropriation. Even the 'resistance' the snow seems to exert over us is made intelligible in the same terms of ontological appropriation:

I have realized this resistance through my fatigue, and I have been able to measure at each instant the progress of my victory. Here the snow is identical with the *Other*, and the common expressions 'to overcome', 'to conquer', 'to master', etc. indicate sufficiently that it is a matter of establishing between me and the snow the relation of *master to slave*. This aspect of appropriation which we find in the ascent, exists also in swimming, in an obstacle course, etc. The peak on which a flag is planted is a peak which has been *appropriated*(585).

Thus everything is set in the same light, and the ontological significance of the particular examples can be brought out in a generalized form:

> . . . a principal aspect of sport—and in particular of open air sports—is the conquest of these enormous masses of water, of earth, and of air, which seem *a priori* indomitable and unutilizable; and in each case it is a question of possessing not the element for itself, but the *type of existence in-itself* which is expressed by means of this element; it is the *homogeneity of substance* which we wish to possess in the form of snow; it is the *impenetrability of the in-itself* and its *non-temporal permanence* which we wish to appropriate in the form of the earth or of the rock, etc. *Art, science, play* are activities of appropriation, either wholly or in part, and what they want to appropriate beyond the concrete object of their quest is *being itself, the absolute being of the In-itself*(585).

And this is the point where the overall design becomes wholly visible, asserting the unity of the particular and the general in the synthesis of existentialist ontology with existential psychoanalysis:

> Thus ontology teaches us that desire is originally a desire of being and that it is characterized as the free lack of being. But it teaches us also that desire is a relation with a concrete existent in the midst of the world and that this existent is conceived as a type of In-itself; it teaches us that the relation of the For-itself to this desired In-itself is appropriation. We are, then, in the presence of a *double determination of desire*: on the one hand, desire is determined as a desire to be a certain being, which is the In-itself-For-itself and

whose existence is *ideal*; on the other hand, desire is determined in the vast majority of cases as a relation with a *contingent and concrete* In-itself which it has the project of appropriating. Does one of these determinations dominate the other? Are the two characteristics compatible? Existential psychoanalysis can be assured of its principles only if ontology has given a *preliminary* definition of the relation of these two beings—the concrete and contingent In-itself or *object* of the desire, and the In-itself-For-itself or *ideal* of the desire—and if it has made explicit the relation which unites appropriation as a type of relation to the In-itself, to being, as a type of relation to the In-itself–For-itself(585-6).

These few pages present to us in a microcosm, as it were, the totality of Sartre's existentialist conception. We can witness the development of the particular themes on the ground of the fundamental existentialist categories. Inevitably, the closer we get in the process of eidetic description to the ontological core, the more the antinomies of its structure are pushed into the foreground, profoundly affecting the character of the particular instances. It is because of the underlying structural antinomies that appropriation must be conceived—in sharpest possible contrast to our empirical notion of it—as nothing but a *symbolic* relation to an ideality, and in its ideality, corresponding to the ultimate ontological structure, it must be envisaged 'simultaneously as something given *at one stroke* . . . and as requiring an *infinite time* to be realized'(592). In other words, we are again confronted with an *impossible realization*, in the truest spirit of the existentialist message:

> . . . it is impossible to realize the relation symbolized by appropriation. In itself appropriation contains *nothing concrete*. It is not a real activity (such as eating, drinking, sleeping) which could serve in addition as a symbol for a particular desire. It exists, on the contrary, only as a *symbol*; it is its symbolism which gives it its meaning, its coherence, its existence. There can be found in it *no positive enjoyment* outside its *symbolic value*; it is only the indication of a supreme enjoyment of possession (that of the being which would be its own foundation), which is *always beyond* all the appropriative conduct meant to realize it(593).

It is not an idosyncratic inclination for paradoxical transformations which produces such antinomous contrasts but, on the contrary, the conceptual framework of structural antinomies tends to articulate itself often through extreme, and sometimes even shockingly extreme, paradoxical formulations: *Destruction* realizes appropriation perhaps more keenly than *creation* does, for the object destroyed is no longer there to show itself impenetrable. . . . to *destroy* is to *recreate* by assuming oneself as solely responsible for the being of what existed for all(593). True enough, no matter how shockingly paradoxical. But of course true only in terms of the fundamental definitions of the overall conceptual framework which must precede it. The particular paradoxes are only instantiations of the conceptual framework of unilateral oppositions: they can be derived from the latter with the ease of the kaleidoscopic transformations which throw at one moment the light of one side of the antinomy, and the next moment the contrasting light of its opposite, on the particular point at issue, and in the most extreme cases they can even combine the two lights into a single beam, so as to display with authenticity the 'uneasy balance' of the existentialist conception.

Contrary to interpretations which arbitrarily isolate the particular descriptions from the philosophical conception and oppose them to the latter, we can clearly identify the determination of even the most minute details by the overall conception. Taken in isolation, assertions like 'the In-itself is transformed into nothingness'(582 – that is, when I pick up some snow and my fingers melt it), or 'the snow solidifies suddenly under the action of my speed; it supports me'(583) are unsustainable absurdities. Melted snow is by no means 'nothingness', and in any case things might turn out the other way round—namely my frozen fingers departing into 'nothingness' from my hand rather than the snow melting away—depending on the outside temperature. Nor is it true that the snow solidifies and supports me 'under the action of my *speed*'. For speed or no speed, what I need, above all, is the *supporting platform* of my skis, or some similar devices, and *they* do the supporting, not my speed which itself must be 'supported': that is, made possible by the underlying support. But obviously such factual trivia cannot be allowed to stand in the way of Sartre's eidetic sweep. All the less so, since admitting that it is the clumsy materiality of my skis which supports me and not the free determination of my elegantly speeding nothingness would undermine the existentialist opposition of sliding to 'taking root', in that one may be compelled to say that skiing is 'a moving concretion of snow' by analogy with root described as 'a living concretion of the earth'(584). For obviously we are talking about the same process of 'material inertia' mastering material inertia: in one case 'it can utilize the earth only by making itself earth'(584), and in the other 'it can utilize for sliding compressed snow only by making itself a kind of compressed snow'. (The liberty involved in calling the ski 'a kind of compressed snow' is not one whit greater than in calling the root 'earth'.)

The selectivity of the particular imagery, with its telling omissions, is dictated by the necessary requirements of the existentialist conception as a whole. The outlines of the particular imagery are speedily sketched in the self-generative process of kaleidoscopic transformations as mediated projections of the basic categorial framework (ultimately identified as symbolic equivalents of the latter) and nothing can be allowed to disturb the picture. If a contrary example crops up in the course of the self-generative transformations—for instance in that as soon as the particular case of skiing is generalized as 'sliding' (and it must be generalized in the process of becoming a symbolic equivalent), it inevitably brings forth to our attention also other forms of sliding—it is categorically dismissed the moment it appears. 'Sliding on ice, which scratches the ice and finds a matter already organized, is *very inferior* [to skiing], and if people continue to do it despite all this, it is for other reasons'(584). Whatever those other reasons might be, we are never told. The kaleidoscopic mode of progression enables Sartre to get out of the difficulty by simply declaring the characteristic that has emerged (scratching the surface) to be inferior. This, however, brings another problem with it, namely the realization (as an afterthought) that in a sense skiing also 'scratches the snow'. But not to worry; another eidetic assertion will help to extricate himself also from this difficulty by nullifying the counter-effect of the disconcerting characteristic and thus by taking back in some form what he was forced to admit by the logic of his own example. He does this by referring to a 'slight disappointment which always seizes us when we see behind us the imprints which our skis have left on the snow. How much better it would be if the snow re-formed itself as we passed over it! Besides, when we let ourselves slide down the slope, we are accustomed to the *illusion* of not making any mark; we *ask* the snow *to behave* like that water which secretly it is'(584).

And this is where Sartre's dominating subjectivity turns out to be the necessary sustaining power of the whole enterprise. For if some people might question the liberties he takes with his own terms of analysis, he will not hesitate for a moment to dismiss his critics just as categorically as he sweeps aside examples and instances perceptibly contrary to his own interpretative direction, saying that his critics have not read his work, or if they did they have not understood it, or that they are *a priori* incapable of understanding it, or even that they are incapable of understanding their own works. This could not be otherwise in a conception in which we set out from a description of skiing and end up with a legislative assertion of how the ideal snow *ought* to behave in the *symbolic* act of appropriation. No philosophical conception can be divorced from its author's specific subjectivity which sustains it in its articulation. This is just as true of Sartre as of Spinoza and Descartes, Hegel and Marx, Wittgenstein and Heidegger. Sartre's overpowering subjectivity is a necessary complement to a conception which must impose on the reader, through whatever liberties its eidetic descriptions might require, the conviction that things *are* in their ontological depth (of which the empirical manifestations and modes of behaviour are only the symbol) as they *ought to be* according to the existentialist 'hermeneutic of existence'.

It is the total context which confers the proper meaning on the particular examples and instantiations. It is the articulation of the overall conception which sustains the particular points, no matter how much they may be 'forced'. All selectivity is necessarily tendentious and therefore it needs a broader frame of reference for its justification than the 'accuracy' of details. Indeed, the selection of 'accurate' particulars is no less in need of a justification than 'taking liberties'. In both cases the criterion of justification can only be the coherence of a significant discourse, and the 'accuracy of details' is no guarantee whatsoever that we are on the right road to the latter, as all depressingly pedestrian varieties of positivism and neo-positivism testify. And equally, the fact that a writer's terms of description or analysis strongly depart from our everyday experience is no evidence by itself against the meaningful coherence of his discourse. Sartre's 'inaccuracies' and 'forced descriptions' are not just inaccuracies and forced descriptions. As we have seen also in the case of 'taking root' as diametrically opposed to 'sliding', they are highly tendentious constituents of the intended meaning. Reading the great majority of his analyses and descriptions we realize their significant departure from our own perception of the same relations, and yet we do not mind this precisely because of the powerfully suggestive coherence of his discourse. We do not mind the liberties he takes precisely because we realize, in relation to the overall conception, 'what he is driving at' as his vision unfolds in front of us in its existentialist coherence and originality.

No one can deny the profound originality of Sartre's discourse in *Being and Nothingness*. But simply to refer to this originality is not enough for identifying its specificity. For there is a fundamental difference between the originality of, say, Marx's *Capital* and Sartre's work. Our concern here is not the question of relative greatness but the determination of a writer's attitude toward his own work as an essential condition of the particular character of that work. In Sartre's case, as a direct manifestation of his dominating subjectivity, originality is not only the type of solution given to some significant problems: it is also a constantly pursued *conscious aim* of the intellectual undertaking. The quest for originality appears to him at a crucial time in his development as an imperative to emancipate himself entirely from the influence of others so as to be able to follow his own unique road. It is in this spirit that he writes in a letter to Simone de Beauvoir in 1940: 'Since I have broken my inferiority complex vis-à-vis the extreme left, I feel a freedom of thought which I never had before. Also vis-à-vis the phenomenologists. It seems to me that I am well on the way of finding myself'.[305] This attitude is strongly reinforced through its elevation to a theoretical status in Sartre's conception of existentialist 'authenticity' as the pursuit of one's unique project; and from that moment on this cardinal tenet of 'the hermeneutic of existence' is inseparable from the radical self-assertion of his dominating subjectivity. Indeed, to be more precise, the Sartrean pursuit of originality as a conscious aim is very much part of his 'original project' from a very early age, as we can see through *Words* and other autobiographic material at our disposal. The change that we can witness around 1940—which happens to coincide with his traumatic experience with the left and consequently with the definition of his own pursuit as a strictly 'individual venture'—is that his attitude as a writer toward his own work is now crystallized around a specific version of the authenticity of individual existence, defined in a diametrical opposition to 'bad faith' seen above all as the 'spirit of seriousness' which dares to presume that the pursuit of social objectives is more commendable than getting drunk alone.

Thus we see a unique fusion of personal determinations with a particular theoretical posture, and this fusion becomes the organizing core of the synthesis of *Being and Nothingness*. As such it determines in the last analysis not only Sartre's attitude to other thinkers, relegating the matter of scholarly considerations to a status of no real importance,[306] but also his relation to the treatment of experience as intepretative evidence. It is Sartre's overpowering subjectivity as embodied in the structural framework of his conception which sharply determines what sort of evidence is admissible at all for consideration and what kind of use is to be made of the admitted data. (Indeed, the term 'data' is rather inadequate. For by the time the empirical particulars are brought into the focus of theoretical generalization they are fundamentally transformed through eidetic description and kaleidoscopic specification.) Marx may spend the greater part of his life, buried in the British Museum, engaged in unearthing evidence which not merely sustains his theoretical conception but expands, modifies and intensifies it as well, displaying thus an inherently dialectical relationship between theory and research. Nothing could be more alien to Sartre's way of proceeding. (Not surprisingly, therefore, he must break off the project of investigating history precisely at the point where the more or less self-generative permutations of 'the formal structures of history' are sketched out and the need for evidence in the form of a sustained historical research unescapably asserts itself.) He maintains the same sort of attitude toward his particulars as the Absolute Monarch toward his subjects: he treats them as he pleases; and quite legitimately so in that, being the categorically self-asserting foundation of legality itself, he constitutes them in such a way that they owe their very existence as subjects to the constitutive framework of the overall conception in which they are allowed to arise. And just as the conscious pursuit of originality has been existentialistically theorized and authenticated as the unique project of a strictly 'individual venture', now the sovereign attitude toward empirical experience is elevated to a theoretical status in the spirit of 'the hermeneutic of existence' that declares its interest only in their *symbolic* meaning which it itself generates, creates, and invents.

What we see then is a unique integration of subjective and objective determinations in a specific type of synthesis which constantly maintains the sovereignty of the overall conception over the particulars of its articulation. The kaleidoscopic mode of development is a most adequate form of manifestation of such a synthesis. For it is simultaneously open and closed. It is breathtakingly open with respect to the possibilities of self-generative *partial* transformations, and it is rigidly closed as regards the fundamental structure and categorial framework of the *whole*. It is for this reason that every new phase in Sartre's development must bring with it a new presentation of detail, coupled with the claim that it amounts to a radically new synthesis. The novelty is both true and wildly overstated. True in the sense that the new phase, inasmuch as it represents a richer experience (e.g. the challenge of politics and 'the experience of society' in the postwar years), requires the reformulation of Sartre's fundamental concerns in relation to the elements of the new experience. And since the specific synthesis of *Being and Nothingness* is complete precisely in its incompleteness and unfinishability, the new experience of politics and society cannot be simply inserted into its categorial framework, which articulated itself as a new treatise of the passions conceived under its individualistic-subjective aspects as 'the eidetics of bad faith'. At the same time, the claim of radical novelty characteristically brushes aside two basic continuities. First, the most important earlier categories are always transferred into the later syntheses (as indeed is the case also in the relationship between *Being and Nothingness* and the earlier studies in philosophical psychology as well as *Nausea*), even if complemented by new ones, establishing thus a most remarkable continuity in the categorial framework of Sartre's philosophy as a whole, notwithstanding its numerous partial transformations. And second, the structural relationship between any given set of categories—in *L'Imaginaire*, in *Being and Nothingness*, in the *Critique of Dialectical Reason*, or, for that matter, in *The Idiot of the Family*—and the empirical particularizations in terms of which they are spelled out, remains essentially the same, whatever field of experience happens to supply the instances of interpretative specification. In other words, we always set out from the sharply defined outlines of the overall conception as the overpoweringly 'übergreifendes Moment' of the given enterprise, which leaves no room for a genuine dialectic between theory and research. Thus Sartre's approach remains the same whether he writes about the experience of anger and skiing, or about 'negritude', or indeed when he invents with sovereign mastery the deeply significant experiences that Flaubert ought to have had. It is the representative value of this unique mode of synthesis, of which *Being and Nothingness* is a supreme example, which working *through*, and not *in spite of*, his overpowering subjectivity, makes Sartre an outstanding figure.

4

Sartre criticizes Heidegger for his failure to concern himself with sexuality, the result of which is that 'his "Dasein" appears to us as asexual'(383). In contrast to this Sartre insists 'that the For-itself is sexual in its very upsurge in the face of the Other and that through it sexuality comes into the world'(406). The problem at stake is therefore not a matter of secondary importance (though this is the impression one would get by reading some books on Sartre's ontology, [307]) but, on the contrary, quite fundamental to the 'hermeneutic of existence' which is concerned with the meaning of the 'human reality' in all its manifestations. For if the For-itself is sexual in its very upsurge in the face of the Other, then sexuality can only be elucidated in terms of the deepest ontological structures. Here, as everywhere else when we reach the ultimate connections, we are invited to grasp the problem not as 'doing' but as the project of *being*. 'To-be-in-the-world is to form the project of possessing the world'(597), and sexuality is an integral part of the realization of this project, and *as such* it occupies a vital place in the existentialist treatise of the passions.

One cannot stress enough that the meaning of these relations is far from being immediate: it is symbolic. Sartre adopts as the point of departure of his own hermeneutic Pascal's insight that 'in an activity [hunting, or playing tennis, for instance] which would be absurd if *reduced to itself*, there was a meaning which transcended it; that is, an indication which referred to the reality of man in general and to his condition'(562). Sartre generalizes this approach and reads the various manifestations of psychic life as 'symbols maintaining *symbolic* relations to the fundamental, *total structures* which constitute the individual person'(569). Thus whatever experience may be under scrutiny—be it fatigue on a mountain climbing expedition, or sexual desire, or play, or nausea, or preference for certain types of food, and so on—our search for meaning must be guided by the same principle: 'it is a matter of rediscovering under the *partial* and incomplete aspects of the subject the veritable concreteness which can be only the *totality of his impulse toward being*, his original relation to himself, to the world, and to the Other, in the unity of internal relations and of a *fundamental project*' (563).

In this sense, sexuality is understood as a fundamental existential project which aims simultaneously (a) at the Other and (b) at being in general. In the first respect: 'in desire I make myself flesh in the presence of the Other in order to appropriate the Other's flesh'(389).

> Desire is an attitude aiming at *enchantment*. Since I can grasp the Other only in his objective facticity, the problem is to *ensnare his freedom* within this facticity. . . . and by touching this body I should finally touch the Other's free subjectivity. This is the true meaning of the word possession'(394).

And in the second respect:

> To plug up a hole means originally to make sacrifice of my body in
> order that the *plenitude of being* may exist; that is, to subject the
> *passion of the For-itself* so as to shape, to perfect, and to preserve
> the totality of the In-itself. . . . A good part of our life is passed in
> plugging up holes, in filling empty places, in realizing and
> *symbolically establishing a plenitude(613).*

But, of course, here as everywhere else the ideal involved
turns out to be an *impossible ideal*: 'desire itself is *doomed to
failure*'(396) in that 'pleasure is the death and the failure of
desire'(397), and the fullness of being is equally unrealizable,
which ultimately makes man a 'useless passion'.

As we can see, the human reality under its aspect of
sexuality corresponds to the same ontological determinations of freedom and passion which we have encountered in other contexts, in the spirit of a truly totalizing
vision. Thus Sartre's involvement in psychological research
already in his student days, which is further intensified in his
literary projects (*Nausea* and the novellas of the 1930s) as
well as in his theoretical writings on *Emotion* and
*Imagination*, reveals itself as incomparably more than a
contingent beginning. Indeed, there is a sense of necessity
about it: an organic development with a crowning achievement in the 1940s. In *Being and Nothingness* the early
psychological insights are integrated with the ontological
categories of a unique brand of existentialist hermeneutic,
and the new treatise of the passions is articulated as an
eidetic of bad faith aimed at unveiling the paradoxical
realities of the ontological structure, thus not only making
intelligible the bewildering ploys and manifestations of bad
faith which escape even the most ingenious psychoanalytic
approaches, but also offering the possibility of an existential
solution to the problems involved.

In the structure of *Being and Nothingness* we can identify
two essentially different, though of course interlinked, lines
of reasoning. *First*, the often explicit polemic thrust in

Sartre's definition of the basic categories and relations. In this respect the most obvious target is constituted by the various psychological theories (especially psychoanalysis and positivist-behaviorist psychology), but all related conceptions, from Descartes's theory of the 'passions of the soul'[308] to Marx as the paradigm of the standpoint of 'seriousness'[309] and to Proust's idea of a 'passional mechanism',[310] are critically dissected by Sartre in accordance with his concept of bad faith. The *second* discernible dimension of analysis is in fact the more fundamental. It consists in Sartre's attempt at defining the basic ontological structures themselves in terms of which the meaning of the human reality can be identified. 'What is the *meaning* of that being which includes within itself two *radically separated* regions of being?' (XLIII), asks Sartre, and he undertakes an elucidation of this meaning strictly in terms of the ontological relationship between the two indicated regions of being: For-itself and In-itself, categorically excluding the possibility of a religious explanation. And he combines the polemical and substantive dimensions of his analysis under the hypothesis that the various theoretical misconceptions arise as *strategies of flight* in the face of the anguishing existentialist choices which man is compelled to confront. The remarkable structural cohesion of *Being and Nothingness*[311]—our impression that the whole massive work is 'made of the same piece' or 'written in the same breath', in that whatever particular problem is at stake, we are always confronting the one central idea: man's quest for the unrealizable totality—is closely connected with this treatment of the theoretical alternatives as subordinate moments of the overall conception of the meaning of the human reality.

The conscious rejection of the religious framework of explanation carries with it the claim that the existentialist meaning of the human reality must be *constituted* by the being who is at the centre of the hermeneutic of existence. The nature of the human enterprise is identified as the self-constitution of meaning and value at all levels, from the everyday projects of 'alarm clocks, sign boards, tax forms, policemen, so many guard rails against anguish'(39) to the ultimate 'desire to be God'(566). If there is a meaning to the human enterprise—and according to Sartre most emphatically there is, although some sectarian religious critics[312] accuse him of nihilism—it must be inherent in *all* facets of experience. Accordingly, Sartre pursues his quest by systematically scrutinizing the most varied forms of life-activity: work, sexuality, play, art, science, and the production and consumption of food. He finds that although the forms and modalities of these activities significantly differ among themselves, so that we can grasp certain specificities of, say, play in comparison to eating, the ultimate existential meaning of all of them is fundamentally the same. It is given in the 'project of possessing the world', which is conceivable only as a possessive appropriation of the world, whether we think of sexuality—as the project 'to possess the Other's transcedence as pure transcendence and at the same time as body'(394)—or of the existential significance of foods described as the *'appropriative choice of being'*(615). We can understand now in this light why for Sartre desire cannot be a desire of *doing*. All activities, in Pascal's sense, refer 'to the reality of man in general and to his condition', and thus they represent merely the form in which a fundamental ontological characteristic of the human reality—*'lack'* asserting itself through *desire*(87)—manifests itself as 'the desire of a transcendent object'(385), that is as a desire of *being*.

In the constitution of meaning through activity, a privileged position is assigned to the constitution of *value*, in that all everyday values 'derive their meaning from an original projection of myself which stands as my choice of myself in the world'(39) and as such it becomes the source of further action. Naturally, the constitution of value is not a separate activity. Rather, it is inherent in all activities as a supportive structure which links the symbolic manifestations of being to their ontological ground. Strategies of bad faith originate in the course of the constitution of these values and, by contrast, in good faith we try to extricate ourselves from the self-imposed trap of bad faith. Characteristically, Sartre not only declares that 'it is indifferent[313] whether one is in good faith or in bad faith'(70), but he goes as far as asserting the primacy of bad faith over against good faith. 'Good faith seeks to flee the inner disintegration of my being in the direction of the In-itself which it should be and is not. Bad faith seeks to flee the In-itself by means of the inner disintegration of my being' (70) Thus the talk about 'authenticity' is bound to remain somewhat vacuous, since the apparent 'positivity' of good faith is nothing but the double negativity of a 'flight from a flight of disintegration' to which it is impossible to assign other than a purely imperatival 'regulative' meaning. As such it has an ontological status radically different from that of bad faith. The latter constitutes 'an immediate, *permanent* threat to every project of the human being', and this permanent threat or risk originates in the 'fact that the nature of consciousness simultaneously is to be what it is not and not to be what it is'(70). Bad faith, therefore, arises from the innermost structure of consciousness itself, whereas good faith is parasitic on the persistent negativity of the disintegrating flight which it tries to flee. Good faith is, in fact, doubly problematical. First because in contrast to bad faith—which emanates from the ontological structure of consciousness itself and thus needs no additional support— good faith has no such obvious ontological underpinning and must be sustained through some well-founded existential motivation which Sartre fails to specify (Significantly, he evades the problem, which is for him structurally insoluble, by rather gratuitously suggesting in a footnote a 'radical escape' from bad faith through self-recovery or authenticity 'the description of which has no place here'(70), nor for that matter anywhere else in *Being and Nothingness*.) And the second problematical feature of good faith is that even if a motivation has been found, given good faith's 'parasitic character' or structural dependency on bad faith, it is bound to remain an 'unrealizable ideal' and a permanently frustrated one.

But whatever one's reservations about Sartre's approach to these problems, no one should fail to see that in the framework of his existential hermeneutic the most varied aspects of experience are synthesized in a powerfully coherent form. All kinds of activity as well as all forms of psychic life are made intelligible in terms of particular existential projects structured around one's fundamental project, which is said to be identical with the original choice of one's being. The concept of 'passion' occupies a strategic position in this hermeneutic of existence; and indeed no other concept could take its place. For Sartre must explain first of all what makes the human reality persist in its quest for being, and he must be able to do this without introducing a *determinism* into the picture. Consciousness, on its own, could not accomplish anything. Nor could the abstract principle of the 'freedom of the will' help, since it could not supply the motivation for its own deliberations. And this is where 'passion' proves its vital importance for Sartre's vision. We shall see in a moment the fundamental ontological meaning of his concept of passion. But first we have to glance at the other sense in which passion is referred to in *Being and Nothingness*. This second sense is much the same as that used in everyday language, or by philosophers and psychologists, and Sartre sets out to extricate it from what he considers to be a network of deterministic misrepresentations:

> There is a fairly common tendency to seek to identify *free acts* with *voluntary acts* and to restrict the deterministic explanation to the world of the *passions*. . . . In this case it would be necessary to conceive of man as simultaneously *free and determined*, and the essential problem would be that of the relations between this unconditioned freedom and the determined processes of the psychic life: how will it master the passions, how will it utilize them for its

own benefit? A wisdom which comes from ancient times—the wisdom of the Stoics—will teach us to come to terms with these passions so as to master them; in short it will counsel us how to conduct ourselves with regard to affectivity as man does with respect to nature in general when he obeys it in order better to control it. Human reality therefore appears as a free power besieged by an ensemble of determined processes. One will distinguish wholly free acts, determined processes over which the free will has power, and processes which on principle escape the human will(441).

Sartre emphatically rejects this view and opposes to it his own conception:

Here as everywhere we assert that the state of consciousness is a pure idol of a positive psychology. If the *will* is to be freedom, then it is of necessity negativity and the *power of nihilation*. But then we no longer can see why *autonomy* should be preserved for the will(442).

But this is not all: the will, far from being the unique or at least the privileged manifestation of freedom, actually—like every event of the for-itself—must presuppose the foundation of an original freedom in order to be able to constitute itself as will. The will in fact is posited as a *reflective decision* in relation to certain ends. . . . Passion can posit the same ends. For example, if I am threatened, I can run away at top speed because of my fear of dying. This *passional fact* nevertheless *posits implicitly* as a supreme end the value of life(443).

Thus since freedom is identical with my existence, it is the foundation of ends which I shall attempt to attain either by the will or by passionate efforts. Therefore it cannot be limited to *voluntary* acts. Volitions, on the contrary, like passions are certain *subjective attitudes* by which we attempt to attain the ends posited by original freedom(444).

Thus passions (in the plural), as subjective attitudes, are on a par with volitions in that they are both manifestations of original freedom. The passional act is that which has a specific passion for its *motive*(445), but it is free none the less. 'It is the ensemble of the desires, emotions, and passions which urge me to accomplish a certain act'(446), but they all arise on the ground of an original freedom.

However, Sartre does not stop at this point but turns the table completely on the will which appeared to have a privileged position in relation to freedom at our point of departure. Now we learn that assigning a privileged position to the will could not be more illusory. For 'a voluntary deliberation is always a *deception*'(450)

> When I deliberate, the *chips are down*. And if I am brought to the point of deliberating, this is simply because it is a *part of my original project* to realize motives by means of deliberation rather than by some other form of discovery (by passion, for example, or simply by action, which reveals to me the organized ensemble of causes and of ends as my language informs me of my thought). . . . When the will intervenes, the decision is taken, and it has no other value than that of *making the announcement*(451).

And this takes us to the fundamental meaning of passion, which is not a subjective attitude but the basis on which all attitudes arise. This is in the last analysis identical to 'original freedom' itself which posits the ends we attempt to attain. It constitutes our very existence as the '*original choice* [an *impulse* toward being] which originally creates all *causes* and all *motives* which can guide us to *partial* actions' (465). If I want to understand the existential-ontological meaning of the fact that I freely abandon myself to *fatigue* (as opposed to some deterministic physiological or psychological hypothesis), I must refer this action to my original choice of being, since 'this *passion of the body* coincides for the For-itself with the *project of "making the In-itself exist"* '(456). To put it in a generalized form:

> The For-itself by its *self-negation* becomes the affirmation of the In-itself. . . . in the quasi-totality of Being, affirmation happens to the In-itself; it is the adventure of the In-itself to be affirmed. This affirmation which could not be effected as the affirmation of self by the In-itself without destroying its being-in-itself, happens to the In-itself as the affirmation is realized by the For-itself. The affirmation is like a passive ecstasis of the In-itself which leaves the In-itself unchanged yet which is achieved in the In-itself and from

the standpoint of the In-itself. All this happens as if the For-itself had a *Passion to lose itself* in order that the affirmation 'world' might come to the In-itself(217).

As we can see, the introduction of passion into the primary set of relations radically modifies everything. It is in virtue of this passion that the human enterprise can take place at all, and assume a character, a direction, and a meaning— without it we would be stuck to 'consciousness' and 'freedom' conceived as an icy abstraction totally devoid of any possibility of development. Through passion, freedom and consciousness acquire a 'body'—and indeed not just in a figurative sense—so much so that it becomes possible to talk about the 'passion of the body' for carrying out the original project of freedom to 'make the In-itself exist': a description which stands in diametrical opposition to the customary view of the body as the depository of physical and physiological determinations. It is thanks to the primary identity of freedom with passion that freedom can be 'situated': that is conceived in such a way that it can be *nothing but situated* (though, of course, with all the ambiguities[314] necessarily involved).

It is through this fusion of freedom with passion that freedom becomes a meaningful existential category. And passion, likewise, through its fusion with freedom acquires a unique character. It is not just any old passion, but the fundamental ontological passion of the human reality which aims at making the existential venture happen through the 'facticity of freedom'[315] tied to an absolute contingency and yet remaining absolutely free. Fundamental ontological passion is thus defined as self-negation and self-sacrifice: a passion to 'lose oneself' so that the 'world' might come to the In-itself, as we have just seen, or 'that the plenitude of being may exist'(613), or again 'so as to found being and by the same stroke to constitute the In-itself which escapes contingency'(615), and so on, and so forth. Fundamental choice is the original choice of our being and as such it 'must of necessity be a conscious choice'(461), although, Sartre hastens to add a few lines later, not a *deliberate* choice. Rather: 'it is the foundation of all deliberation' in that 'a deliberation requires an interpretation in terms of an original choice'(461-2).

Consciousness, in this Sartrean sense – which makes the firm distinction between 'conscious choice' and '(deliberate) conscious choice', so as to be able to dismiss the idea of the 'unconscious'—is 'non-positional consciousness'.[316] Corresponding to non-deliberate conscious choice, non-positional consciousness is

> . . . we-as-consciousness since it is not distinct from our being. And as our *being* is precisely our *original choice*, the consciousness (of) the choice is identical with the *self-consciousness* which we have. One must be conscious in order to choose, and one must choose in order to be conscious. *Choice and consciousness* are one and the same thing. . . . to be conscious of ourselves and to choose ourselves are one and the same(462).

Sartre insists that there can be no such thing as an 'unconscious psychic phenomenon'(44), and later he adds that the proponents of the psychoanalytic theory have hypostasized and reified bad faith, 'they have not escaped it'(54). It goes without saying, the problematic of the unconscious is far too complex to be dissolved by any particular formula, since an adequate treatment requires the development of a coherent theory of ideology, spelled out not simply in general terms but in great concreteness and specificity directly applicable to particular individuals. And whatever one may discover in Sartre's philosophy, given its individualistic framework of categories, it certainly cannot be an adequate theory of ideology. But this need not concern us here. For the point at issue in this particular context is that his existentialist equation of choice and being, choice and consciousness, choice of ourselves and consciousness of ourselves in the non-positional mode, enables Sartre to suggest a non-deterministic solution to the psychoanalytic problem of the unconscious. For a start, the unconscious is ruled out by definition as *a priori* impossible, since we set out from the original identity of fundamental passion - choice of being (freedom) - non-positional consciousness, and all the specific structures of consciousness, whether affective (like desires, emotions and passions), or volitional, reflective, etc., are constituted on the ground of this original identity, and therefore fully share the burden of absolute responsibility as specific modes of manifestation of the original synthesis. The phenomenon of the unconscious is accounted for as *bad faith* which pretends to itself (in the non-positional mode of 'fundamental unreflective consciousness'(473) as contrasted to the 'consciousness reflected-on') to be 'unconscious' in order to be able to flee 'anguish' (namely the burden of inescapable freedom). The possibility of such a strategy is not proved but obliquely assumed by analogy with Gestalt psychology which couples the primacy of the total form with the variability of the secondary[317] structures. Accordingly, Sartre asserts that it is possible for me 'to impose upon myself *reflectively*—that is, on the *voluntary* plane—projects which *contradict* my initial project without, however, fundamentally *modifying* the initial project'(471). Thus it is possible to talk even about 'the bad faith of the will'(473), in the sharpest possible contrast to any theory of the unconscious.

To be sure, Sartre must consider the psychoanalytic hypothesis an absolute outrage, in that it diametrically contradicts his own conception of our absolute freedom and absolute responsibility which insists that we are totally responsible not only for the wars from which we suffer but even for our birth, race, nationality, place of living and past.[318] All this would sound a thousand times more absurd than the fateful laments of a demented prophet of doom if Sartre could not sustain at least in the form of a subjective authentication his shocking assertions. We have seen briefly in an earlier section the reasons why, given his individualistic conception of the human reality as a strictly individual venture, he must content himself with a subjective authentication and construct a 'phenomenological ontology' in the mould of an existential anthropology, and the concluding section of this chapter will be dedicated to a closer investigation of this crucial problem. At this point the issue is not the determination of the existentialist limits of Sartre's conceptual framework as a whole, that is, the question *why* it *must* articulate itself the way it actually does, but the identification of the structural links and conceptual interconnections: that is, the question of *how* it works and *what* makes possible the manifold 'kaleidoscopic' transformations which we have already witnessed.

As we have seen, the most fundamental ontological relations are defined by Sartre in terms of the identity of freedom and passion in the self-constitution of the human reality which also corresponds to the primary identity of being, choice, and self-consciousness. This ultimate ontological equation proves to be extremely fruitful because its terms are defined in such a way that they become interchangeable right from the beginning, thus establishing the possibility of virtually endless variations and self-generative transformations. The primary concepts can be combined in the first place among themselves, and all additional conceptual derivations can be fused with the preceding ones, resulting in an ever-enlarging circle[319] of relations and sets of definitions. We may be taken aback when we read the apparently arbitrary suggestion that *being* is the same as *being free*. If, however, we grasp the meaning of Sartre's assertions, 'there is no difference between the being of man and his being free'(21), in the context of the original equation of freedom and passion as its fundamental ontological ground, it ceases to be shocking and appears as a quasi-analytic specification of the original terms of reference, in that the being of man as 'being free' is merely another way of asserting the inextricable unity of 'freedom and situation' according to the rules of an existentialist hermeneutic. The same procedure is followed in asserting the identity of freedom and obligation(35), being and choice(440), choice and consciousness(462), choice and action(484), consciousness and desire(391), situation and motivation(487), contingency and facticity(486), and a great many other combinations (such as intention and action, consciousness and consciousness of freedom, facticity of freedom and contingency of freedom, etc.), including at times even the most unexpected ones, like play and anguish(581).

On the ground of Sartre's fundamental ontological equation some rather unorthodox logical procedures become thoroughly legitimate: such as, for instance, the establishment of *lack* as the fundamental ontological characteristic of the human reality with reference to the existence of *desire*(87). While 'strictly speaking' it is taking liberties with logic to say that since desire is a lack therefore man is a lack, nevertheless it is perfectly tenable on the ground on which this equation arises, namely the fundamental definition of the human reality as an ontologically meaningful passion to lose itself so that the original lack should be remedied through the establishement of the plenitude of being. In a discourse which is structured in this way, there can be nothing wrong with saying that '*consciousness* chooses itself as *desire*'(391), or indeed much more shockingly that '*my body* is a conscious structure of my consciousness'(329). The Sartrean discourse is structured the way it is in order to be able to impose on us its own framework and terms of reference, and consequently to make acceptable the 'shocking' assertions of the existentialist hermeneutic. And the close integration of metaphors into the discourse as a whole, as well as the use of the method of kaleidoscopic transformations which we have seen in the preceding sections, serve precisely the same purpose.

Seen in this light, the insistence on 'absolute freedom' and 'absolute responsibility' is far from being as absurd as even Sartre suggests sometimes in his relatively recent interviews.[320] His extreme statements on the absoluteness of freedom are integral parts of a highly complex discourse which must be read within its own terms of reference, whether one agrees with the principal tenets of this philosophy or not. Partly this is a question of remembering the direct or indirect qualifications which one can find elsewhere in the work and which constitute the necessary complement to the extreme formulations. And partly it is a matter of appreciating the moralist-exhortative function which claims on the strength of an 'ontological description' man's absolute freedom so as to be able to address to him the obligation of an absolute responsibility. But more than anything else, the legitimacy of reading Sartre within his own terms of reference concerns the fundamental coherence of a representative philosophical discourse which obeys its inner determinations. Once the core of a significant conception is constituted—as a result of an 'original choice' or 'fundamental project', or whatever other name we care to give to those existential-social determinations which ultimately structure a coherent world view—everything else follows with an 'iron necessity' even if one is the champion of absolute freedom. (Departure from this inner necessity is either some kind of inconsistency, whatever its reasons, or a step toward a meaningful transformation and restructuring of the original conception. In this sense the idea of a 'radical conversion' is certainly feasible, but an adequate treatment of its conditions would require some very precise definitions in the framework of a totalizing theory.)

In this sense, given certain propositions and fundamental definitions, one must insist not only that '*motivation* is not *causation*'(27), but also that 'the structure of motives as *ineffective* is the condition of my freedom. . . . there is never a motive *in* consciousness; motives are only *for* consciousness' since consciousness has the '*task* of conferring on the motive its *meaning* and its *importance*'(34). We should also notice here the imperatival structure of this element of Sartre's discourse: the definition of consciousness in terms of its *task*. Just as in an earlier

mentioned passage freedom–anguish is said to be 'characterized by a constantly renewed obligation to remake the self
which designates the free being' (35), the fundamental
ontological passion of the human reality, 'losing itself', is
sustained through an *as if* clause. Sartre explicitly turns
away from Kantian morality, which is orientated toward
'doing' (action), in the name of an existentialist ontology
whose ultimate point of reference is 'being'(431), and near
the end of *Being and Nothingness* he declares that 'we
cannot possibly derive *imperatives* from ontology's *indicatives*'(625). The problem is, though, that the alleged
indicatives of 'phenomenological ontology' (existential
anthropology) are deeply impregnated with imperatives at
all levels, from the most fundamental sets of relations to the
secondary structures and partial descriptions, and the
'*being*' in question is a '*choice of being*' which 'ought to be
constantly renewed': that is, a 'doing', in the Kantian sense
of the term. Also, when he claims that the existentialist
hermeneutic succeeds in eliminating the distinction between
the intention and the act, the actual state of affairs is far more
problematical than the claim suggests. For the 'act' in
question is *choosing*, which is said to be by definition
identical to 'doing' (484), and the freedom of our action is
made subjectively plausible merely in terms of the possibility of an *authentic choice*—the choice of our being.
Kantian philosophy 'haunts' *Being and Nothingness* from
beginning to end (and not just *Being and Nothingness*, of
course), even if the Kantian constituents are fully integrated
into Sartre's unique mould of discourse.

The 'ontological indicatives' of absolute freedom and
responsibility arise in Sartre's philosophy under the sign of
the strictest 'ought', and they operate in the context of the
most severe contingency. And of course all this is articulated
in characteristically Sartrean terms. The absoluteness of
freedom is established through its definitional identity with
the *unavoidability of choice* even in the circumstances of a
deliberate refusal to choose, and the categories of 'con-

tingency' and 'facticity' are brought into the foreground in order to remind us that we should not have any voluntaristic illusions as to the possible impact of our actions. Sartre goes as far as he possibly can in acknowledging the 'force of circumstance', in talking about the 'necessity of fact' and the inherent ambiguity of 'freedom in situation', as we have seen above. To concede more than that would not just qualify his conception of freedom but undermine and ultimately destroy his philosophical framework as a whole. He must go on insisting that we are absolutely free and absolutely responsible, adding that 'it is the contingency of freedom and the contingency of the In-itself which are expressed in situation by the *unpredictability* and the *adversity* of the environment.'(509), meaning that the adversity of my environment imposes on me the absolute obligation of carrying the full burden of responsibility also for my situation *which* I therefore must *be*, rather than just being *in it*. And so it goes to and fro, emphasizing now one side and then the other. He is fully aware of the extremely uneasy balance which threatens to precipitate the whole structure in one moment on one side and the next moment on the other: that is why he must be constantly engaged in re-balancing and re-qualifying, so as to maintain the integrity of the fundamental conception. 'I am responsible for everything, in fact, *except for my very responsibility, for I am not the foundation of my being*.'(555) Quite so. But then ultimately I am not responsible for anything at all! It shows Sartre's great honesty as a thinker that he makes no attempt at hiding this unpalatable dilemma. Obviously, however, he cannot allow it to remain the final word on the subject. And since there is no other way out, the Kantian 'as if' comes again to the rescue. Just as the fundamental passion of the human reality for losing itself for the plenitude of being could only be established in terms of 'as if', here, in the sentence that immediately follows the one just quoted, we are confronted with the ultimate qualification: 'Therefore everything takes place *as if* I were *compelled* to be responsible.' The imperatival underpinnings of the whole structure reveal themselves in an unmistakeable fashion. I am absolutely free in virtue of being compelled to choose (condemned to be free), and because everything happens as if the human reality through the free exercise of its fundamental passion decided to lose itself so that the plenitude of being might exist. And likewise, I am absolutely responsible because in my absolutely free being I am identical with my situation, no matter how devastating the 'coefficient of adversity'[321] might be, and therefore everything happens as if I were compelled to be absolutely responsible, whether I assume the awesome burden of this responsibility or try to run away from it through the ruses of bad faith.

On which side is Sartre's heart in this balancing of freedom and responsibility against contingency and adversity? The answer is revealed by an astonishing inconsistency: surely an existentialist version of the 'Freudian slip' for a man of Sartre's stature. It occurs in the context of Sartre's discussion of death and suicide. He rightly takes Heidegger to task for the latter's treatment of 'death', insisting that in view of the fact that death is a radical contingency, it cannot belong to the ontological structure of the For-itself, and consequently it must be ruled out of all ontological conjectures(545). Death cannot be my possible, since it is the *nihilation* of *all* my possibles, 'which is outside my possibilities'(537). Similarly, '*suicide* is an *absurdity* which causes my life to be submerged in the absurd', and of course it carries with it the nihilation of all my possibilities. And yet, when it comes to dealing with a situation of extreme gravity in which the possibilities of an authentic choice are suffocated by adversity, Sartre does not hesitate for a moment to elevate one's death by suicide to the dignity of an authentic ontological possibility. Thus we are told that 'there are *no accidents* in a life; . . . If I am mobilized in a war, this is my war; it is in my image and *I deserve it*. I deserve it first because I could always get out of it by suicide or by desertion; these *ultimate possibles* are those which must always be present for us when there is a question of envisaging a situation. For lack of getting out of it, *I have chosen it*'(554). Desertion, yes, but suicide? Such a view is no less grotesque than Locke's theory of a 'tacit consent', and the 'ideological interest' is equally visible in it. The only difference is that we are much more favourably disposed toward the ideology of assuming one's responsibility in a fight for freedom than toward the 'liberal legitimation' of institutionalized wage-slavery. But we can entertain Sartre's view only as a moral 'ought' which requires, of course, an appropriate justification—one which suicide cannot be given even in his own terms of reference—and definitely not as an 'indicative of ontology'. The assertion: 'suicide is one mode among others of being-in-the-world'(556), far from being one of 'ontology's indicatives', is a mere rationalization of extreme voluntarism, no matter how much we might sympathize with the underlying intent.

However, the need to assert the existentialist message in *Being and Nothingness* at the price of such inconsistency is extremely rare. As a matter of course the delicate balancing enterprise is successfully accomplished through those legitimate and powerfully original methods of articulation which we have seen above. Inevitably, the discourse on absolute freedom and absolute responsibility deeply marks *Being and Nothingness*, in its all-pervasive negativity, with a character of *abstract heroism*. According to this passionate eidetic of bad faith, it is in the innermost nature of our ontological conditions, which trascend temporality and hold for feudalism just as much as for our present-day predicament, that we have '*infinite* possibilities of choice'(522), and therefore we should not resign ourselves to the choice of disintegrating flight in an attempt at escaping from the responsibility of freedom. And no degree of adversity or failure is allowed to invalidate the abstract heroism of this imperative of authenticity which remains undefined as a generic choice of being, necessarily devoid of any indication of what might constitute a tangibly authentic form of action. For the imperative is coupled with a revealing qualification that blends perfectly with both the abstract heroism and the subjective authenticity of Sartre's existentialist hermeneutic: 'There can be a free For-itself only as engaged in a resisting world. . . . *Success is not important to freedom*'(483). We are presented with the abstract imperative of 'engagement' generically confronting 'a resisting world', and the enterprise remains a strictly individual venture, struggling against the 'Other' or capitulating to the illusions of collective solidarity in the 'spirit of seriousness' on the barren road of disintegrating flight. If this is the relation of forces, if this is how the lines of demarcation are drawn in the eidetic of bad faith, obviously success must not be important to freedom. What counts is the authenticity of the undertaking itself: a principle which is compatible not only with the assertion of the ontological 'equivalence' of all kinds of endeavour,[322] but even with the gloomy forecast of the ultimately necessary failure of all projects of the human reality: a forecast which is not really a forecast but the acknowledgement of an absolute certainty, inherent in the fundamental ontological structure of being which itself defines man as a 'useless passion'. We are bound to fail in our attempt at dominating others just as much as in the project of love which 'holds in its being-for-others the seed of its own destruction'(377).

And yet, 'if to will oneself free is to choose to be in the world confronting Others, then the one who wills himself such must will also the passion of his freedom'(526). This is why 'whether in fury, hate, pride, shame, disheartened refusal or joyous demand, it is necessary for me to *choose* to *be* what I *am*'(529). Which sums it all up again, in a characteristically Sartrean fashion. And in the ultimate re-balancing effort we are also given a glimmer of hope, though only as the promise of the possibility of a 'radical conversion'.[323] Again we are really presented with the imperatival 'conditions of possibility' of this radical conversion, although it appears as an 'indicative of ontology'. And again it is authenticated in strictly individual terms, on the strength of the subjective integrity of a particular example, taking its inspiration from the world of the 'imaginary' (l'imaginaire), especially the world of Dostoevsky's and Gide's heroes. The concept which is meant to convey the glimmer of hope in a Delphic form, anticipating Sartre's postwar cult of 'the adventurer', is the '*instant* as a beginning which is given as the end of a prior project', and we are told that 'it is precisely this which is produced in the case of a radical modification of a fundamental project'(466). In truth, the condition of possibility of a radical conversion is the suspension of the temporal determinations specified by my earlier choice, and this may be envisaged in the framework of the Sartrean hermeneutic of existence only as the infinitesimal instant which interposes itself between two radically different fundamental projects. But it must be presented as an 'indicative of ontology': we are told that it *is produced* in the case of a radical modification of a fundamental project. In other words, the condition of possibility of a radical conversion is the radical modification of the fundamental project through the instant. The change is envisaged as a 'liberating instant' in which I am 'suddenly exorcized' and become 'radically other', accomplishing a total metamorphosis of my original project(475). And if Sartre paradoxically also maintains that 'we must conceive of the original choice as unfolding time'(465), that only brings to the fore the often forbidding complexities of an antinomous structure of thought, without invalidating the primary importance of the liberating instant which puts the chips down in an exhilarating moment and allows unfolding time merely to make the more or less prosaic announcements:

> These extraordinary and marvellous instants when the prior project collapses into the past in the light of a new project which rises on its ruins and which as yet exists only in outline, in which humiliation, anguish, joy, hope are delicately blended, in which we let go in order to grasp and grasp in order to let go—these have often appeared to furnish the clearest and most moving image of our freedom(476).

A movingly poetical description indeed of the existentialist unity of freedom and passion. As to what it is which we grasp when we let go in order to grasp and grasp in order to let go, or where it will all take us on the necessary premise of our 'useless passion', or again what the value is of this 'radical conversion' while the Other remains the ontologically established permanent threat and perverter of even the most authentic project, all such questions are permanently banished from the horizon of a hermeneutic of existence conceived as an inescapably individual venture.

5

The standpoint from which Sartre articulates his hermeneutic of existence is that of an anarchistic individualism,[324] and its ultimate point of reference is 'the *ontological solitude* of the For-itself'(456). In this spirit he insists that what he calls the impulse toward being 'can be only purely individual and unique'(563). Understandably, therefore, Sartre's ontology of solitude assumes the dimensions of an eidetic of bad faith which can be coherently formulated from the standpoint of isolated individuality. And in keeping with this character of the work, the proofs we are presented with in *Being and Nothingness* are either analytic-deductive[325] or appear as subjectively authentic and plausible representations of an existential predicament.

Sartre's individualistic ontological posture asserts itself through ascribing to the 'Other' a radically different ontological status from the For-itself, with far-reaching consequences for all aspects of his conception. According to Sartre, 'the Other is an *a priori* hypothesis with *no justification* save the unity which it permits to operate in our experience'(227).

> Human reality remains *alone* because the Other's existence has the nature of a contingent and irreducible fact. We encounter the Other; we do not constitute him. And if this fact still appears to us in the form of a necessity, yet it does not belong with those 'conditions of

the possibility of our experience' or—if you prefer—with *ontological necessity'* (250).

Like Marx, Sartre owes a great deal to Hegel's characterization of the Master–Slave relationship in *The Phenomenology of Mind*. However, they develop Hegel's original insights in diametrically opposite directions. Marx's criticism of Hegel's approach aims at intensifying the historical dynamism inherent in this relationship, rectifying the ideologically determined violation of the inner logic of his own conception by Hegel himself.[326] Sartre, by contrast, radically eliminates the historical dimension from the relationship and transforms it into a timeless existential structure. And by denying to the Other a proper ontological status, he renders the whole relationship extremely problematical, determining in a peculiar way not only the character of the Other but also the nature of self-consciousness, especially in its collective form (the 'We-subject'), as we shall see in a moment.

To be sure, the assertion of the fundamental ontological solitude of the For-itself cannot be sustained in isolation. Consequently, the whole range of categories to which the For-itself is closely connected must be defined in structurally identical terms. In other words, the categories are arranged as ontologically primary or fundamental on one side, and as derivative or parasitic on the other. This is how the most important relations are depicted in *Being and Nothingness*:

| *Ontologically primary* | *Derivative or parasitic* |
| --- | --- |
| Consciousness | The World |
| Individual point of view | Global point of view |
| Negation | Affirmation |
| For-itself | In-itself |
| Ontological solitude | Togetherness |
| Self | Other |
| Individual totality | Humanity |
| Conflict | Solidarity |

| | |
|---|---|
| Incomparable uniqueness | We-subject and Us-object |
| Bad faith | Good faith |
| Lack | Realization |
| Possibility | Probability |
| Freedom and passion | Causality and necessity |
| Contingency and facticity | *Ens causa sui* |
| Detotalized totality | Totalized totality |
| Missing God | Ideal or value |
| The Imperative (to realize the unrealizable) | Society's demands |
| Imperfection and fragmentation | The Imaginary Synthesis (Beauty) |

Inevitably, if this is the ontological structure of being, then the deepest ontological meaning of the human reality cannot be other than *suffering*, and the consciousness of this human reality must be defined as an *ontologically unhappy* consciousness: an approach which, again, radically liquidates all historical connotations of Hegel's concept of 'unhappy consciousness':

> . . . human reality arises as such in the presence of its own totality or self as a lack of that totality. . . . it combines in itself the *incompatible* characteristics of the In-itself and the For-itself. . . . The being of human reality is *suffering* because it rises in being as perpetually haunted by a totality which it is without being able to be it, precisely because it could not attain the In-itself without losing itself as For-itself. Human reality therefore is by nature an *unhappy consciousness* with *no possibility* of surpassing its unhappy state(90).

Sartre constructs an ontological framework from a set of antinomously structured relations, and consequently, situating himself on one side, he can argue that the unification of one side with the other is impossible because they are structurally incompatible. Thus, what may very well be an antinomous relationship in virtue of some identifiable historical determinations, is transformed into an absolute. In the spirit of his ontological commitment to an individualistic standpoint, coupled with an *a priori* exclusion of the possibility 'to take a *global* point of view'(359), Sartre insists, as if it were a matter of absolute self-evidence, that 'the *self is individual*; it is the *individual completion* of the self which haunts the For-itself(91). It is not difficult to agree that so long as the ontological project is conceived as the individual completion of the self, such a completion can only 'haunt' the For-itself. Equally, if I adopt as my absolute point of departure 'the ontological solitude of the For-itself', I can only ascribe a derivative and hypothetical ontological status to the Other. But, of course, this whole procedure is extremely problematical. For it is only 'analytically' (tautologically) true that 'the self is individual' in so far as the 'individual self' is certainly individual. But such 'individual self' is nothing more than a one-sided philosophical construct. The real self, by contrast, is the dialectical unity of individual and social determinations, hence both individual and non-individual, and therefore it cannot conceivably have a merely 'individual completion'. Since, however, I started out from a purely individualistic ontological conception of the self, the idea of a completion must and can only arise as the abstract imperative of an unrealizable totality. Furthermore, since the 'Other' could only be given a totally inadequate ontological status as a mere hypothesis, all possible combinations of the self with the Other must suffer the consequences of the latter's problematical ontological determination. As a result, the self's social dimension appears as an ontological afterthought which arises on the derivative ground of the hypothesis of the Other, transforming the For-itself into a degraded, petrified and reified being: 'The For-itself when *alone* transcends the world; it is the nothing by which there are things. The Other by rising up confers on the For-itself a being-in-itself-in-the-midst-of-the-world as a *thing among things*. This *petrification* in In-itself by the Other's look is the profound meaning of the myth of Medusa'(430).

We should notice a significant change of emphasis in comparison to Sartre's early essay on Husserl's idea of intentionality which ends with some enthusiastic words, in the spirit of an epistemological and ontological optimism: we discover ourselves on the highway, in the city, in the middle of the crowd, *'thing among things, man among men'*[327]. Now the last three words are revealingly eliminated, and the suffocating atmosphere of reification is all-pervasive. Besides, the epistemological and ontological optimism which characterized not only the essay on Husserl but also *The Transcendence of the Ego*[328] now becomes an existentialist target to fire at, condemning Hegel in the name of a fundamental conception of the human predicament ruled by irreconcilable conflict:

> In the first place Hegel appears to us to be guilty of an epistemological optimism. It seems to him that the truth of self-consciousness can appear; that is, that an objective agreement can be realized between consciousnesses—by authority of the Other's recognition of me and my recognition of the Other(240).
>
> But there is in Hegel another and more fundamental form of optimism. This may be called an ontological optimism. For Hegel indeed truth is truth of the Whole. And he places himself at the vantage point of truth—i.e., of the Whole—to consider the problem of the Other. . . .individual consciousnesses are moments in the whole, moments which by themselves are *unselbständig* (dependent), and the whole is a mediator between consciousnesses. Hence is derived an ontological optimism parallel to the epistemological optimism: plurality can and must be surpassed toward the totality(243).
>
> [By contrast] . . . the sole point of departure is the interiority of the cogito. . . . No logical or epistemological optimism can cover the *scandal* of the plurality of consciousnesses. If Hegel believed that it could, this is because he never grasped the nature of that particular dimension of being which is self-consciousness. . . .[For] even if we could succeed in making the Other's existence share in the apodictic certainty of the cogito— i.e., of my own existence—we should not thereby "surpass" the Other toward any inter-monad totality. So long as consciousnesses exist, the separation and conflict of consciousnesses will remain; . . . (244).

Thus, the plurality of consciousnesses is a 'scandal', and 'conflict' is a primary and insurmountable ontological condition. 'Conflict is the original meaning of being-for-others'(364), and unity with the Other is radically impossible(365). The relationship is conceived in the *formal* structure of reciprocity, understood as symmetry, obliterating the dimension of an actual social-historical genesis. 'I seek to enslave the Other, the Other seeks to enslave me'(364). The plain and bitterly unpalatable truth of the matter is, though, that only one side of the conflict is successful in enslaving the other, and even then not in virtue of some abstract ontological reciprocity, but because as a matter of 'brute existence', he historically gains control of the conditions of work and thus destroys even the semblance of formal reciprocity, realizing the structure of domination not as an ontological imperative but as a *historically* persistent, and therefore at least in principle also historically *surmountable*, set of actual social relations. Sartre's formal reciprocity, however, which is constituted on the ontological premise of antagonistically opposed 'individual thises'—much like Hobbes's *bellum omnium contra omnes*—can only be depicted as a fateful existential-ontological circle: 'the circle of relations with the Other'(408). 'My project of recovering myself is fundamentally a project of absorbing the Other'(364), but the formal structure of reciprocity makes sure that the project fails and perpetually reproduces itself as unrealizable, thus *a priori* denying all possibility of escape from the ontologically dignified circle. The idea of a *dialectical* relationship with the Other is categorically rejected in favour of the existential circularity, stipulating that 'we can never get outside the circle'(363), as we have already seen. And even the most fundamental strategies of excape, *sadism* and *masochism*, are condemned to futility. Nor does *hate* fare any better:

> Hate does not enable us to get out of the circle. It simply represents the final attempt, the attempt of despair. After the failure of this attempt nothing remains for the For-itself except to *re-enter the*

*circle* and allow itself to be indefintely tossed from one to the other of the two fundamental attitudes(412).

If the fundamental ontological conditions and determinations are depicted in this way, how could the idea of 'an ethics of deliverance and salvation', achieved 'after a radical conversion which we cannot discuss here'(412), be more than a gratuitous postulate encapsulated in a three line footnote? For how could *my* 'radical conversion'[329] fundamentally change the 'ontological structure of being' which is defined as *a priori* incompatible with the idea of a change, in the sharpest possible contrast to the '*psychological* experience of an *historic* man'(429)? And what about the Other? In this respect either I must envisage the simultaneous 'radical conversion' of all—which is *a priori* rejected eleven pages after the footnote as 'an abstract, unrealizable project of the For-itself toward an absolute totalization of itself and of all others'(423)—or I must take refuge in the mythical idea of the '*instant*', coupled with the enthusiasm of the equally mythical '*Apocalypse*', an idea that appears in Sartre's work immediately after the war.

As things stand in *Being and Nothingness*, the existential–ontological circle defines the character and limits of the human enterprise.

> We work to live and we live to work. The question of the meaning of the totality 'life-work'—'Why do I work, I who am living? Why live if it is in order to work?'—this can be posited only on the *reflective level* since it implies a *self-discovery* on the part of the For-itself(201).

This passage follows Sartre's description of the roof repairer's workclothes as an example of how the 'being-for-others' refers us to the 'infinite regress of instrumental complexes', pictured as a chain of which the 'for whom' is merely a link incapable of breaking the chain itself. Understandably, therefore, the ontological determination of the structures of reification confines the search for meaning to the *reflective* level of a discovery of one's own 'incomparable uniqueness'. And this is where the limitations of the individualistic stance become painfully visible. For obviously the chain of capitalistic reification must be broken if I want to constitute a meaning which is refused to me within the circle, while, to be sure, it is impossible to envisage the realization of this task through a purely individual action. Sartre is, of course, far too great a thinker to settle for such an absurdly individualistic solution, which would elevate Don Quixote to the stature of all positive heroes of world literature rolled into one, from Hercules and El Cid to Figaro and Julien Sorel. Sartre's sense of realism not only specifies the necessary inseparability of Don Quixote (absolute freedom) from Sancho Panza (absolute contingency and facticity), but also produces a complete fusion of the two in the stipulated identity of 'authentic *choice*' with 'radical *action*': a full-blooded Don Quixote who carries *in* him, and not just *with* him, his Sancho panza. (No danger, therefore, of a head-on collision with the windmill of society. Our fused hero is not interested in the success of freedom but in the possibility of action. And he can always succeed in acting, for whatever he does or does not do is necessarily an action, even when it all amounts to no more than the choice of refusing to choose.) But even so, the enterprise remains problematical. For one's individual self-discovery, no matter how authentic the choice, cannot significantly affect the massive structures of domination, with all their antagonisms and instrumental complexes. This is why the search for meaning cannot be made intelligible 'on the *reflective* level': the terrain of isolated individuality. 'We work to live and we live to work' is not just a circle, but the most vicious of all conceivable vicious circles in the circumstances of alienated labour, precisely because as the circularity of a 'brute existent' it constitutes the material foundation of all domination, and hence is radically incompatible with a meaningful life. Thus the search for meaning is identical with *breaking* the vicious circle of alienated self-objectification, which implies not a 'self-discovery on the part of the For-itself' but the practical breaking up and radical restructuring of the whole immense chain of instrumental complexes in relation to which the isolated individual in all his 'incomparable uniqueness' is nothing but a helpless victim. And given the sheer size of the undertaking, not to mention its inherent character, this means that the realization of the task involved can only be envisaged as a radical intervention at the level of *social praxis,* with the aim of bringing under conscious social control the crucial material, human, institutional and instrumental determinations: a task which implies a viable *social consciousness* in charge of the situation, in contrast to the purely *individual* self-consciousness concerned with its own authentic self-discovery on the reflective-contemplative level.

However, the world of *Being and Nothingness* is radically incompatible with this social consciousness. Setting out from the 'ontological solitude of the For-itself', the existence of the Other is established at the price of identifying *objectivity* with *alienation* and stipulating the *absolute insurmountability* of this alienation:

> My original fall is the existence of the Other. . . . I grasp the Other's look at the very center of my act as the *solidification* and *alienation* of my own possibilities(263). . . . my *possibility* becomes *probability* which is *outside me.*(265) Thus being-seen constitutes me as a defenseless being for a freedom which is not my freedom. . . . this slavery is not a *historical* result—capable of being *surmounted*(267). My being for-others is a fall through absolute emptiness toward *objectivity*(274-5). Shame is the feeling of an original fall, . . . I have 'fallen' into the world in the midst of things and I need the *mediation* of the Other in order to be what I am(289). . . . by the fact of the Other's existence, I exist in a situation which has an *outside* and which *due to this very fact* has a dimension of *alienation* which I can in *no way remove* from the situation any more than I can act directly upon it. This limit to my freedom is, as we see, posited by the Other's *pure and simple existence*(510). Thus the very meaning of our free choice is to cause a situation to arise which expresses this choice, a situation the

*essential* characteristic of which is to be *alienated*; that is, to exist as a form in itself for the Other. *We cannot escape this alienation* since it would be absurd to think of existing otherwise than in situation(526).

How could one get out of the circle through solidarity arising on the foundation of a shared predicament if the 'pure and simple existence' of the Other turns objectivity into permanent slavery by defining the 'essence' of all situation as alienation? How could one even conceptualize the possibility of a social struggle against reified objectivity if reification is given the ontological dignity of 'solidification' and 'petrification' as contained in 'the profound meaning of the myth of Medusa'?[330] And how could one envisage an end to the helplessness of isolated individuality through a *dialectical* reciprocity and *mediation* with others if the dialectic of reciprocity is turned into a self-defeating circularity and mediation is *a priori* condemned as the rule of the Other in my very being, after I have mythically fallen through 'absolute emptiness' into the objectivity–alienation–petrification of my situation?

By adopting the standpoint of anarchistic individualism, Sartre imposes on himself the characteristic limitations of this framework as a range of possible conceptualizations to the exclusion of others: an approach the salient feature of which is the *a priori* rejection of the possibility of a historical supersession of alienation through a conscious social disentanglement of objectivity from reification, in a radical reversal of the original historical process of entanglement corresponding to the 'unconscious condition' of human development hitherto. Sartre's individualistic stance, however, deprives him of the conceptual tools required for envisaging a solution to such problems. In the conceptual framework of *Being and Nothingness* the possibility of a genuine collective consciousness is an *a priori* non-starter, since self-consciousness is by definition purely individual, and the idea of an unconscious is categorically rejected already at the level of individual consciousness. Thus we can

see again that Sartre goes in a direction diametrically
opposed to Marx's way of developing these problems. While
he adopts the Hegelian identification of alienation and
objectivity, which is inherently ahistorical, he goes a great
deal further, liquidating even the remnants of historicity
from these relations by declaring the emptiness of the
concept of a historically developing humanity. Anticipating
Althusser's laments by more than two decades Sartre
writes:

> But if God is characterized as radical absence, the effort to realize
> *humanity as ours* is forever renewed and forever results in *failure*.
> Thus the humanistic 'Us'—the Us-object—is proposed to each
> individual consciousness as an ideal *impossible* to attain although
> everyone keeps the *illusion* of being able to succeed in it by
> progressively enlarging the circle of communities to which he does
> belong. This humanistic 'Us' remains an *empty concept*, a pure
> indication of a possible extension of the ordinary usage of the 'Us'.
> Each time that we use the 'Us' in this sense (to designate suffering
> humanity, sinful humanity, to determine an *objective historical
> meaning* by considering man as an object which is *developing its
> potentialities*) we limit ourselves to indicating a certain concrete
> experience to be undergone in the prescence of the absolute Third;
> that is, of God. Thus the limiting-concept of humanity (as the
> totality of the Us-object) and the limiting-concept of God imply one
> another and are correlative(423).

The fact is, though, that 'humanity as ours' does very much
exist in alienated form and practically asserts itself as world
history through the world market and the division of labour
on a world scale.[331] Furthermore, the concept of man
developing his potentialities does not imply in the least the
formulation of an impossible ideal, viewed from the illusory
standpoint of the absolute Third, God, but requires grasping
the disconcerting reality of the structures of domination in
the dynamic process of their objective unfolding and
potential dissolution, from the standpoint of a self-
developing collective subject.[332] In the absence of such
social consciousness the structures of alienation remain 'in
dominance' over against the isolated individual who is lost in

the jungle of an unstructured totality and in the 'infinite regress of instrumental complexes'. And history, deprived of its fundamental dimension of 'continuity in change and change in continuity' through the categorical negation of the possibility of an actual collective subject, ceases to exist in a meaningful sense of the term and becomes an ontologically insignificant dimension of individual existence, affecting only the thinnest layer of the psychological surface. The multiplicity of individual ventures cannot be united even at a given point in time: how could it be united then through history? Human agency is conceived as purely individual, and the direction of a series of actions is defined through the structural coherence of the primary and secondary structures of the fundamental project. As to change, or indeed radical change, we are presented with the mysterious 'moment' or 'instant' which is put forward to provide its own explanation in virtue of its simple occurrence, without any possibility of prior determinations. The definition of the human enterprise as a strictly individual venture and the radical negation of the possibility of a meaningful social consciousness arising on the real ground of history leaves us with the 'ultimate Fourth': the contemplative philosopher, who negating the position of the 'absolute Third' and its necessary correlative, the 'humanistic Us', announces the deepest ontological meaning of the human reality: 'man is a useless passion'. And he does that by *directly* identifying isolated *individuality* with the *universality* of 'ontological man'—in sharp contrast to the alienated objectivity of 'historical man' representing the degraded mediation of the For-itself with the Other—through stipulating a fundamental *symbolic* relationship of equivalence between the two.

In the context of Sartre's individualistic presuppositions, the ontological solitude of the For-itself and the essentially degraded character of the Other's mediatory function, there can be no other way than that. There can be no genuine social consciousness, not only at the level of 'humanity as ours' but equally in the domain of class relations. We are either confronted with the direct *symbolic manifestations* of profound ontological relationships, or with the 'psychological experience of historic man'. Accordingly, the idea of a 'class consciousness' is relegated to the position of a derivative and 'strictly psychological experience' which cannot significantly affect the fundamental ontological relations:

Class consciousness is evidently the assɥming of a particular 'Us' on the occasion of a collective situation more plainly structured than usual. . . . the situation of the oppressing classes presents the oppressed classes with the image of a perpetual Third who considers them and transcends them by his freedom(420). The primary fact is that the member of the oppressed collectivity, who as a simple person is engaged in fundamental conflicts with other members of this collectivity (love, hate, rivalry of interests, etc.) apprehends his condition and that of other members of this collectivity as looked-at and thought-about by a consciousness which escapes him. . . . I discover the 'Us' in which I am integrated or 'the class' outside, in the look of the Third, and it is this collective alienation which I assume when saying 'Us'(421). The oppressed class can, in fact, affirm itself as a We-subject only in relation to the oppressing class(422). But the experience of the 'We' remains on the ground of individual psychology and remains a simple symbol of the longed-for unity of transcedences. . . . the subjectivities remain out of reach and radically separated(425). . . . the experience of the We-subject has no value as a metaphysical revelation; it depends strictly on the various forms of the for-others and is only an empirical enrichment of certain of these forms. It is to this fact evidently that we should attribute the extreme instability of this experience. It comes and disappears capriciously, leaving us in the face of others-as-objects or else of a 'They' who look at us. . . .We should hope in vain for a human 'we' in which the intersubjective totality would obtain consciousness of itself as a unified subjectivity. Such an ideal could be only a dream produced by a passage to the limit and to the absolute on the basis of fragmentary, strictly psychological experiences. Furthermore this ideal itself implies the recognition of the conflict of transcendences as the original state of being-for-others(428). . . .the We-subject is a psychological experience realized by an historic man immersed in a working universe and in a

> society of a definite economic type. It reveals nothing particular; it is a purely subjective *Erlebnis* (experience). . . .the We-subject is a psychological experience which supposes one way or another that the Other's existence as such has been already revealed to us. It is therefore useless for humanity to seek to get out of this dilemma: one must either transcend the Other or allow oneself to be transcended by him. The essence of the relations between consciousnesses is not the *Mitsein* (being-with); it is conflict(429).

Here we have a succession of extremely problematical principles which spell out the 'hermeneutic of existence' on the social plane as a system of total immobility. In this system the 'collective situation' is not a primary ontological condition but merely an 'occasion' in relation to which the consciousness of a particular 'Us' may be assumed if the situation is 'more plainly structured than usual'. (What makes it become more plainly structured we are never told.) This derivative situation is contrasted with the 'primary fact' of 'fundamental conflicts' (love, hate, rivalry of interests, etc.) in which *all* individuals are involved (*bellum omnium contra omnes*) as a matter of ontological determination, and therefore any conceivable solidarity of the members of the oppressed class, who are among themselves necessarily torn by ontologically fundamental conflicts, must remain secondary, hopelessly unstable, and ultimately illusory. Furthermore, 'collective situation' is not an objective determination but merely an assumed one which I bring upon myself when I say 'Us' under the gaze of the 'perpetual Third'.[333] Consequently, the 'We-subject', in its capricious instability must necessarily posit the permanence of the oppressing class on which it structurally depends in this upside-down ontology of *Being and Nothingness*, in sharp contrast even to Hegel's insights on this point in his account of the Master–Slave relationship, not to mention Marx. This means that we are forever locked into the structures of the 'class in-itself'[334] which derives its identity and consciousness from its mere negation of the opposing class, and the constitution of the 'class for-iself'[335] through which an end to class antagonism and class existence may be envisaged is declared to be *a priori* impossible. The experience of *collective* solidarity is confined to *individual* psychology, and the inherent contradiction is explained away by gratuitously suggesting a *symbolic* relationship of identity between this paradoxical manifestation of 'individual psychology' and longing for the 'impossible unity of radically separate transcendences'. The 'strictly psychological' character of these relations is reiterated again and again, and it is sharply contrasted with the 'original state of being-for-others' defined as insoluble conflict to be perpetually acted out within the confines of the existential–ontological circle. Thus the psychological experiences of historic man, trapped in a working universe of alienated objectivity, yield the inescapability of impotence as a degraded mirror-image of the ultimate ontological uselessness of human passion.

But again we should ask the question: how could all this be different on the premise of the ontological solitude of the For-itself which stipulates the *a priori* impossibility of a unity of the self with others through meaningful social mediation? So long as totality is defined as 'an internal ontological relation of "thises" which can be revealed only in and through the individual "thises" '(180), and so long as the human reality is conceived as a 'detotalized totality which temporalizes itself in a perpetual incompleteness'(*id.*), just as long all possible combinations for the For-itself with others must remain secondary and problematical. The *a priori* rejection of interpersonal-social mediation as 'objectivity-alienation' condemns the possibility of combinations to the futility of mere exteriority (while in fact one would need a precise definition of the criteria which can separate the meaningful combinations from their reified counterparts) and dismisses the idea of constituting ontologically significant relationships on their basis

'Being a 'group of three' is not a concrete property of the group. Neither is it a property of its members. . . . The relation of *quantity* is therefore a relation In-itself but a *purely negative and external* relation . . . . it is isolated and detached from the surface of the world as a reflection (reflet) of nothingness cast on being'(191).

But since the 'relation of quantity' is a necessary pre-requisite to the constitution of a viable social mediation and collective consciousness, the step from the self-oriented *one* to the self-conscious *many* surely amounts not to a 'purely negative and external' relation but to the challenging positivity of a different kind of internal relation: one made possible by the dialectic of quantity and quality inherent in an effective social mediation. Consequently, it cannot be subsumed under the model of a 'detotalizing totalization of the individual thises' aimed at preserving in the 'unrealizable totality of an impossible unification' the incomparable uniqueness of the ontologically solitary For-itself. By contrast, in the framework of Sartre's individualistic ontological presuppositions the step from the 'I' to the 'We' that appears in 'our freedom itself creates the obstacles from which we suffer'(495) represents an arbitrary conflation of the individual and collective subjects into an entity of *extreme ambiguity*: a quasi-collective subject which becomes intelligible only as an inherently historical being,[336] and yet he transcends all history in the abstract-ontological discourse on absolute freedom and absolute responsibility. And the procedure which produces this ahistorical and curiously plural subject is all the more suspect since Sartre dismisses the 'We-subject' of actual social-historical action as a 'strictly psychological experience' devoid of a proper ontological status.

If, as Sartre admits, his proposed method for an existential psychoanalysis leaves 'much to be desired', this is not simply, as he suggests, 'because everything remains to be done in this field'(457), but because of the problematical character of the methodological principles themselves inherent in its ontological standpoint. The assertions that 'in *each* inclination, in *each* tendency the person expresses himself *completely*'(363) in that 'each drive or tendency *is* the *entire* person'(364) may well agree with the principle according to which 'the being of the For-itself is an individual venture' and 'the choice of the For-itself is always the choice of a concrete situation in its incomparable uniqueness'(598), but they produce a method of analysis which tends to disintegrate in the interminable particularization[337] of a 'bad infinity' (Hegel). The definition of the original project as 'the center of reference for an *infinity* of *polyvalent* meanings'(570) is coupled with the idea that 'the for-otself in its freedom *invents* not only primary and secondary ends; by the same stroke it *invents* the whole *system of interpretations* which allows their interconnections. . . . the subject must furnish his touchstone and his personal criteria'(471). Accordingly, the analyst 'will have to rediscover at *each* step a *symbol* functioning in the *particular* case which he is considering'(573). For 'the choice is living and consequently can be *revoked* by the subject who is being studied. [Revoked through] *abrupt* changes in orientation. . . . Our concern here is to understand what is *individual* and often even *instantaneous*. The method which has served for one subject will not necessarily be suitable to use for *another* subject or for the *same* subject at a *later* period'(*id.*). Needless to say, it is the rejection of a dialectical social mediation which brings with it the dispersive particularization of this method. And the latter, far from following the way in which the subject itself is supposed to invent the appropriate system of interpretations and provide 'his personal touchstone and his personal criteria', ends up, on the contrary, inventing*for* the subject a quasi-fictional framework of interpretation, as Sartre himself is later forced to admit[338] with respect to the actual realization of his long-standing project on Flaubert.[339] The methodologically explicit rejection of generalization produces both the dispersive particularization of the underlying ontological generalities of the claimed 'fundamental choice of being',[340] as well as the quasi-fictional framework of interpreation, which in Sartre's own words invents even the subject, in a desperate attempt at encapsulating the bad infinity of dispersive particularization in a world of its own invention. Thus even in this respect the adoption of an extreme individualistic standpoint makes Sartre pay very dearly for maintaining the absolute ontological primacy of solitude over against the merely psychological experience of historic man and his social mediations.

Paradoxically, however, some of the greatest insights of Sartre's philosophy arise on the same ground in *Being and Notingness* as its problematical features. And while it is certainly true that the historical and social dimension would greatly enhance their significance, it is equally arguable that Sartre's conscious distancing of himself from the prevailing social and historical theories was an essential condition of the production of these insights. In this respect the profoundly imaginative depiction of the complex man-ifestations of individual existence in Sartre's 'eidetic of bad faith' which we have looked at above need not detain us here any further, save just to mention that his almost fanatical insistence on the freedom of the For-itself was an essential condition of undertaking at all such an enquiry in the circumstances of apparently uncontrollable collective forces. We must now look, even if only briefly, at some less obvious instances, in which Sartre's insight is produced in virtue of the vantage point of his ontological presupposi-tions, and not in spite of them. Furthermore it must be stressed that these acquisitions of the Sartrean philosophy do not simply provide a welcome corrective to the prevailing varieties of mechanical 'vulgar Marxism' but represent a potential enrichment even to the most subtle dialectical approach. The fact that there is no evidence of a serious acquaintance with Marx's thought in *Being and Nothing-ness*, indeed that the available evidence shows rather the opposite,[341] need not concern us here. For it makes only more remarkable Sartre's achievements, arising almost in isolation in the process of single-mindedly carrying to their utmost conclusions the far-reaching implications of his own ontological principles.

The first point concerns the definition of the human reality in relation to the whole network of 'instrumental complexes'—from the most primitive tool to the 'monstrous materiality of the crowd-instrument'—without which human existence is simply inconceivable. While the necessary social-historical embeddedness of all instrumentality cannot be stressed enough, there is also a dimension of 'instrumentality *as such*' which transcends all particular phases of history. Understandably, the historical conditions under which Marxist theory was originally constituted pushed this transhistorical dimension into the background. However, the original historical contingency cannot change the fact that an adequate treatment of this dimension is a vital part of elaborating a coherent theory of instrumentality without which even the most dedicated social enterprise is bound to remain under the threat of utter failure. To be sure, Sartre tends to emphasize only this dimension, or rather, he tends to transform all aspects of instrumentality into an ahistorically defined ontological dimension. None the less, through his overpowering stand against the almost universally prevailing tide, he achieves in this respect single-handed more than anyone else in the twentieth century.

The same goes for the problematic of the 'instant'. We have seen the dubious uses to which Sartre puts this concept in *Being and Nothingness* in order to fill the immense lacunae produced by the missing social dimension of his ontology. But even so, his recurrent amplification of the ontological importance of the instant pushes to the forefront of our attention a major factor without which the structure of historical change itself remains unintelligible. Naturally, the category has important individual and social applications whose manifold specificities cannot be subsumed under a single model. And, of course, an adequate solution presupposes its treatment in the dialectic of continuity and change for which one would look in vain in *Being and Nothingness*. But again, what we actually do find there is both illuminating and challenging enough to provide a major inspiration to some long overdue research. For it is not enough to insist on the necessary social conditions of a radical historical change. Stalinism simply assumed the radical novelty of its own reality, while its opponents, like Lukács, tended to overemphasize the element of continuity in historical change. Sartre's great insight, which insists both on the being of the instant as a structure *sui generis* and on its *structuring* function as the centre of reference of the new fundamental project, offers a great deal for a better understanding of social causation and social consciousness.

The assessment of the nature of structural dependency is closely connected with the previous point. We have seen Sartre's problematical approach to interpersonal and social relations and its consequences for the articulation of his philosophy as a whole. And yet, in his analysis of the way in which 'the Other determines me', he suddenly confronts us with a tremendous insight: 'Our relation is not a *frontal opposition* but rather an *oblique interdependence*' (246). We must appreciate the importance of this insight in contrast to many theories which picture social conflict on the model of a frontal opposition and heavily contribute to the generation of disappointed expectations. But surely, the concept of an irreconcileable *structural antagonism* should not be confused with that of a *frontal opposition*. 'Oblique interdependence' is not only thoroughly compatible with the persistence of a structural antagonism but may very well constitute its fundamental modality, as Sartre tells us. Indeed, the explanatory value of the 'instant' is precisely this, that it suggests a *radical restructuring* of the normally prevailing modality of *oblique interdependence* into the transient modality of a *frontal opposition*: a restructuring both on the plane of the key material and instrumental complexes and at the level of social consciousness. An adequate social strategy, arising on the basis of a correct historical understanding, requires the precise definition of the 'moment' of a major historic change together with its 'before' and 'after', in terms of the complex modalities of the prevailing structural relations and their dialectical trans-formations. History has its structures just as much as anything else: if this were not the case, it would hopelessly escape us. Thus whatever we may think of the defects of Sartre's conception of history, insights like the one just quoted—which paradoxically arise out of an individualistic project of defining his own position in the form of an 'equidistance' from the major social forces, ontologically fixing their relations in the ahistorical immobility of the existential circle—represent a major contribution to a deepening historical understanding.

The final point in this survey concerns the problem of appropriation. And this is where we can see perhaps most clearly the way in which the individualistic stance produces the paradoxical unity of the depth of Sartre's insights and the limitations which determine the various conceptual com-binations, including the *symbolic* claims of his existential heuristic. Reflecting on the problem of appropriation from the standpoint of a radical individualism, Sartre perceives an elemental contradiction between ownership and utilization: an insight which would be obviously denied to all those who situate themselves at the standpoint of a utilitarian liberalism. Since, however, Sartre cannot transcend his ontological presuppositions, he produces a characteristic solution of this contradiction:

> *ownership* appears to the owner simultaneously as something given *at one stroke* in the eternal and as requiring an *infinite time* to be realized. No *particular* act of *utilization* really realizes the enjoyment of *full possession* . . . handing over a bank-note is enough to make the bicycle belong to me, but my *entire life* is needed to realize this possession. In acquiring the object, I perceive that possession is an enterprise which *death* always renders still *unachieved*. Now we can understand why; it is because it is

*impossible* to realize the relations *symbolized* by appropriation. In itself appropriation contains nothing concrete. It is not a real activity (such as eating, drinking, sleeping) which could serve in addition as a symbol for a particular desire. It exists, on the contrary, only as a symbol; it is its symbolism which gives it its meaning, its coherence, its existence. There can be found in it no positive enjoyment outside its symbolic value; it is only the indication of a supreme enjoyment of possession (that of the being which would be its own foundation), which is *always beyond* all the appropriative conducts meant to realize it (592-3).

Thus the symbolic solution of the insoluble contradiction between the 'eternality' of the act of ownership and the 'disintegrating' limitedness of appropriation in the particular acts of utilization becomes the paradigm of Sartre's explanatory framework. The ultimate meaning of the human reality is, as we have seen above, the appropriation of being in the form of the world. Since, however, appropriation cannot be other than *symbolic*, my appropriative relation to being must be also symbolic in every significant respect. Thus we are given a heuristic framework in the form of symbolic relations which both pinpoint (even denounce) and preserve the inherent contradictions. The ultimate meaning of the human reality is tantamount to revealing the insoluble character of contradictions (hence all the categories of 'unrealizable totality', 'impossible unification', 'impossible ideal', 'insoluble dilemma of radically separated trans-cendences', the 'circle of relations with the Other', and the like): which is both profoundly true and radically prob-lematical. For it is true only with a vital social-historical qualification which, however, appears as ontologically insignificant in the form of 'historic man immersed in a working universe of a definite economic type'. And the missing elements of the theory speak equally loud. For the 'world' which we must *appropriate* must also be *produced*, in the dialectic mode of a 'productive appropriation and appropriative production'. And while it is still plausible to envisage the act of appropriation as a *symbolic* act of an isolated individuality, the *production* of the world as a totality of appropriative relations and corresponding objects cannot conceivably be envisaged from the standpoint of an isolated individuality. Thus *work* appears only marginally, if at all (significantly, its instances are confined to some highly selective individualistic manifestations, from the waiter to the roof-repairer, both 'productive' only in the sense of being producers of surplus value in the economically 'tertiary' sphere of services) and the 'working universe' occupies an ontologically insignificant status, in the sharpest possible contrast to the fundamental ontological significance of symbolic appropriation. There is an alternative solution, namely an approach according to which the act of appropriation need not be conceived as a symbolic act if we remove the contradiction between ownership and utilization through the abolition of ownership and the simultaneous collective accessibility of utilization, together with the harmonization of the totality of *actual* appropriative relations with the totality of *productive* relations in the self-realization of the transindividual and transhistorical agency. But such a solution is radically incompatible with the ontological horizons of *Being and Nothingness*, no matter how intensely it is animated in its search for freedom by an authentic passion.

As we can see, then, Sartre's undertaking produces as many illuminating insights as major question marks, in a synthesis full of tensions. No one is supposed to feel comfortable in the presence of his conclusions, least of all the author himself. The restlessness and the determination to move forward appears to be an integral part of his fundamental project.

How far can Sartre go in his postwar development in resolving the tensions we have encountered in his ontological framework, and to what extent is it possible for him to modify his original ontological conception through 'the experience of society' and the challenge of history? The investigation of these questions will be the task of the volume that follows.

# NOTES

*Unless otherwise stated, translations are my own.* I.M.

1   'L'alibi', interview, *Le Nouvel Observateur*, 19 Nov. 1964; reprinted in *Situations*, VIII, 127-45; quotation from p. 142. *Les Écrits de Sartre: chronologie, bibliographie commentée* by Michel Contat and Michel Rybalka (Gallimard, Paris, 1970) is invaluable for all those interested in Sartre's development. In addition to a complete bibliography of his works, up to 1969, it contains excellent summaries, with extracts from his numerous interviews, as well as nearly 300 pages of rare texts. Henceforth this book will be referred to as C/R.

2   'La nationalisation de la littérature' (1945), *Situations*, II, 35, 43. And in the same article he remarks on the absurdity of being called 'the Master of neo-surrealism' who is supposed to have under his command Eluard and Picasso, while in reality 'I was still wearing short pants when they were already masters of themselves' (*ibid.*, p 37).

3   Cf. Henri Lefèbvre, 'Existentialisme et marxisme: réponse à une mise au point', *Action*, 8 June 1945.

4   Gabriel Marcel, 'Prise de position', *Nouvelles Littéraires*, 29 Oct. 1964.

5   Cf. C/R, p. 329.

6   On the occasion of the publication of Sartre's *Entretiens sur la politique* (Gallimard, Paris, 1949) with David Rousset and Gérard Rosenthal; cf. *Le Figaro*, 25 April 1949.

7   'Réponse à François Mauriac', *Le Figaro Littéraire*, 7 May 1949.

8   The exchange started with Sartre's letter dated 13 April 1967, followed by de Gaulle's reply on 19 April 1967, and published in *Le Monde*, 25 April 1967. Sartre's answer to de Gaulle took the form of an interview in *Le Nouvel Observateur*, 26 April – 3 May 1967; the whole exchange is reprinted in *Situations* VIII, 42-57.

9   Sartre's letter to the Swedish Academy, in which he tried to prevent their decision in his favour, was later published in *Le Monde*, 24 Oct. 1964. The complete text of this letter, together with an account of the debate that followed his refusal, is given in C/R; pp. 401-8.

10  André Breton, 'Le rappel de Stockholm', *La Brèche*, Dec. 1964.

11  *Le Figaro Littéraire*, 4-10 May 1970.

12  *Le Monde*, 6 June 1970.

13  'Writing for one's age' (1946), in *What is Literature?*, trans. Bernard Frechtman, Methuen, London, 1950, p. 238.

14  *Ibid.*, p. 233.

15  Interview by Jacqueline Piatier, *Le Monde*, 18 April 1964.

16    *Ibid.*
17    'La nationalisation de la littérature', p. 38.
18    'The purposes of writing' (1959), Jean-Paul Sartre, *Between Existentialism and Marxism*, trans. John Matthews, NLB, London, 1974, pp. 13-14.
19    *Ibid.*, p. 25.
20    *Ibid.*, p. 14
21    From a poem by Endre Ady (1877-1919).
22    'The purposes of writing', p. 26.
23    I have discussed these problems in my book on *Attila József e l'arte moderna*, Lerici, Milano, 1964.
24    A fragment by Attila József.
25    'The purposes of writing', p. 29.
26    *Ibid.*, p. 14.
27    Interview by Christian Gisoli, *Paru*, December 1945.
28    Interview by Jacques-Alain Miller, *Les Cahiers libres de la jeunesse,* 15 Feb. 1960.
29    'The purposes of writing', p. 19.
30    *Ibid.*, p. 19.
31    Cf. 'Détermination et liberté' (1966); C/R, pp. 735-45.
32    Interview by Pierre Lorquet, *Mondes Nouveaux*, 21 Dec. 1944.
33    'The purposes of writing', p. 22.
34    Interview by Gabriel d'Aubarède, *Les Nouvelles littéraires*, 1 Feb. 1951.
35    'Réponse à M. Mauriac', *L'Observateur*, 19 March 1953.
36    'Of rats and men' (1958), Jean-Paul Sartre, *Situations*, trans. Benita Eisler, Fawcett Publications, Greenwich, Conn., 1965, p. 242. Sartre's footnote about the 'accidental individual' refers to Marx's *German Ideology*. See also note 37.
37    Marx, *Critique of the Hegelian Philosophy of Right* (1843), Marx-Engels, *Werke*, I, 284.
38    'Itinerary of a thought' (1969), *New Left Review*, Nov-Dec. 1969, p. 59.
39    'Forgers of myths: the young playwrights of France', *Theatre Arts*, June 1946.
40    'The purposes of writing', p. 27.
41    'A propos de l'existentialisme: mise au point', *Action*, 29 Dec. 1944; reprinted in C/R pp. 653-8 (quotation from p. 654).
42    Interview by Claude Sarraute, *Le Monde*, 17 Sept. 1959.
43    'Je-tu-il', preface to André Puig's novel, *L'Inachevé* (The Unfinished), Gallimard, 1970; reprinted in *Situations*, IX, 277-315 (quotation from p. 281).
44    'Itinery of a thought', p. 55.
45    Interview by Gabriel d'Aubarède, *Les Nouvelles littéraires*, 1 Feb. 1951.

46    Simone de Beauvoir, *La Force des choses*, p. 466.

47    To maintain a killing rhythm of work while writing his *Critique of Dialectical Reason*, he consumes a tubeful of corydrone each day; de Beauvoir, *La Force des choses*, p. 407.

48    Simone de Beauvoir, 'Jean-Paul Sartre: strictly personal', *Harper's Bazaar*, January 1946; a major portion is reprinted in C/R, pp. 418-20.

49    Published in *The New Ambassador / Revue Universitaire internationale*, Jan. 1927; reprinted in C/R, pp. 517-30.

50    'Enquête auprès des étudiants d'aujourd'hui', by Roland Alix, *Les Nouvelles littéraires*, 2 Feb. 1929. Parts of Sartre's letter are reprinted in Simone de Beauvoir, *Memoirs of a Dutiful Daughter*, Penguin edn, 1963, pp. 342-3.

51    'Si grand que soit mon admiration pour Proust, il m'est *tout opposé*: il se complait dans l'analyse, et je ne tend qu'à la synthèse' (interview by Pierre Lorquet, *Mondes Nouveaux*, 21 Dec. 1944).

52    'It is perfectly true, isolated subjectivity is, in the opinion of the age, evil; but "objectivity" as a cure is not one whit better. The only salvation is subjectivity, i.e. God, as infinite compelling subjectivity' (*The Journals of Kierkegaard: 1834-1854*, ed. and trans. Alexander Dru, Fontana Books, p. 184).

53    'The paintings of Giacometti' (1954), *Situations* (English), pp. 124-5.

54    de Beauvoir, *Memoirs of a Dutiful Daughter*, p. 342.

55    'Jean-Paul Sartre has done the finest of critical appreciations of [Césaire's] *Cahier* as poetry, but his explanation of what he conceives Negritude to mean is a disaster' (C.L.R. James, *The Black Jacobins*, 2nd rev. ed, Vintage Books, New York, 1963, p. 401).

56    *Les Temps Modernes*, Dec. 1957, p. 1137.

57    'L'écrivain et sa langue' (1965), interview by Pierre Verstraeten, *Revue d'Esthétique*, July-December 1965; reprinted in *Situations*, IX, 40-82 (quotation from p. 75). It is worth stressing that Lukács deals in much the same way with this problem in his Correspondence with Anna Seghers.

58    'The paintings of Giacometti', p. 132; I have changed 'supra-determination' to 'overdetermination'—the generally accepted term for 'surdetermination', the term used by Sartre; cf. French edition of this essay in *Situations*, IV, 359.

59    'The paintings of Giacometti', p. 132.

60    See C/R, p. 429.

61    Interview by Alain Koehler, *Perspectives du Théâtre*, March-April 1960.

62    Interview by Robert Kanters, *L'Express*, 17 Sept. 1959.

63 'A friend of the people', interview by Jean-Edern Hallier and Thomas Savignat, *L'Idiot International*, October 1970; reprinted in *Situations*, IX, 456-76 and in NLB volume, *Between Existentialism and Marxism*, pp. 286-98 (quotation from p. 295 of the latter).

64 This is recognized to some extent when Sartre declares: 'If I had to rewrite *Roads to Freedom*, I'd try to present every character without commentary, without showing my feelings' (interview by Jacqueline Autrusseau, *Les Lettres françaises*, 17-23 Sept. 1959).

65 '*Nausea* has been accused of being too *pessimistic*. But let's wait for the ending. In a forthcoming novel, which will be the continuation, the hero shall redress the machine. We shall see existence rehabilitated, and my hero act, tasting action' (interview by Claudine Chonez, *Marianne*, 7 Dec 1938).

66 Cf. above, pp. 80-81.

67 This is how Sartre describes in an interview the relationship between *Being and Nothingness* and *Huis Clos*: 'This story of mine about souls in torment was not symbolic — I had no wish to "repeat" *Being and Nothingness* in different words. What would have been the point? I simply made up some stories with an imagination, sensibility and thought that the conception and writing of *Being and Nothingness* had united, integrated and organized in a certain way' ('The purposes of writing', p. 10).

68 Interview by Jacqueline Autrusseau, *Les Lettres Françaises*, 17-23 September 1959.

69 Interview by Bernard Dort, *Théâtre Populaire*, Winter 1959.

70 'Sartre talks to Tynan', *The Observer*, 18 and 25 June 1961, reprinted in Kenneth Tynan, *Tynan Right and Left*, Longmans, London, 1967, pp. 302-12. reference is to pages 310-11. Other relevant passages are as follows: 'the theatre is not concerned with reality: it is only concerned with truth. The cinema, on the other hand, seeks a reality which may contain moments of truth. The theatre's true battlefield is that of tragedy — drama which embodies a *genuine myth*. There is no reason why the theatre should not tell a story of love or marriage, as long as it has *a quality of myth*; in other words, as long as it occupies itself with something more than conjugal disagreements or lovers' misunderstandings. By seeking *truth through myth*, and by the use of forms as non-realistic as tragedy, the theatre can stand up against the cinema' (p. 304). 'I don't think theatre can be directly derived from political events. For instance, I would never have written *Altona* if it was merely a simple question of a conflict between Left and Right. For me, *Altona* is tied up with the whole evolution of Europe since 1945, as much with the Soviet concentration camps as with the war in Algeria. The theatre must take all these problems and *transmute them into mythic form*

(p. 307). 'I am always looking for *myths*; in other words, for subjects so sublimated that they are *recognizable to everyone*, without recourse to minute psychological details' (p. 310). Furthermore, there are also gradations or varieties of myth on the subjective to objective scale: the work of Tennesse Williams is 'permeated with *subjective myths*'. (p. 308). And the whole category of 'myth', subjective as much as objective, is opposed to symbolism: 'I have not liked Beckett's other plays [other than *Waiting for Godot*, that is] particularly *Endgame*, because I find the *symbolism* far too inflated, far too *naked*' (*ibid*., p. 307).

71  In *Theatre Arts* (New York), June 1946.
72  In *Le Point*, Jän. 1967.
73  Interview by Nicole Zand, *Bref*, Feb.-March 1967.
74  Interview by Alain Koehler, *Perspectives du Théâtre*, March-April 1960.
75  'Itinerary of a thought', p. 56.
76  'La recherche de l'absolu' (1948), *Situations*, III, 300-1.
77  *Ibid*.,p. 301.
78  'Masson' (1960), *Situations*, IV, 389.
79  *Ibid* p. 401.
80  'La recherche de l'absolu', p. 293.
81  'Les mobiles de Calder' (1946), *Situations*, III, 308-11. And he writes on Giacometti that his works, constantly in the course of making, are 'always half-way between nothingness and being' ('La recherche de l'absolu', p. 293).
82  'The purposes of writing', pp. 11-12.
83  'Le choix libre que l'homme fait de soi-même s'identifie absolument avec ce qu'on appelle sa destinée' (Jean-Paul Sartre, *Baudelaire*, Gallimard, Paris, 1947, p. 224). And another important passage concerning this problem: 'nous touchons ici au *choix originel* que Baudelaire a fait de lui même, à cet *engagement absolu* par quoi chacun décide dans une situation particulière de ce qu'il *sera* et de ce qu'il *est*.' (*ibid*., p. 20).
84  Interview by Claudine Chonez, *L'Observateur*, 31 May 1951.
85  'Défense de la culture française par la culture européenne', *Politique étrangère*, June 1949.
86  Interview by Françoise Erval, *Combat*, 3 Feb. 1949.
87  Interview by Alain Koehler, *Perspectives du Théâtre*, March-April 1960.
88  'The purposes of writing', p. 12.
89  'Itinerary of a thought', p. 55.
90  'Légende de la vérité', *Bifur*, June 1931; reprinted in C/R, pp. 531-45.
91  'Itinerary of a thought', p. 56.

92    Interview by Claudine Chonez, *Marianne*, 23 Nov. and 7 Dec. 1938.
93    'Of rats and men', *Situations*, 245.
94    See note 33.
95    Jean-Paul Sartre, *Saint Genet: comédien et martyr*, Gallimard, Paris, 1952, p. 536.
96    'La nationalisation de la littérature', *Situations*, II, 53.
97    'La Libération de Paris: une semaine d'Apocalypse', *Clartés*, 24 Aug. 1945; reprinted in C/R, pp. 659-62.
98    'Gribouille', *La Rue*, Nov. 1947.
99    'L'imagination au pouvoir, entretien de Jean-Paul Sartre avec Daniel Cohn-Bendit', *Le Nouvel Observateur*, Special Supplement, 20 May 1968.
100   Interview by Serge Lafaurie, *Le Nouvel Observateur*, 17 March 1969; reprinted in *Situations*, VIII, 239-61 (quotation from p. 254).
101   'La libération de Paris: une semaine d'Apocalypse', C/R, p. 661.
102   'Détermination et liberté', C/R, p. 745.
103   'L'Art cinématographique' (1931), first published in a brochure of the Lycée of Le Havre, *Distribution solennelle des prix*, Le Havre, 12 July 1931; reprinted in C/R, pp. 546-52 (quotations from pp. 548-52).
104   Interview by Yvon Novy, *Comoedia*, 24 April 1943.
105   'Quand Hollywood veut faire penser – *Citizen Kane* d'Orson Welles', *L'Ecran français*, 1 Aug. 1945.
106   'L'Art cinématographique', C/R, p. 551.
107   *Ibid*, p. 549.
108   Interview by Yvon Novy, *Comoedia*, 24 April 1943.
109   'A propos de *Le Bruit et la Fureur* – la temporalité chez Faulkner' (July 1939), *Situations*, I, p. 68.
110   *Ibid*, p. 71.
111   *Ibid*, p. 72.
112   *Ibid*, p. 73.
113   *Ibid*, p. 73.
114   *Ibid*, p. 74.
115   Lucien Goldmann has discussed in several of his works the relationship between Lukács and Heidegger, cf. *Mensch, Gemeinschaft und Welt in der Philosophie Immanuel Kants* (Europa-Verlag, Zürich, 1945), *Recherches dialectiques* (Gallimard, Paris, 1959), and in particular his posthumous volume, *Lukács et Heidegger*, ed. and with an introduction by Youssef Ishaghpour (Denoël/Gonthier, Paris, 1973).
116   Heidegger's preface to the seventh German edition of *Being and Time*, trans. John Macquarrie and Edward Robinson, Blackwell, Oxford, 1967, p. 17.

117 'La temporalité chez Faulkner', p. 73.
118 *Ibid*, pp. 74-5.
119 *Ce Soir*, 16 May 1938.
120 'Quand Hollywood veut faire penser . . . ' cf. note 105.
121 'Qu'est-ce-que l'existentialisme? Bilan d'une offensive' (interview by Dominique Aury, *Les Lettres françaises*, 24 Nov. 1945).
122 Interview by Jacques-Alain Miller, *Les Cahiers libres de la Jeunesse*, 15 Feb. 1960.
123 Simone de Beauvoir, *La Force des choses*, p. 214.
124 Interview by Robert Kanters, *L'Express*, 17 Sept. 1959.
125 'Itinerary of a thought', p. 52.
126 Quoted by Thomas Mann in his *Essay in Autobiography*.
127 'The purposes of writing', p. 31. The same view is expressed in *Words*: 'I have renounced my vocation, but I have not unfrocked myself. I still write. What else can I do? *Nulla dies sine linea*. It is my habit and it is also my profession. For a long while I treated my pen as a sword: now I realize how helpless we are. It does not matter: I am writing, I shall write books; they are needed; they have a use all the same' (Penguin edn. p. 157).
128 Sartre quoting Isaac Deutscher in 'A friend of the people', pp. 292-3.
129 *Ibid*, pp. 293-5.
130 'Itinerary of a thought', pp. 51.
131 *Ibid.*, p. 45.
132 'A friend of the people', pp. 293 and 295.
133 Interview by Jacqueline Piatier, *Le Monde*, 18 April 1964.
134 'L'ange du morbide', published in *La Revue sans titre*, 15 Jan. 1923.
135 'Jésus la Chouette, professeur de province', *La Revue sans titre*, 10 and 25 Feb. and 10 Mar. 1923.
136 His *Esquisse d'une théorie des émotions* (*Sketch for a Theory of the Emotions*) was written in 1936 but probably revised before publication in 1939. *L'Imagination* (English title: *Imagination: a psychological critique*) was written in 1935 and published in 1936. And *L'Imaginaire* (English title: *The Psychology of Imagination*) was written and in part published in 1939, and as a book in 1940.
137 'Meanwhile Sartre was writing a treatise on phenomenological psychology which he entitled *La Psyché*, and of which in the end he published an extract only, calling it *Esquisse d'une théorie phénoménologique des émotions* (*The Emotions: Outline of a theory*). Here he developed his theory of 'psychic objectivity', which had been sketched out in the essay on *The Transcendence of the Ego*. But to his way of thinking this was little more than an exercise, and after writing four hundred pages he broke off to complete his collection of stories' (Simone de Beauvoir, *The Prime of Life*, Penguin edn, p. 318).

138    Cf. for instance the following passage: 'The third reason for choosing Flaubert is that he represents a sequel to *L'Imaginaire*. You may remember that in my very early book *L'Imaginaire* I tried to show that an image is not a sensation reawakened, or reworked by the intellect, or even a former perception altered and attenuated by knowledge, but is something entirely different—an absent reality, focused in its absence through what I called an *analogon*; that is to say, an object which serves as an analogy and is traversed by an intention. For example, when you are going to sleep, the little dots in your eyes—phosphenes—may serve as an analogy for every kind of oneiric or hypnagogic image. Between waking and sleeping, some people see vague shapes pass, which are phosphenes through which they focus on an imagined person or a thing. In *L'Imaginaire*, I tried to prove that imaginary objects—images—are an absence. In my book on Flaubert, I am studying *imaginary persons*—people who like Flaubert act out roles. A man is like a leak of gas, escaping into the imaginary. Flaubert did so perpetually; yet he also had to see reality because he hated it, so there is the whole question of the relationship between the real and the imaginary which I try to study in his life and work' ('Itinary of a thought', p. 53).

139    'Intimacy', 'The Wall', 'The Room', 'Erostratus', and 'The Childhood of a Leader'.

140    'Itinerary of a thought', p. 44.

141    *Action*, 29 Dec 1944; reprinted in C/R, pp. 653-8.

142    A lecture delivered on 28 Oct. 1945, and published as a volume by Nagel, Paris, 1946.

143    Written in 1945 and published in 1946.

144    'Le R.D.R. et le problème de la liberté', *La Pensée socialiste*, Spring 1948.

145    'Faux savants ou faux lièvres?' (1950), *Situations*, Vol. VI, p. 28.

146    'Pourtant, après avoir applaudi à la victoire du militant, c'est l'aventurier que je suivrai dans sa solitude. Il a vécu jusqu'au bout une condition impossible: fuyant et cherchant la solitude, vivant pour mourir et mourant pour vivre, convaincu de la vanité de l'action et de sa nécessité, tentant de justifier son entreprise en lui assignant un but auquel il ne croyait pas, recherchant la totale objectivité du résultat pour la diluer dans une absolue subjectivité, voulant l'échec qu'il refusait, refusant la victoire qu'il souhaitait, voulant construire sa vie comme un destin et ne se plaisant qu'aux moments infinitésimaux qui séparent la vie de la mort. Aucune solution de ces antinomies, aucune synthèse de ces contradictoires. . . . Pourtant, au prix d'une tension insupportable, cet homme les a maintenus ensemble et tous à la fois, dans leur incompatibilité même; il a été la conscience permanente de cette

incompatibilité. . . . je pense qu'il témoigne à la fois de l'existence absolue de l'homme et de son impossibilité absolue. Mieux encore: il prouve que c'est cette impossibilité d'etre qui est la condition de son existence at que l'homme existe parce qu'il est impossible. . . une cité socialiste où de futurs Lawrence seraient radicalement impossibles me semblerait stérilisée' ('Portrait de l'aventurier; 1950, *Situations*, VI, 20-1). It is worth remembering that in 1945, in his lecture *Existentialisme est un humanisme* Sartre characterized Lawrence as an existentialist. No doubt as a result of criticism received from his socialist friends, Sartre omitted such references from the published text.

147　*Saint Genet*, p. 177.

148　*Ibid*. A substantial part of *Saint Genet* appeared in 1950, in several issues of *Les Temps Modernes*.

149　'La bombe H, une arme contre l'histoire', *Défense de la Paix*, July 1954.

150　Cf. 'Ce que j'ai vu à Vienne, c'est la Paix', *Les Lettres françaises*, 1-8 Jan. 1953; and an interview by Marcel Saporta, *Cuadernos Americanos*, Jan.-Feb. 1954.

151　'La pensés et la politique d'aujourd'hui nous mènent au massacre parce qu'elles sont abstraites. . . . Chacun est *l'Autre*, l'ennemi possible, on s'en mefie. Il est rare, en France, mon pays, de rencontrer des hommes; on rencontre surtout des étiquettes et des noms. Ce qu'il y a de neuf et d'admirable dans ce congrès de la Paix, c'est qu'il réunit des hommes. . . . Nous avons résolu, non de nous substituer à nos gouvernements, mais de communiquer entre nous, *sans eux*' (Sartre's intervention at the opening session of the Vienna meeting, on 12 Dec. 1952; published in *Congrès des Peuples pour la Paix, Vienne, 12-19 Dec. 1952*, Paris, 1953).

152　'The purposes of writing', p. 13.

153　*Les Temps Modernes*, Feb. 1956.

154　Interview by Simon Blumenthal and Gérard Spitzer, *La Voie communiste*, new series, June-July 1962.

155　*Les Temps Modernes*, Nov.-Dec. 1956 – Jan. 1957, pp. 577-697.

156　'Itinerary of a thought', p. 46.

157　'The purposes of writing', p. 9.

158　Echoing his own earlier hopes about a broadly based yet effective political *rassemblement* (cf. his participation in the R.D.R.), he sees the militancy of *La Cause du Peuple* in a similar light: 'the militants of *La Cause du Peuple* do not constitute a party. It is a political group [rassemblement] which can always be dissolved. . . . This procedure allows a way out of the rigidity in which the Communist Party has imprisoned itself. . . . Today, the Maoists criticize and break out of the notion of *leftism*: *they want to be the left* and to create a broad political organization [*rassemblement*]'(Interview by Michel-Antoine Burnier, *Actuel*, No. 28, and *Tout va Bien*, 20 Feb.-20 March 1973; trans. Robert d'Amico, *Telos*, Summer 1973; quotations from pp. 93 and 95 of *Telos*.) It does not matter here that leftism is often characterized precisely by a voluntaristic 'wanting to be the left' which disregards the objective relation of forces. Nor are we concerned with the question whether or not the reality of French Maoism corresponds to Sartre's description. What matters is the reassertion of Sartre's ideal of a broadly based and extremely flexible political organization: a *rassemblement* of individuals as opposed to a highly disciplined and structured political party.

159   'Itinery of a thought', pp. 58-9
160   Of course Sartre's works are inherently problematical, but not in such a way that the later works might be considered less problematical than the earlier ones. *Roads to Freedom* is not a more 'mature' novel than *Nausea* (in the sense in which Thomas Mann's *Magic Mountain* is incomparably more mature than his *Royal Highness*), nor is *Critique of Dialectical Reason* more 'mature' than *Being and Nothingness* in the field of philosophy, or *The Idiot of the Family* than *Saint Genet* in the field of biography. In the later works there are some new principles at work—alongside with a great many they share with the earlier ones—that is all. It is Sartre's lifework as a whole which is problematical, with its overpowering negativity, and not one or two of its limited phases that might be characterized in relation to one another in terms of 'radical breaks'. We cannot stress enough, Sartre—in some ways like Picasso—produces not so much 'representative works' as a *representative lifework*. If we want a great parallel from the past—keeping in mind, of course, all the differences and specificities—we may think of Voltaire, with his all-embracing negativity. Situated at another juncture of great socio-historical transformation and transition, Voltaire subjects the old order to the most devastating criticism and satire—quite unlike Rousseau, who organically complements his radical negativity with anticipations of a new order. As we all know well, only a tiny fraction of Voltaire's immense lifework is read today. But if we try to imagine the eighteenth century without his contribution we must immediately realize how much the poorer it would be for that.

161   Interview by Dominique Aury, *Les Lettres françaises*, 24 Nov. 1945.
162   *Being and Nothingness: an essay on phenomenological ontology* (1943), trans. Hazel E. Barnes, Methuen, London, 1969, pp. 526 and 529 (henceforth referred to as *B & N*).

163 Interview by Robert Kanters, *L'Express*, 17 Sept. 1959. The theme of 'being judged' appears many times in Sartre's writings, including an interview with Kenneth Tynan in which he says: 'The point is that we know we shall be judged, and not by the rules we use to judge ourselves.' And he adds: 'In that thought there is *something horrific*' (K. Tynan, *Tynan Right and Left*, 1967, p. 304) Thus there is always something threatening, sinister, tragic on the horizon. Even when Sartre declares that he has 'always been an optimist, indeed too much of an optimist', he does this in conjunction with some sombre metaphysical statements: 'The Universe remains dark. We are sinister animals.' And although he insists in the same interview that alienation, exploitation and hunger are the evils we should be concerned about because they 'relegate to the second plane the metaphysical evil', the latter remains menacingly looming in the background in the Sartrean 'dark Universe' (interview by Jacqueline Piatier, *Le Monde*, 18 April 1964).

164 'La recherche de l'absolu' (1948), *Situations* III, 293.

165 Interview by Michel-Antoine Burnier, *loc. cit.*, p. 99.

166 'La question' (1965), *Théâtre vivant*, Sept. 1965.

167 Preface for *Portrait of a Man Unknown* by Nathalie Sarraute (1948), trans. by Maria Jolas, *Situations*, Fawcett, Greenwich, Conn., 1965. p. 139.

168 *Ibid.*, p. 141.

169 *Ibid.*, p. 139.

170 'Merleau-Ponty' (1961), *Situations*, (English ed.) p. 185.

171 *The Problem of Method* (1959), trans. Hazel E. Barnes, Methuen, London, 1963, p. 20 (henceforth referred to as *Method*).

172 See the description of his prisoner of war camp experience (see chapter 1, note 18) which is used to authenticate his analysis of 'distance' as a concept meaningful only in a human context. That he contradicts elsewhere the statement that close proximity to others in the camp 'was never disturbing, as the others were a part of me', only underlines the fact that such personal references do not appear in his work for the sake of their *descriptive content* but for their *authenticating function*. It does not really matter whether or not Sartre *actually* had the experiences he describes. What is structurally important is that his crucial *theoretical* propositions are coupled and integrated with *existentially authenticating* subjective references.

173 'Je le dis tout de suite: vos attaques me paraissent inspirés par la mauvaise foi et l'ignorance. Il n'est même pas sûr que vous avez *lu aucun des livres* dont vous parlez' (Sartre, 'A propos de l'existentialisme: mise au point', pp. 653-4).

174 'Ses [Lukács's] arguments sont nuls et non avenus: *il n'a pas lu*

*L'Étre et le Néant'* (interview by François Erval, *Combat*, 3 Feb. 1949). On the other hand, when the principal object of his criticism is the French C. P., Sartre completely reverses this severe judgment and refers to Lukács in the highest terms of praise: 'Le seule qui tente en Europe, d'expliquer par leurs causes les mouvements de pensée contemporains, c'est un communiste hongrois, Lukács' ('Le Réformisme et les fétiches', *Les Temps Modernes*, Feb. 1956, p 1159).

175  'I have at least this in common with Hegel. *You have not read either of us*. You have such a mania for not going to the source' ('Reply to Albert Camus' (1952), *Situations*, p. 66.

176  *Les Temps Modernes*, Dec. 1957, p. 1137.

177  'Une idée fondamentale de la phénoménologie de Husserl: l'Intentionnalité' (January 1939), *Situations*, I, 30. (henceforth referred to as 'Une idée').

178  *The Transcendence of the Ego*, trans. Forrest Williams and Robert Kirkpatrick, The Noonday Press, New York, 1957, pp. 39-40; (henceforth referred to as *Transcendence*).

179  *Ibid*, pp. 87-8.

180  *Ibid*, p. 103.

181  'The refutation [of solipsism] that Husserl presents in *Formale und Transzendentale Logik* and in *Cartesianische Meditationen* does not seem to us capable of unsettling a determined and intelligent solipsist. As long as the I remains a structure of consciousness, it will always remain possible to oppose consciousness, with its I, to all other existents' (*Ibid*, p. 103).

182  *Ibid*, pp. 103-4.

183  *Ibid*, pp. 104-6.

184  This is how Simone de Beauvoir describes Sartre's encounter with Husserl's philosophy: 'Sartre was coming to realize that in order to give the ideas dividing his mind some coherent organization, help was essential. The first translations of Kierkegaard appeared about this time: we had no particular incentive to read them, and left them untouched. On the other hand, Sartre was strongly attracted by what he had heard about German phenomenology. Raymond Aron was spending a year at the French Institute in Berlin and studying Husserl simultaneously with preparing a historical thesis. When he came to Paris he spoke of Husserl to Sartre. We spent an evening together at the Bec de Gaz in the Rue Montparnasse. We ordered the speciality of the house, apricot cocktails; Aron said, pointing to his glass: "You see, my dear fellow, if you are a phenomenologist, you can talk about this cocktail and make philosophy out of it!" Sartre turned pale with emotion at this. Here was just the thing he had been longing to achieve for years—to describe objects just as he

saw and touched them, and extract philosophy from the process. Aron convinced him that phenomenology exactly fitted in with his special preoccupations: by-passing the antithesis of idealism and realism [materialism], affirming simultaneously both the supremacy of reason and the reality of the visible world as it appears to our senses. On the Boulevard Saint-Michel Sartre purchased Lévinas's book on Husserl, and was so eager to inform himself on the subject that he leafed through the volume as he walked along, without even having cut the pages'(*The Prime of Life*, trans. Peter Green, Penguin edn, pp. 135-6). The contrast with Lukács couldn't be greater. As Sartre from Raymond Aron twenty years later, Lukács gets an enthusiastic account of phenomenology during the first world war from Max Scheler, but he reacts to it with extreme scepticism. This is how Lukács himself describes the incident: 'Als mich zur Zeit des ersten Weltkrieges Scheler in Heidelberg besuchte, hatten wir hierüber ein interessantes und charakteristisches Gespräch. Scheler vertrat den Standpunkt, die Phänomenologie sie eine universale Methode, die alles zum intentionalen Gegenstand haben könne. "Man kann zum Beispiel", führte Scheler aus, "über den Teufel phänomenologische Untersuchungen machen, man muss nur zunächst die Frage der Existenz des Teufels in Klammer setzen." – "Freilich", antwortete ich, "und wenn sie dann mit dem phänomenologischen Bild üben den Teufel fertig geworden sind, dann öffnen Sie die Klammer – und der Teufel steht leibhaftig vor uns." Scheler lachte, zuckte mit den Achseln und antwortete nichts' (Georg Lukács, *Existentialismus oder Marxismus*? Aufbau-Verlag, Berlin, 1951, pp. 36-7). Lukács's early philosophy has been constituted on the basis of a positive response to Plato, Kant and Hegel, in accordance with his fundamental interest in finding a secure way of transcending the world of deceptive appearances while remaining on the ground of reality, and therefore the idea of phenomenological bracketing and reduction had to be totally alien to him.

185   *The Psychology of Imagination*, trans. Bernard Frechtman, Washington Square Press, New York, 1966, p. 233 (henceforth referred to as *L'Imaginaire*).
186   'Une idée', p. 32.
187   *Ibid.*,
188   *B & N.*, p. 626.
189   Eugen Fink, 'Die phänomenologische Philosophie Edmund Husserl in der gegenwartigen Kritik', *Kantstudien*, 1933.
190   *Transcendence*, pp. 102-3.
191   *Sketch for a Theory of the Emotions*, trans. Philip Mairet, Methuen, London, 1962, p. 81 (henceforth referred to as *Emotions*).

192   *Imagination: a psychological critique*, trans. Forrest Williams, The
      University of Michigan Press, Ann Arbor, 1962, pp. 141-3
      (henceforth referred to as *Imagination*).
193   *L'Imaginaire*, pp. 241-2.
194   *Ibid.*, p. 243. Also, we should bear in mind the following
      qualifications: 'In an imaginary world, there is no dream of
      possibilities since possibilities call for a real world on the basis of
      which they are thought of as possibilities. Consciousness cannot get
      perspective on its own imaginations in order to imagine a possible
      sequence to the story which it is representing to itself: that would be
      to be awake. . . . All anticipation at a given moment if a story
      derives from the very fact that the anticipation appears as an
      episode of the story. I cannot entertain, conceive another ending. I
      have no choice, no recourse, I am compelled to narrate the story to
      myself: there is no "blow for nothing". So each moment of the story
      occurs as having an imaginary future, but a future I cannot foresee,
      which will come of its own accord, in its own time, to haunt
      consciousness, against which consciousness will be crushed. So,
      contrary to what could be believed, the imaginary world occurs as a
      *world without freedom*: *nor is it determined*, it is the opposite of
      freedom, it is *fatal*' (*ibid*, pp. 220-1). 'We can conclude that the
      dream—contrary to Descartes—does not at all occur as an
      apprehension of reality. On the contrary, it would lose all its sense,
      its own nature if it could posit itself as real even for a moment. It is
      primarily a story and our strong interest in it is of the same sort as
      that of the naïve reader in a novel. It is lived as a fiction . . . Only it
      is a *"spell-binding" fiction*: consciousness . . . has become
      knotted. And what it lives, at the same time as the fiction
      apprehended as a fiction is the impossibility of emerging out of the
      fiction. Just as King Midas transformed everything he touched into
      gold, so consciousness is itself determined to transform into the
      imaginary everything it gets hold of: hence the *fatal* nature of the
      dream. It is the seizure of this fatality as such which has often been
      confused with an apprehension of the dreamed world as *reality*'
      (*ibid.*, p. 228). 'The dream is a privileged experience which can help
      us to conceive what a consciousness would be which *would have
      lost its "being-in-the-world"* and which would be, by the same
      token, *deprived of the category of the real*' (*ibid.*, p. 229). The last
      remark is particularly important for understanding Sartre's way of
      asserting the function of the real in relation to consciousness while
      rejecting all deterministic accounts.
195   *Emotions*, p. 93.
196   *Imagination*, pp. 115-16.
197   See in particular *Emotions*, pp. 32-48.

198 Simone de Beauvoir, *The Prime of Life*, p. 128.
199 See the last section of this chapter.
200 For a classic analysis of these problems, see Lukács's essay on 'Reification and the Consciousness of the Proletariat' (1922), *History and Class Consciousness*, trans. Rodney Livingstone, Merlin Press, London, 1968, pp. 83-222.
201 *L'Imaginaire*, pp. 240-1.
202 *Ibid.*, p. 245.
203 *Ibid.*, p. 241.
204 *Ibid.*, pp. 243-4.
205 See notes 212 and 214.
206 *L'Imaginaire*, p. 241.
207 *Ibid.*, p. 245.
208 *Ibid.*, p. 244.
209 *Nausea*, trans. Robert Baldick, Penguin edn, p. 22.
210 'His blue cotton shirt stands out cheerfully against a chocolate-coloured wall. That too brings on the Nausea. Or rather it is the Nausea. The Nausea isn't inside me: I can feel it over there on the wall, on the braces, everywhere around me. It is one with the café, it is I who am inside it' (*ibid.*, p. 35).
211 'The Nausea hasn't left me and I don't believe it will leave me for quite a while; but I am no longer putting up with it, it is no longer an illness or a passing fit: it is me' (*ibid.*, p. 182).
212 *Ibid.* pp. 182-3.
213 We should recall here Sartre's early critique of the notions of 'will to power' etc., in his contribution to the student enquiry; See note 50.
214 *Nausea*, pp. 183-92.
215 *Emotions*, p. 90.
216 See note 163.
217 *Emotions*, pp. 84-5.
218 *Ibid.*, pp. 90-1.
219 *Method*, p. 130.
220 *Ibid.*, p. 59.
221 *Ibid.*, p. 152.
222 *Ibid.*, p. 94.
223 *Ibid.*, p. 95.
224 *Ibid.*, p. 80.
225 See in particular, pp. 77-9 of *Method*.
226 'Itinery of a thought', p. 58.
227 *Method*, p. 88.
228 *Ibid.*, p. 78.
229 *Ibid.*, p. 115.
230 Interview by Michel-Antoine Burnier, p. 99.
231 *Method*, p. 90.

232  *Ibid.*, p. 79.
233  There are some important changes in method in the development of Husserl and Heidegger, as well as of Merleau-Ponty. I shall attempt their characterization on some future occasion.
234  Simone de Beauvoir, *The Prime of Life*, p. 136.
235  *Method*, p. 52. (Sartre's reference is to Henri Lefèbvre's 'Perspectives de sociologie rurale', *Cahiers de sociologie*, 1953.)
236  *Ibid.*, p. 52.
237  'We shall define the method of the existentialist approach as a *regressive-progressive* and *analytic-synthetic* method. It is at the same time an enriching *cross-reference* between the object (which contains the whole period as *hierarchized significations*) and the period (which contains the object in its totalization)' (*ibid.*, p. 148).
238  *Emotions*, pp. 93-4.
239  *Imagination*, p. 128.
240  *Method*, p. 135.
241  According to Heidegger 'Because Marx, through his experience of the *alienation of modern man*, is aware of a *fundamental dimension of history*, the Marxist view of history is superior to all other views'. (See Iring Fetscher, *Marxismusstudien*, in: *Soviet Survey*, No. 33, July-Sept. 1960, p. 88) It goes without saying, Marx did not experience alienation as 'the alienation of modern man', but as the alienation of man in capitalist society. Nor did he look upon alienation as a 'fundamental dimension of history', but as a central issue of a given *phase* of history which can be historically transcended. The Heideggerian idea of alienation as a 'fundamental dimension of history' is in fact profoundly anti-historical.
242  The concept of 'non-positional self-consciousness' plays a very important part in Sartre's thought. See in this respect also note 326.
243  *Transcendence*, pp. 105-6.
244  *Ibid.*, p. 100.
245  *Ibid.*, p. 100.
246  *Ibid.*, p. 100.
247  *Ibid.*, pp. 101-2.
248  The phenomenologist 'will interrogate *consciousness, the human reality* about emotion' (*Emotions*, p. 26).
249  *Ibid.*, p. 63.
250  *Ibid.*, p. 78.
251  *Ibid.*, p. 78.
252  *Ibid.*, p. 80.
253  See *L'Imaginaire*, p. 199, for instance.
254  See note 146.
255  *Transcendence*, pp. 104-5.
256  Even in the 'Itinerary of a thought', where Sartre is critical of the

extreme form in which he stressed in some earlier works man's freedom and responsibility, he reasserts this fundamental idea in a somewhat different form: 'the idea which I have never ceased to develop is that in the end one is always responsible for what is made of one. Even if one can do nothing else besides assume this responsibility. For I believe that a man can always make something out of what is made of him' (*ed. cit.*, p. 45).

257 *Emotions*, pp. 24-5.
258 'M. Rubel criticizes me for not making any allusion to this "Marxist materialism" in the article I wrote in 1946, "Materialism and Revolution". But he himself supplies the reason for this omission. "It is true that this author is directing his comments at Engels rather than at Marx". Yes, and even more at contemporary French Marxists' (*Method*, p. 34; see also p. 100 of *Method* for Sartre's critique of Engels).
259 This is one of the principal themes of the *Method*.
260 'Itinerary of a thought' (*ed. cit.*, p. 46).
261 ' . . . cela [his preoccupation 'to provide a philosophical foundation to realism'] m'a permis, plus tard, d'assigner certaines limites au materialisme dialectique—en validant la dialectique historique tout en rejetant une dialectique de la nature qui *réduirait l'homme*, comme toute chose, à un simple produit des lois physiques'. 'Sartre par Sartre' (Itinerary of a thought), *Situations*, IX, 104-5.
262 See, for instance, Mary Warnock, *The Philosophy of Sartre*, Hutchinson, London, 1965, Chapter 6: 'The radical conversion', pp. 135-81.
263 *Method*, p. 181.
264 Marx, *Economic and Philosophic Manuscripts of 1844*, trans. Martin Milligan, Lawrence & Wishart, London, 1959, p. 136.
265 'L'Anthropologie' (1966), *Situations*, IX, 93.
266 Marx, *Capital*, trans. Samuel Moore and Edward Aveling, I, 486.
267 *What is Literature?* p. 157.
268 Both quotations; *ibid.*, p. 159.
269 *Emotions*, p. 16.
270 Both quotations; *ibid.*, p. 51.
271 *Ibid.*, pp. 53-4.
272 ' . . . this language produces a mythology of the unconscious which I cannot accept. I am completely in agreement with the facts of disguise and repression, as facts. But the words "repression", "censorship", or "drive"—words which express one moment a sort of *finalism* and the next moment a sort of *mechanism*, these I reject. Let us take the example of "condensation", for instance, which is an ambivalent term in Freud. One can interpret it simply as a phenomenon of association, in the same way as your English

# NOTES

philosophers and psychologists of the 18th and 19th centuries. Two images are drawn together externally, they condense and form a third: this is classical psychological atomism. But one can also interpret the term on the contrary as expressive of a finality. Condensation occurs because two images combined answer a desire, a need. This sort of ambiguity occurs again and again in Freud. The result is a strange representation of the unconscious as *a set of rigorous mechanistic determinations*, in any event a *causality*, and at the same time as a *mysterious finality*, such that there are "ruses" of the unconscious, as there are "ruses" of history; yet it is impossible to reunite the two in the work of many analysts—at least early analysts. I think that there is always a *fundamental ambiguity* in them; the unconscious is one moment another consciousness, and the next moment other than consciousness. What is other than consciousness then becomes simply a mechanism ('Itinerary of a thought', pp. 46-7).

273    Simone de Beauvoir, *The Prime of Life*, p. 128.
274    *B & N*, p. 626.
275    Simone de Beauvoir, *The Prime of Life*, p. 134.
276    *Ibid.*, p. 135.
277    To use a later expression which—looking back upon the existentialist venture—sums up well the meaning of Sartre's early concern too (*Method*, p. 9).
278    *Ibid.*, p. 10.
279    *Ibid.*, p. 10.
280    It is a clear example of the internal tensions of Sartre's philosophy that while on *page 10* of the *Method* he admits that the existentialist thesis holds only to the degree to which knowledge remains powerless to transform being, on *page 181* he reasserts in an unqualified form the separation of 'being from Knowledge' and, without evidence, claims that Marx, as opposed to later marxists, holds the same existentialist view.
281    Numbers standing alone in brackets in this chapter refer to *Being and Nothingness (B & N)*.
282    *L'Existentialisme est un humanisme*, Nagel, Paris, 1946, p. 62.
283    *Ibid.*, p. 63.
284    'Merleau-Ponty', in *Situations*, p. 161. Sartre's text speaks of 'eidetics' (eidetique), not of an 'eidetic imagery'. I modified the translation accordingly.
285    'The Writer and his Language' (an interview with Pierre Verstraeten, 1965), in Sartre, *Politics and Literature*, trans. J. A. Underwood, Calder & Boyars, London, 1973, p. 112.
286    ' . . . philosophy is a matter of borrowing and inventing concepts which progressively, through a kind of dialectic, bring us to a

broader awareness of ourselves on the experiential level. Ultimately philosophy is always designed to cancel itself out. . . . What this amounts to is that philosophy must continually be destroying itself and being reborn. Philosophy is thought in so far as thought is invariably already the dead moment of praxis since, by the time it occurs, praxis is already framed. To put it another way, philosophy comes after, while none the less constantly looking forward. It must not allow itself to dispose of anything other than concepts, i.e. words. Yet even so what counts in philosophy's favour is the fact that those words are not completely defined. The *ambiguity of the philosophical word* does after all offer something which can be used to go further. It can be used in order to mystify, as Heidegger often does, but it can also be used for the purposes of prospecting, as he uses it also. . . . Philosophy is concerned with the creator of the sciences and it cannot deal with him in *scientific words*; it can only deal with him in *ambiguous words*'. 'The Writer and his language', pp. 110-11.

287   *Ibid.*, p. 96.

288   This is true, of course, not only of Sartre's *Critique of Dialectical Reason*, but of his later work in general. For instance, in 'The Writer and his Language' he takes up an important theme from *B & N*, without referring to it explicitly. The issue concerns the existential significance of wish: 'for me the concrete universal must always imply a kind of self-awareness that is other than conceptual, a kind of self-awareness that is awareness of Wish, awareness of History. Take awareness of Wish, for example. As I see it, a wish necessarily utilizes the force of need, but whereas need is a simple requirement—the need to eat, and to eat no matter what so long as it is edible—wish is on the level of Epicurus' titillation, i.e. I need to eat this rather than that. As soon as I want to eat this rather than that, the thing I want to eat inevitably refers me back to the universe. Because basically if I detest oysters but love lobster, or *vice versa*, it is always for a reason which goes beyond oyster or lobster themselves; there are certain relationships to life, relationships to whole hosts of things, which refer us back to ourselves at the same time as referring us back to the universe' (103). The statement that our taste refers us back to ourselves and to the universe is both monumentally vague and opaque. If we want to find out the meaning of the relationships hinted at, we have to go back to *B & N* which gives as examples even the same types of food: 'To eat is to appropriate by destruction; it is at the same time to be filled up with a certain being. And this being is given as a synthesis of temperature, density, and flavour proper. In a word, this synthesis signifies a certain being; and when we eat, we do not limit ourselves

to knowing certain qualities of this being through taste; by tasting them we appropriate them. . . . Certain tastes give themselves all at once, some are like delayed action fuses, some release themselves by degreees, certain ones dwindle slowly until they disappear, and still others vanish at the very moment one thinks to possess them. . . . We conclude that flavour . . . has a complex architecture and differentiated matter; it is this structured matter—which represents for us a particular type of being—that we can assimilate or reject with nausea, according to our original project. It is not a matter of indifference whether we like oysters or clams, snails or shrimps, if only we know how to unravel the existential significance of these foods. Generally speaking there is no irreducible taste or inclination. They all represent a certain appropriative choice of being. It is up to existential psychoanalysis to compare and classify them. Ontology abandons us here; it has merely enabled us to determine the ultimate ends of human reality, its fundamental possibilities, and the value which haunts it' (614-5). As we can see, the suggestion that our preference for certain types of food 'refers us back to ourselves and to the universe' does not represent any advance on *B & N*. Indeed it may be argued that while in the context of Sartre's existentialist theory of a symbolic appropriation of being the problem can be discussed with a high degree of suggestive particularization which aims at establishing the existentially significant identity of particular instances of action and the appropriation of being, the later work suffers from the vagueness of simply referring the issue to the poles of individuality ('ourselves') and universality ('the universe'). Sartre's greater social awareness brings with it a new problem, but not necessarily its solution. For while the original formulation in *B & N* bypasses the problem of mediation by stipulating a direct relationship of identity between the particular examples of appropriative behaviour and the universality of a symbolic appropriation of being ('there is no irreducible taste or inclination'), the later work, by shifting its frame of reference in the direction of a greater social concretization, imposes upon itself the burden of providing the categories of an adequate social mediation between particularity and universality. The vagueness could be removed only by filling the rather forbidding gap between 'ourselves' and 'the universe' through a well defined social mediation.

289   See in this respect section 2 of the previous chapter: 'In Search of the Individual: The Early Works'.

290   These expressions refer to essentially the same thing.

291   Again we can note both the similarities with and the differences from Kant. Just as in Kant 'ought implies can', in Sartre 'the force of

circumstance' is never allowed to challenge the existentialist demand for authenticity. At the same time, the fact that Sartre's frame of reference is existential-ontological, and not trans-cendental, significantly modifies the function of 'ought' in his system. The Sartrean 'ought' is subsumed under the general demand for authenticity which in its turn is spelled out in direct opposition to the various existing systems of value, including of course all forms of religious axiology. However, this is a much more complex problem than it would appear at first sight. See in this respect also note 312.

292    Notice the ambiguity of syntax in this sentence, which is just as evident in the French original as in the translation: 'La causalité première, c'est la saisie de l'apparu avant qu'il apparaisse, comme étant déjà là dans son propre néant pour préparer son apparition', (259). The 'appeared' is said to be already there 'in *its own* nothingness' before it appears so as to prepare 'its (?) apparition'. If it is the appeared which prepares 'its' apparition, then 'it' must really prepare *its own* apparition. The ambiguity of syntax, coupled with the vaguely undefined character of 'prepares', radically exclude any deterministic reading. This is why the 'appeared' must first exist in the mode of 'its own nothingness' which in its turn is called upon to 'prepare' its own apparition as actually appeared. Such a conception of causality (as the apprehension of the preparatory, but of course not determining, function of nothingness in the apparition of the appeared) brings with it a few pages later a definition of *motion* as 'the least being of a being which can neither arrive, nor be abolished nor wholly be' (213).

293    See the chapter on 'Individual and Society: the "Formal Structures of History" ' in volume two.

294    Here is a representative selection of metaphorical imagery from *B & N* in the order in which the particular metaphorical concepts appear: 'Consciousness is a *plenum of existence*' (XXXI). 'the preceding reflections have permitted us to distinguish two absolutely separated *regions of being*; . . . two *regions without communication*' (XXXIX). 'being is *opaque* to itself precisely because it is *filled* with itself' (XLI). 'The necessary condition for our saying not is that non-being be a *perpetual presence* in us and outside of us, that nothingness *haunt* being' (11). 'Negation cannot *touch* the *nucleus* of being of Being, which is absolute *plenitude* and entire positivity. By contrast Non-being is a negation which *aims* at this *nucleus of absolute density*. Non-being is denied at the *heart of being*' (15) 'Non-being exists only on the *surface of being*' (16). '*Nothingness carries being in its heart*' (18). 'If I emerge in nothingness beyond the world, how can this extra-mundane

nothingness furnish a foundation for those *little pools of non-being* which we *encounter* each instant in the *depth of being*' (19). 'There is an infinite number of realities which are not only objects of judgement, but which are experienced, opposed, feared, etc., by the human being and which in their inner structure are *inhabited by negation*, as by a necessary condition of their existence' (21). '*Nothingness lies coiled in the heart of being – like a worm*' (21). The questioner 'nihilates himself in relation to the thing questioned by *wrenching himself from being* in order to be able to bring out of himself the possibility of non-being' (23). 'Human freedom *precedes* essence in man and makes it possible; the essence of the human being is *suspended* in his freedom' (25). 'Every psychic process of nihilation implies then a *cleavage* between the immediate psychic past and the present. This cleavage is precisely nothingness' (27). 'Freedom is the human being *putting his past out of play by secreting his own nothingness*' (28). '*Anguish* is precisely my consciousness of *being my own future, in the mode of not-being*' (32). 'The immediate is the world with its urgency; and in this world where I engage myself, *my acts cause values to spring up like partridges*' (38). Bad Faith provides us with 'a *permanent game of excuses*' (40). 'If *I am anguish in order to flee it,* that presupposes that I can *decenter myself* in relation to what I am, that I can be anguish in the form of "not-being it", that I can dispose of a nihilating power at the *heart of anguish* itself' (44). 'a *perpetually distintegrating synthesis* and a *perpetual game of escape* from the For-itself to the For-others and from the For-others to the For-itself'. (58). 'One puts oneself in bad faith as one goes to *sleep* and one is in bad faith as one *dreams*. Once this mode of being has been realized, it is as difficult to get out of it as to *wake oneself up*' (68). 'This *perpetual act* by which the *In-itself degenerates into presence to itself* we shall call an ontological act' (79). 'as a *perpetually evanescent totality*, being-in-itself must be given as the *evanescent contingency of my situation*' (83). 'the contingency which *paralyzes these motivations* to the same degree as they totally found themselves is the facticity of the For-itself' (83-4). Facticity '*resides* in the For-itself as a *memory of being*, as its *unjustifiable presence* in the world' (84). 'Value is everywhere and nowhere; at the *heart* of the nihilating relation "reflection-reflecting", it is *present* and *out of reach*, and it is simply lived as the concrete meaning of that *lack* which makes my present being' (95). 'We shall use the expression Circuit of Selfness for the relation of the For-itself with the possible which it is, and "world" for the totality of being in so far as it is *traversed by the Circuit of Selfness*' (102). 'The world is mine because it is *haunted by possibles*' (104).

'memory presents to us the being which we were, *accompanied by a plenitude of being* which confers on it a *sort of poetry*. That grief which we had—although fixed in the past—does not cease to present the meaning of a For-itself, and yet it exists in itself with the *silent fixity of the grief of another*, the *grief of a statue*' (119). 'The For-itself is present to being in the form of *flight;* the Present is a *perpetual flight* in the face of being' (123). 'The Future is the *ideal point* where the *sudden infinite compression* of facticity (Past), of the For-itself (Present), and of its possible (a particular future) will at last cause the Self to arise as the existence in-itself of the For-itself' (128). 'To be free is to be *condemned to be free*' (129). The mode of being of the For-itself 'is *diasporatic*' (136). 'the For-itself, *dispersed in the perpetual game* of reflected-reflecting, *escapes itself* in the unity of one and the same flight. Here being is everywhere and nowhere: wherever one tries to seize it, it is there before one, it has escaped. It is this *game of musical chairs at the heart of the For-itself* which is presence to being' (142). 'Thus the time of consciousness is human reality which temporalizes itself as the totality which is to itself its own incompletion; it is *nothingness slipping into a totality* as a *detotalizing ferment*. This totality which *runs after itself* and *refuses itself* at the same time, . . . can under no circumstances exist within the limits of an instant' (149). '*Impure reflection* is an *abortive effort* on the part of the For-itself to be another while remaining itself' (161). 'We use the term Psyche for the organized totality of these virtual and transcendent existents which form a *permanent cortege for impure reflection*' (163). The psychic object 'appears as an unachieved and probable totality there where the For-itself makes itself exist in the *diasporatic unity of a detotalized totality*' (165). 'It is precisely because it [quantity] does not belong either to things or to totalities that it is *isolated and detached from the surface of the world* as a *reflection of nothingness cast on being*' (191). 'The *ideal fusion* of the lacking with the one which lacks what is lacking is an *unrealizable totality which haunts the For-itself* and constitutes its very being as a nothingness of being' (194). 'Thus the world is revealed as *haunted by absences* to be realized, and each "this" appears with a *cortège of absences* which point to it and determine it. . . . Since each absence is being-beyond-being—i.e., an absent-in-itself—each "this" points toward another state of its being or toward other beings. But of course this organization of indicative complexes is *fixed and petrified* in In-itself; hence all these *mute and petrified indications,* which *fall back into the indifference of isolation* at the same time that they arise, resemble the *fixed, stony smile in the empty eyes of a statue*' (199). 'This connection in isolation, this inert relation within the dynamic is what we call the relation of means to end. It is a being-for which is *degraded, laminated by exteriority*' (200). 'the For-itself apprehends temporality *on* being, as a pure reflection which *plays on the surface of being* without any possibility of modifying being'. (206). 'This exteriority-to-self . . . appears as a *pure disorder of being* (212). 'Motion is the *upsurge of the exteriority of indifference* at the very *heart* of the In-itself. This *pure vacillation of being* is a contingent venture of being' (213). 'universal time is revealed as *present vacillation;* already in the past it is no longer anything but an *evanescent line,* like the *wake of a ship which fades away;* in the future it is not at all, for it is unable to be its own project. It is like the *steady progression of a lizard on the wall*' (213). 'time appears as a finite, organized form in the *heart of an indefinite dispersion.* The lapse of time is the result of a *compression of time at the heart of an absolute decompression* and it is the project of ourselves toward our possibilities which realizes the compression' (215). 'Thus time appears through *trajectories.* But just as spacial trajectories *decompose and collapse* into pure static spatiality, so the temporal trajectory collapses as soon as it is not simply lived as that which objectively implies our expectation of ourselves . . . time is revealed as the *shimmer of nothingness on the surface of a strictly a-temporal being*' (216). 'To the extent that the Other is an absence he *escapes nature*' (228). 'Consciousnesses are directly supported by one another in a *reciprocal imbrication of their being*' (236). The Other 'is the test of my being inasmuch as he *throws me outside of myself* toward structures which at once both *escape me* and define me' (245). 'The appearance of the Other in the world corresponds therefore to a *fixed sliding of the whole universe,* to a *decentralization* of the world which *undermines the centralization* which I am simultaneously effecting' (255). 'it appears that the world has a kind of *drain hole in the middle of its being* and that it is *perpetutally flowing off through this hole*' (256). 'My *original fall* is the existence of the Other' (263). 'My being for others is a *fall through absolute emptiness* towards objectivity. . . . Thus myself-as-object is neither knowledge nor a unity of knowledge but *an uneasiness, a lived wrenching away* from the ecstatic unity of the For-itself, a limit which I cannot reach and which yet I am' (275). 'When objectivized the prenumerical reality of the Other is *decomposed and pluralized*' (282). 'Shame is the feeling of an *original fall,* not because of the fact that I may have committed this or that particular fault but simply that I have "fallen" into the world in the midst of things and that I need the mediation of the Other in order to be what I am' (289). 'Modesty and in particular the fear of being surprised in a state of nakedness are only a *symbolic specification of original shame'* (289). 'It is precisely through its results that we apprehend fear, for it is given to us as a *new type of internal haemorrhage in the world*—the passage from the world to a type of *magical existence'* (295). 'Thus the Other-as-object is an *explosive instrument* which I handle with care because I foresee around him the permanent possibility that *they* are going to make it explode and that with this explosion I shall suddenly experience the *flight of the world away from me* and the alienation of my being' (297). 'The relations which I establish between the Other's body and the external object are really existing relations, but they have for their being the being of the for-others; they suppose a *center of intra-mundane flow* in which knowledge is a *magic property of space,* "action at a distance" ' (305). 'knowledge can be only an *engaged upsurge* in a determined point of view which one is' (308). 'the world as the correlate of the possibilities which I am appears from the moment of my upsurge as *the enormous skeletal outline of all my possible actions. . . .* The world is revealed as *an "always future hollow",* for we are always future to ourselves' (322). 'A *dull and inescapable nausea* perpetually reveals my body to my consciousness. . . . We must not take the term nausea as a metaphor derived from our physiological disgust. On the contrary, we must realize that it is on the foundation of this nausea that *all concrete and empirical nauseas* (nausea caused by spoiled meat, fresh blood, excrement, etc.) are produced and make us vomit' (338-9). 'The *flesh is the pure contingency of presence'* (343). 'motion is a *disorder of being'* (348). 'this instrument which I am is made-present to me as *an instrument submerged in an infinite instrumental series,* although I can in no way view this series by "surveying" it' (352). 'But precisely because I exist by means of the Other's freedom, I have no security; I am *in danger* in this freedom. It *moulds* my being and makes me be, it confers values upon me and removes them from me; and my being receives from it a *perpetual passive escape from self '* (366). 'In love it is not a determinism of the passions which we desire in the Other nor a freedom beyond reach; it is a freedom which *plays the role* of a determinism of the passions and which is *caught in its own role'* (367). 'in desire there is an attempt at the *incarnation of consciousness* (this is what we called earlier the *clogging of consciousness,* a *troubled consciousness,* etc.) in order to realize the *incarnation of the Other'* (391). 'The world is made *ensnaring; consciousness is engulfed in a body* which is *engulfed in the world'* (392). 'Desire is an attitude aiming at *enchantment.* Since I can grasp the Other only in his objective facticity, the problem is to *ensnare his freedom* within this facticity. It is necessary that he be *"caught"* in it as the *cream is caught up* by a person *skimming milk*. So the Other's For-itself must come to *play on the surface of his body*, and be extended all through his body; and by touching this body I should finally *touch the Other's free subjectivity*' (394). 'Thus the other meaning of *my incarnation*—that is, of *my troubled disturbance*—is that it is a *magical language*' (396). 'sadism and masochism are the *two reefs* on which desire may founder. . . . It is because of this inconsistency on the part of desire and its *perpetual oscillation* between these two perils that "normal" sexuality is commonly designated as "sadistic-masochistic" ' (404). 'this *explosion of the Other's look* in the world of the sadist causes the meaning and goal of sadism to *collapse*' (406). 'The person who says "Us" then reassumes in the *heart of the crowd* the original project of love, but it is no longer on his own account; he asks a Third to save the whole collectivity in its very object-state so that he may *sacrifice his freedom* to it. Here as above disappointed love leads to masochism. . . .The *monstrous materiality of the crowd* and its profound reality (although only experienced) are fascinating for each of its members; each one demands to be *submerged in the crowd-instrument by the look of the leader*' (422). 'When I deliberate, the *chips are down*. . . . When the will intervenes, the decision is taken, and it has no other value than that of *making the announcement*' (451). 'By the sole fact that *our choice is absolute*, it is *fragile*' (465). 'If the given cannot explain the intention, it is necessary that the intention by its very *upsurge* realize a *rupture with the given*, whatever this may be' (478). '*my freedom eats away my freedom*' (480). 'The For-itself discovers itself as *engaged* in being, *hemmed in* by being, *threatened* by being' (487). 'the *upsurge* of freedom is the *crystallization of an end across a given* and the *revelation of a given* in the light of an end' (508). 'death is a *boundary*, and every boundary (whether it be final or initial) is a *Janus bifrons*' (531). '*freedom enchains itself* in the world as a free project toward ends' (551). 'man condemned to be free *carries the weight of the whole world* on his shoulders' (553). 'In knowing, consciousness *attracts* the object to itself and *incorporates it* in itself. Knowledge is *assimilation* . . . to know is to *devour* it yet without consuming it. We see here how the sexual and alimentary currents mingle and interpenetrate in order to constitute the *Actaeon complex* and the *Jonah complex;* we can see the *digestive and sensual roots* which are reunited to give birth to the desire of knowing' (579). 'all serious thought is *thickened by the world;* it *coagulates;* it is a dismissal of human reality in favour of the world' (580). '*sliding* appears as identical with a continuous creation. The *speed* is comparable to consciousness and here *symbolizes consciousness*' (584). 'But creation is an *evanescent concept* which can exist only through its movement. If we stop it, it disappears' (591). 'No particular act of utilization really realizes the enjoyment of full possession; but it refers to other appropriative acts, each one of which has the value of an *incantation*' (592). 'my freedom is a *choice of being God* and all my acts, all my projects *translate* this choice and *reflect* it in a thousand and one ways' (599). 'A psychoanalysis of things and of their matter ought above all to be concerned with establishing the way in which *each thing is the objective symbol of being* and of the relation of human reality to this being' (603). 'What is the *metaphysical purport of yellow,* of red, of polished, of wrinkled? And after these elementary questions, what is the *metaphysical coefficient of lemon,* of water, of oil, etc.?' (604). 'slimy . . . represents in itself a dawning triumph of the solid over the liquid—that is, a tendency of the indifferent In-itself, which is *represented by the pure solid,* to fix the liquidity, to *absorb the For-itself* which ought to *dissolve* it. Slime is the *agony of water*' (607). 'Here we can see the symbol which abruptly discloses itself: there exists a *poisonous possession*; there is a possibility that the *In-itself might absorb the For-itself,* that is, that a being might be constituted in a manner just the reverse of the In-itself . . . *Slime is the revenge of the In-itself.* A *sickly-sweet, feminine revenge* which will be symbolized on another level by the quality "sugary" ' (609). 'Thus in the project of appropriating the slimy, the sliminess is revealed suddenly as a *symbol of antivalue:* it is a type of being not realized but *threatening* which will *perpetutally haunt* consciousness as the *constant danger which it is fleeing,* and hence will suddenly transform the project of appropriation into a project of flight' (611). '*Man is a useless passion*' (615). 'The For-itself, in fact, is nothing but the pure nihilation of the In-itself; it is like a *hole of being at the heart of being. . . .* The For-itself is like a *tiny nihilation* which has its origin at the heart of Being; and this nihilation is sufficient to cause a *total upheaval* to happen to the In-itself. *This upheavel is the world*' (617-18). 'The real is an *abortive effort* to attain to the *dignity of the self-cause.* Everything happens as if the world, man, and man-in-the-world succeeded in realizing only a *missing God.* Everything happens as if the In-itself and the For-itself were presented in a *state of disintegration* in relation to an ideal synthesis' (623). 'Man *pursues being blindly* by *hiding* from himself the free project which is this pursuit. He makes himself such that he is *waited for* by all the tasks placed along his way' (626).

295  There is a great deal of uneasiness even in the inspired 1965 interview on 'The Writer and his Language' in Sartre's discussion of the relationship between philosophy and literary prose. After

condemning the use of a 'literary turn of phrase in a philosophical work' as a breach of trust in the name of 'strictly philosophical terms' (*loc cit.*, p. 96), he goes on to contrast philosophy and prose like this: 'literary prose seems to me to be the still immediate, not yet self-aware, totality, and philosophy ought to be powered by the ambition to attain that awareness while disposing only of concepts' (p. 108). Yet a few pages later, in the context of dismissing Husserl's idea of philosophy as a 'rigorous science' as 'the idea of a madman genius, but a mad idea none the less', he not only exalts ambiguity but also the literary element by saying that 'philosophy always contains *concealed literary prose*' (p. 112). And when towards the end of the interview Pierre Verstraeten tries to pin him down on some specific points, he produces some curious answers: 'I don't believe I have ever used the word "will" without giving it *inverted commas*—that is to say *theoretical* inverted commas, *invisible ones*' (p. 122). And again: 'I write in so many different languages that *things pass from one to another*; I write the language of prose, I write the language of philosophy, I write the language of theatre, and so on' (p. 123). The latter is very true, but of course it cannot constitute an answer to the question of relationship between philopsical language and literary prose.

296  'To believe is to *know* that one believes, and to know that one believes is no longer to believe. Thus *to believe is not to believe any longer* because that is only to believe—this is the unity of one and the same non-thetic self-consciousness. *To be sure, we have here forced the description* of the phenomenon by designating it with the word *to know*; non-thetic consciousness is not to know. But it is in its very translucency at the origin of all knowing. Thus the non-thetic consciousness (of) believing is *destructive of belief*' (69).

297  'übergreifendes Moment'—the moment of overriding importance.

298  *Emotions*, pp. 59-61.

299  Interview by Jacques-Alain Miller, *Les Cahiers Libres de la Jeunesse*, 15 February 1960.

300  *On Page XLII of B & N* Sartre insists that 'Necessity concerns the connection between ideal propositions', and on pages 469-70 he writes that 'the connection between the derived possible (to resist fatigue or to give in to it) and the fundamental possible is not a connection of deducibility. It is the connection between a *totality* and a *partial* structure. The view of the total project enables one to "understand" the particular structure considered. But the Gestalt School has shown us that the *Prägnanz* of the total forms does not exclude the variability of certain secondary structures. There are certain lines which I can add or subtract from a given figure without altering its specific character. There are others, on the contrary,

which cannot be added without involving the immediate disappearance of the figure and the appearance of another figure. The same thing is true with regard to the relation between the *secondary possibles* and the *fundamental possible* or the *formal totality* of my possibles'.

301    Indeed, this 'hermeneutic of existence' is envisaged as the 'sufficient *foundation for an anthropology*' (*Emotions*, pp. 24-5): a recurrent theme of Sartre's philosophy, from the early works to his *Critique of Dialectical Reason*.

302    In the same way, the concept of 'seriality' in the *Critique of Dialectical Reason* is not *derived* from the graphic situation of the bus queue; on the contrary, it *produces* the latter and other similar examples.

303    The idea that an organic totality transforms itself into inert matter, in accordance with the objective requirements of its location, so as to be able to function in its material environment, is an important theme in Sartre's discussion of 'Need' in his *Critique of Dialectical Reason*. A related idea is Sartre's definition of analytical thought as 'thought that renders itself inert so as to be competent to deal with the inert'. 'The Writer and his Language', p. 119.

304    '*Glissez, mortels, n'appuyez pas*'. See also Sartre, *Words*, Penguin edn, p. 178.

305    Letter to Simone de Beauvoir, 6 January 1940, published in *Magazine Littéraire*, No. 103-104, September 1975, p. 24.

306    Sartre himself never paid much attention to such considerations (see, for instance, his encounter with Husserl's thought), and it would be quite wrong to use the measure of scholarly accuracy in evaluating his work. Sartre's references to other thinkers are always strictly subordinate to his own immediate concerns, and major shifts in evaluation (from an essentially negative to a highly positive and then again back to an almost completely negative assessment of Marx, for instance) are likewise the result of his changing preoccupations. Consequently our attitude toward Sartre's work must hinge on the validity of his concerns inasmuch as they can be sustained on their own ground, and should not be clouded over by our disagreement with his highly self-oriented interpretations of other thinkers.

307    See, for instance, Klaus Hartmann, *Sartre's Ontology*, Northwestern University Press, Evanston, 1966.

308    'There is a fairly common tendency to seek to identify free acts with voluntary acts and to restrict the deterministic explanation to the world of the passions. In short the point of view of Descartes. The Cartesian will is free, but there are "passions of the soul". Again, Descartes will attempt a physiological interpretation of these passions' (441).

309 'It is not by chance that materialism is serious; it is not by chance that it is found at all times and places as the favourite doctrine of the revolutionary. This is because revolutionaries are serious. They come to know themselves first in terms of the world which oppresses them, and they wish to change this world. . . . Marx proposed the original dogma of the serious when he asserted the priority of object over subject. Man is serious when he takes himself for an object'. (580) Here we can see a good example of the problem mentioned in note 306. Marx proposed nothing of the kind attributed to him by Sartre whose strictures apply to the worst kind of vulgarization of Marxism. However, this crude distortion of Marx's thought does not affect the validity of Sartre's idea that 'man is serious when he takes himself for an object'.

310 In contrast to Descartes' physiological determinism, 'Later there will be an attempt to instate a purely psychological determinism. Intellectualistic analyses such as Proust, for example, attempts with respect to jealousy or snobbery can serve as illustrations for this concept of the passional "mechanism". In this case it would be necessary to conceive of man as simultaneously free and determined, and the essential problem would be that of the relations between this unconditioned freedom and the determined processes of the psychic life: how will it master the passions, how will it utilize them for its own benefit?' (441).

311 Sartre's *Critique of Dialectical Reason* is very different indeed in this respect, as we shall see in Chapter 9. However, no one should conclude that for this reason *Critique of Dialectical Reason* is a less important work.

312 In point of fact, religious references in *B & N* are numerous, and none of them could be described as nihilistic. On the contrary, Sartre is anxious to account for the meaning of many religious categories—from 'sin' and 'original sin' to 'pride', 'shame', 'fall from grace', 'ideal being', 'passion of Christ', etc.—in terms of his own discourse, instead of just dismissing them, as a nihilist would. Notwithstanding his severe critical references to religious axiology as the 'loss' and 'sacrifice' of the human reality in the interest of the 'ens causa sui', the religious problematic constitutes a vitally important element in Sartre's reasoning in Marx's sense, according to which 'the negation of the negation' (i.e. the negation of religion as a negation and alienation of man) remains inextricably intertwined with and necessarily dependent on what it negates, in that it is unable to define 'the human reality' in positive, self-sustaining terms.

313 Again, this position should not be confused with nihilism. For Sartre goes on to say that this indifference 'does not mean that we

cannot radically escape bad faith. But this supposes a self-recovery of being which was previously corrupted. This self-recovery we shall call authenticity, the description of which has no place here' (70). The difficulty with Sartre's position is that since he has established the ontological primacy of bad faith over good faith, he cannot attempt a positive description of good faith and authenticity without the danger of falling into bad faith. Thus coming to grips with authenticity and good faith, in an 'ethics of deliverance and salvation', remains the elusive promise of some other work.

314 ' . . . the situation, the common product of the contingency of the In-itself and of freedom, is an ambiguous phenomenon in which it is impossible for the For-itself to distinguish the contribution of freedom from that of the brute existent. In fact, just as freedom is the escape from a contingency which it has to be in order to escape it, so the situation is the free coordination and the free qualification of a brute given which does not allow itself to be qualified in any way at all' (488; see also pages 483-7 and 509).

315 ' . . . the fact of not being able not to be free is the facticity of freedom, and the fact of not being able not to exist is its contingency. Contingency and facticity are really one; there is a being which freedom has to be in the form of non-being (that is, of nihilation). To exist as the fact of freedom or to have to be a being in the midst of the world are one and the same thing, and this means that freedom is originally a relation to the given' (486).

316 Also called 'unreflective consciousness', 'non-thetic consciousness' and 'pre-reflective cogito'. As we have seen in note 296, though this non-thetic consciousness does not give us knowledge, 'it is in its very translucency at the origin of all knowing'.

317 See in this respect the quotation in note 300.

318 'The *past* which I am, I have to be with no possibility of not being it. I assume the *total responsibility* for it *as if* I could change it, and yet I cannot be anything other than it' (116). 'we must proceed from this *antinomy*: human-reality originally *receives* its *place* in the midst of things; human-reality is that by which something we call place *comes* to things' (490). 'I exist my place *without choice, without necessity* either, as the pure absolute fact of my being-there. I am there, not here but there. This is the absolute and incomprehensible fact which is at the origin of extension and consequently of my original relations with things (with these things rather than with those). A fact of *pure contingency—an absurd fact*' (491). 'facticity is the only reality which freedom can discover . . . freedom is the apprehension of my facticity' (494). 'To be sure, in being born I take place, but *I am responsible for the place* which I take. We can see clearly here the inextricable connection of freedom and facticity in

the situation' (495). 'the irremediable quality of the past comes from my actual choice of the future; . . . while freedom is the choice of an end in terms of the past, conversely the past is what it is only in relation to the end chosen' (497). 'the order of my choices of the future is going to determine an order of my past, and this order will contain nothing of the chronological' (499). 'A living past, a half-dead past, survivals, ambiguities, discrepancies: the ensemble of these layers of pastness is organized by the unity of my project' (500). 'Thus *we choose our past* in the light of a certain end, but from then on it imposes itself upon us and *devours us*' (503). 'Thus like place, the past is integrated with the situation when the For-itself by its choice of the future confers on its past facticity a *value*, an hierarchical order, and an urgency in terms of which this *facticity motivates* the act and conduct of the For-itself' (504).

319 Sartre is by no means embarrassed by the circularity involved. He asserts that it is in the nature of consciousness to exist 'in a circle' (XXIX), and in another context he defines the world as 'a synthetic complex of instrumental realities inasmuch as they point one to another in *ever widening circles*' (17). Similarly, the relations with the Other are characterized by the circle (408), and Sartre reiterates again and again that we can never get out of the circle (e.g., 412).

320 See for instance 'Itinerary of a Thought', *New Left Review*, 58, Nov.-Dec. 1969.

321 'Coefficient of adversity'—a term adopted from Gaston Bachelard's *L'Eau et les rêves*, ed. José Corti, Paris, 1942. It stands for the resistance of things or objects *vis-à-vis* human projects.

322 In *L'Existentialisme est un humanisme* Sartre writes that if one day men decided to establish fascism and other men were 'coward and crippled enough to let them do it, from that moment fascism would be the human truth, and all the worse for us' (pp. 53-4). Despite the fact that Sartre's own position is clearly visible as opposed to fascism, the underlying principle is extremely problematical. It is very similar to Bertrand Russell's paradoxical predicament toward the end of his life. For having spent the greater part of his life totally relativizing value judgments as a form of emotionalism, he found his own commitment to nuclear disarmament and to many other worthy causes totally unsustainable in terms of his own philosophy.

323 The question of a major conversion is realistically formulated in some particular contexts. For instance, when Sartre writes: 'There is no doubt that I could have done otherwise, but that is not the problem. It ought to be formulated rather like this: could I have done otherwise without perceptibly modifying the *organic totality of the projects which I am? . . . at what price?*' (456). And later on, writing about yielding to fatigue, he makes the point that 'This does

not imply that I must necessarily stop but merely that I can refuse to stop only by a *radical conversion* of my being-in-the-world; that is, by an abrupt metamorphosis of my initial project—i.e., by another choice of myself and of my ends. Moreover this modification is always possible' (464). This is all very clear and feasible, in that the 'radical conversion' in question only implies switching from one set of personal policies and strategies to another while many of the particular projects can belong to both, in accordance with the principle of *Prägnanz* which defines the relationship between the 'secondary possibles' and the 'fundamental possible'. However, there is a world of difference between this kind of 'radical conversion' and the one merely postulated in the apocalyptic footnote on the ethics of salvation.

324    Sartre quite openly acknowledged his own anarchistic liber-tarianism in some recent interviews. Simone de Beauvoir's description of their experience in a café in Rouen (see note 275) when they decided that the proletarian struggle was not their struggle, is highly relevant in this respect, though of course the roots of such a decision go much further back in the past. In *B & N* Sartre attributes anarchism to the bourgeoisie: 'the weakness of the oppressing class lies in the fact that although it has at its disposal precise and rigorous means for coercion, it is within itself profoundly anarchistic. The "bourgeois" is . . . a consciousness which does not recognize its belonging to a class' (428).

325    See for instance Sartre's 'ontological proof' on page XXXVII.

326    In this respect see my essay on 'Marx's relation to philosophy', in *Ideology and Social Science, and Other Essays,* Harvester Press, 1980.

327    *Situations,* I., 32.

328    The same epistemological optimism is in evidence in *The Transcendence of the Ego.* By contrast now the *crowd* becomes a '*monstrous materiality*' and the helpless individual is depicted as 'submerged in the crowd-instrument by the look of the leader' (422).

329    In his essay on 'Sartre's existentialism' Marcuse writes: 'It was said in a note in *L'Être et le Néant* that a morality of liberation and deliverance was possible, but that it would require a "radical conversion". Sartre's writings and the stands he has taken over the last two decades are a conversion of this kind' (*Studies in Critical Philosophy,* NLB, London, 1972, p. 189). This may be true of Sartre personally, but such a personal conversion (if, that is, we may describe Sartre's development in those terms) does not resolve the contradiction between the postulated ethics of deliverance and salvation and the ontological structure of being as articulated in *B & N*.

330 The fact that the myth of Medusa (430) is turned 'the other way round' in order to fit the theory (for in the original it is not the mythical Other's look at me which causes my petrification but *my own* forbidden look at Medusa) need not worry us unduly. Much more important is the general use to which the claimed symbolic relations are put. Ultimately they all hinge on the question of appropriation: on Sartre's individualism preventing him from conceiving appropriation in other than symbolic terms, since a full appropriation in relation to the isolated individual is clearly inconceivable. This position is mythically projected into a past which precedes the division of labour, and there we meet Sartre's existentialist version of the 'Robinsonade' which is designed to bring *production* in line with *appropriation* as individualistic, and as such ontologically fundamental. We are presented with a fictitious armchair anthropology, in the name of an ontological description of the fundamental relations, and we end up with a perverse conclusion which identifies 'luxury' as closest to original ownership: *'originally it is I* who make for myself the object which I want to possess. *My bow and arrows* [Friday comes later] . . . *Division of labour* can dim this original relation but cannot make it disappear. *Luxury* is a degradation of it; in the primitive form of luxury I possess an object which *I have had made (done) for myself* by people belonging to *me* (slaves, servants born in the home). Luxury therefore is the form of ownership closest to primitive ownership' (589).

331 See Marx's discussion of these problems in *The German Ideology*, especially pp. 84-86.

332 *Ibid.*, especially pp. 78, 86, 87, 88.

333 This 'perpetual Third' should not be confused with the 'absolute Third', nor with the 'neutral Third' (429).

334 See Marx's discussion of the 'class for-itself' in his 'Introduction to the Critique of the Hegelian Philosophy of Right'.

335 See my essay on 'Contingent and necessary class consciousness', in *Aspects of History and Class consciousness*, Routledge & Kegan Paul, London, 1971.

336 See Marx's discussion of generations of men inheriting determinate conditions of existence and proceeding from there toward their transformation, in *The Poverty of Philosophy*, 1847.

337 In *B & N* Sartre is very critical of Paul Bourget's *Essai de Psychologie Contemporaine: G. Flaubert*, saying that 'such a psychological analysis proceeds from the postulate that an individual fact is produced by the intersection of abstract, universal laws. The fact to be explained—which is here the literary disposition of young Flaubert—is resolved into a combination of

typical, abstract desires such as we meet in "the average adolescent". What is concrete here is only their combination; in themselves they are only possible patterns. The abstract then is by hypothesis prior to the concrete, and the concrete is only an organization of abstract qualities; the individual is only the intersection of universal schemata. But—aside from the logical absurdity of such a postulate—we see clearly in the example chosen, that it simply fails to explain what makes the *individuality* of the project under consideration. . . . In addition this method rejects the *pure individual* who has been banished from the *pure subjectivity* of Flaubert into the external circumstances of his life' (558-9). Later he addresses the same criticism to Marxism in general.

338    'In my book on Flaubert, I am studying imaginary persons—people who like Flaubert act out roles. A man is like a leak of gas, escaping into the imaginary. Flaubert did so perpetually; . . . Writing on Flaubert is enough for me by way of *fiction*—it might indeed be called a *novel*. Only I would like people to say that it was a true novel. I try to achieve a certain level of comprehension of Flaubert by means of hypotheses. Thus I use fiction—guided and controlled, but nonetheless fiction—to explore why, let us say, Flaubert wrote one thing on the 15th March and the exact opposite on the 21st March, to the same correspondent, without worrying about the contradiction. My hypotheses are in this sense a sort of *invention of the personage*', 'Itinerary of a Thought', *loc cit.,* pp. 53 and 55. Many years earlier, in *Nausea*, very similar ideas are put forward by Roquentin in his reflections on the problems of a biography which he plans to write: 'Well, yes: he may have done all that, but there is *no proof* that he did: I am beginning to believe that nothing can ever be proved. These are reasonable *hypotheses* which take the facts into account: but I am only too well aware that they come from me, that they are simply a way of unifying my knowledge. Not a single glimmer comes from Rollebon's direction. Slow, lazy, sulky, the facts adapt themselves at a pinch to *the order I wish to give them*, but it remains outside of them. I have the impression of doing *a work of pure imagination*. And even so, I am certain that characters in a *novel* would appear *more realistic*' (p. 26).

339    This project is spelled out in a fairly detailed form in *B & N* (559-62), in the context of 'existential psychoanalysis'. And Sartre concludes: 'This psychoanalysis has not yet found its Freud. At most we can find the foreshadowing of it in certain particularly successful biographies. We hope to be able to attempt elsewhere two examples in relation to Flaubert and Dostoevsky' (575).

340    In this sense the 'particularization' is in fact the most abstract of all

possible generalizations since it aims at establishing a *symbolic relationship of identity* between the 'incomparably unique' and the 'ontological absolute', a priori excluding all categories of social mediation which belong to the sphere of the 'strictly psychological experience of historic man immersed in a working universe' of alienated objectification on the surface of being.

341  Anybody who can lump together Marx, Halbwachs and de Man—as Sartre does in *B & N* (513), in the name of an alleged 'inferiority complex'—demonstrates a singular incomprehension of Marx. Likewise in his description of Marx as the orginator of the 'dogma of seriousness' mentioned above.